Basic Wiring

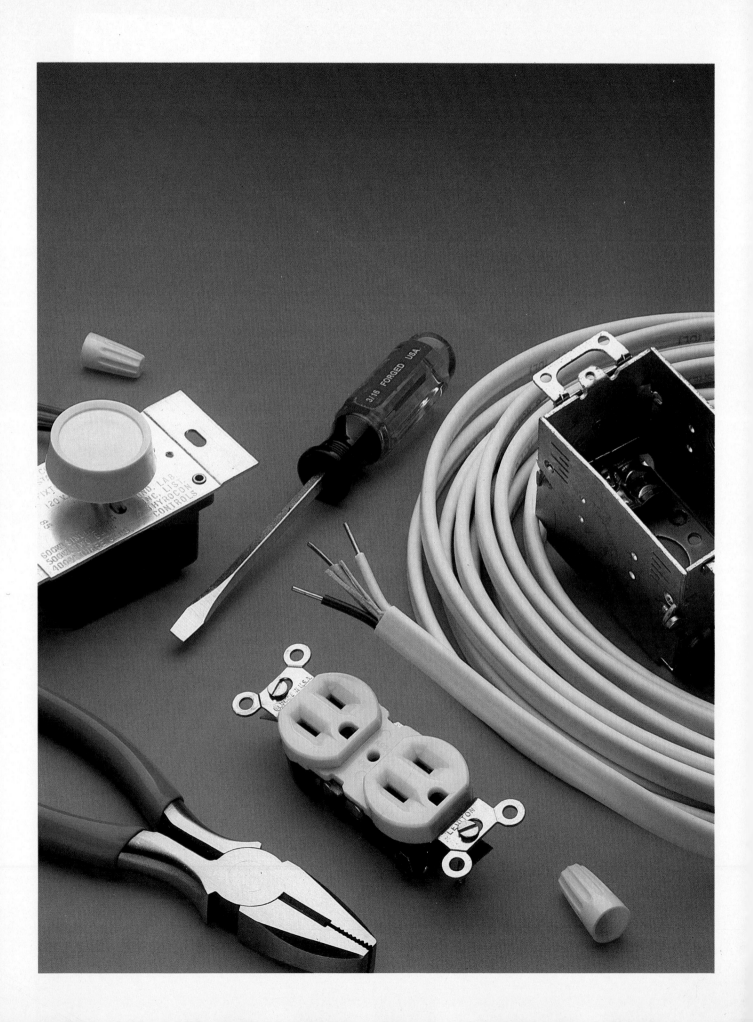

Basic Wiring

The Editors of Creative Homeowner Press

CREATIVE HOMEOWNER PRESS®

Wire Nut® is a registered trademark of Ideal Industries, Inc.
Molly® is a registered trademark of the Emhart Corporation.

Manufactured in United States of America.

Current printing (last digit)
10 9 8 7 6 5 4 3 2

Produced by Roundtable Press, Inc.

Project editor: Donald Nelson
Managing editor: Marguerite Ross
NEC consultant: Joseph A. Tedesco
Editorial consultant: William Broecker
Technical advisors: Bill Fischer, Clayton Eurich
Illustrations: Norman Nuding
Design: Jeffrey Fitschen
Jacket design: Jerry Demoney
Jacket photo: David Arky
Art production: Nadina Simon

LC: 88-15035
ISBN: 0-932944-82-5 (paper)
       0-932944-88-8 (hardcover)

CREATIVE HOMEOWNER PRESS®
BOOK SERIES

A DIVISION OF FEDERAL MARKETING CORPORATION
24 PARK WAY, UPPER SADDLE RIVER, NJ 07458

Introduction

Most do-it-yourselfers don't give a second thought to doing repairs or projects around their homes—until it comes to an electrical project. Then confidence ceases, and licensed electricians are called in to do the work—even the simplest projects. This causes unnecessary expense in most cases; many homeowners are as capable as many professional electricians. Fear often is behind their reluctance. Many homeowners feel uncomfortable dealing with something that can't be seen, especially when that something is powerful enough to injure or kill. Electricity certainly should be respected, but not feared. A simple flip of a switch or removal of a fuse can eliminate any element of danger so that work can proceed without risks of any kind.

You might think that replacing an electrical switch or wiring a table lamp is more difficult than replacing a kitchen sink or paneling a room. Just the opposite is true. Electrical repairs and projects can be as easy to do as anything else, and, in many cases, even easier. In fact, the most difficult aspects have nothing to do with electricity. They involve opening and closing up walls before and after doing the basic wiring project.

This book provides simple step-by-step instructions for electrical repairs and projects. The first three sections explain how electricity works in your home, the terms you will need to know to buy the right electrical materials for the job and follow the instructions presented here, and the tools that you will need to properly and safely make the repairs. The chapters that follow cover basic electrical projects in order of difficulty, throughout your home, such as working with wire; switches and outlets; replacing cords, plugs, and sockets; installing lighting; and working with electricity in new and existing construction.

This book is not intended to make you into a professional electrician. In fact, you will find notations every so often that advise you to call in a professional to handle special procedures. In some areas of the nation, local codes require that you have your work inspected by a professional once you complete a project. This is the smart, safe way to handle it, and you almost always will find that the cost of professional help is not prohibitive.

For all your electrical projects, we strongly recommend that you buy and use only quality electrical materials—those that bear the UL (Underwriters' Laboratories) label and are appropriate for the project. Don't try to innovate with substitute products and techniques. Use the right stuff the first time. Finally, after completing a project, double-check your work carefully against the information in this book and any data provided by materials manufacturers before restoring electrical power to the circuit.

Contents

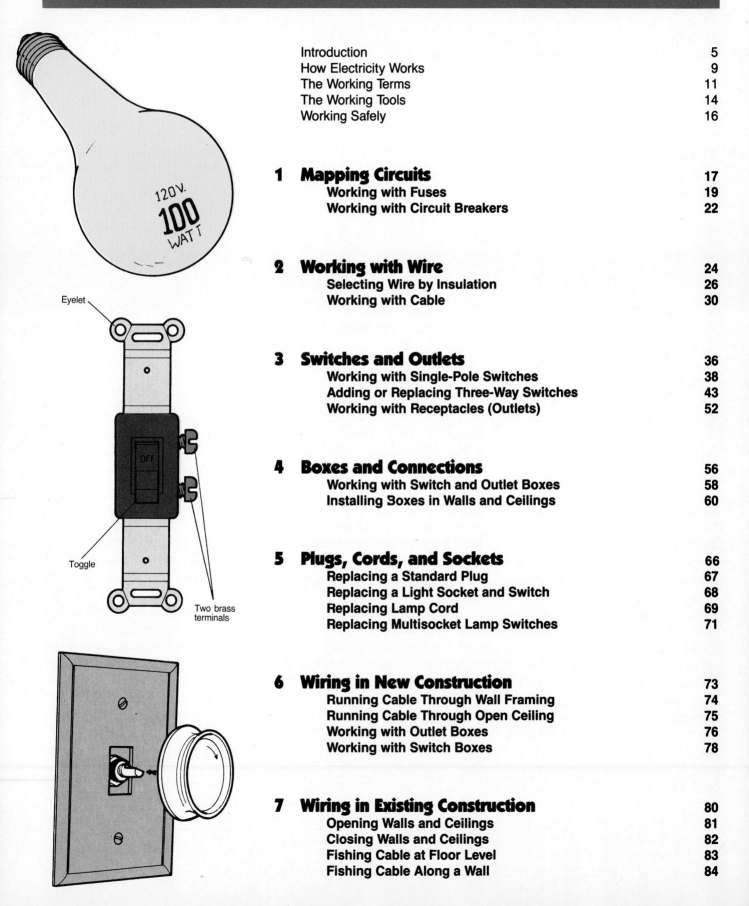

Eyelet

Toggle

Two brass terminals

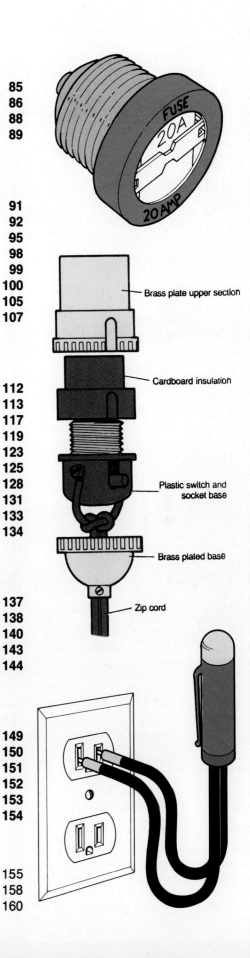

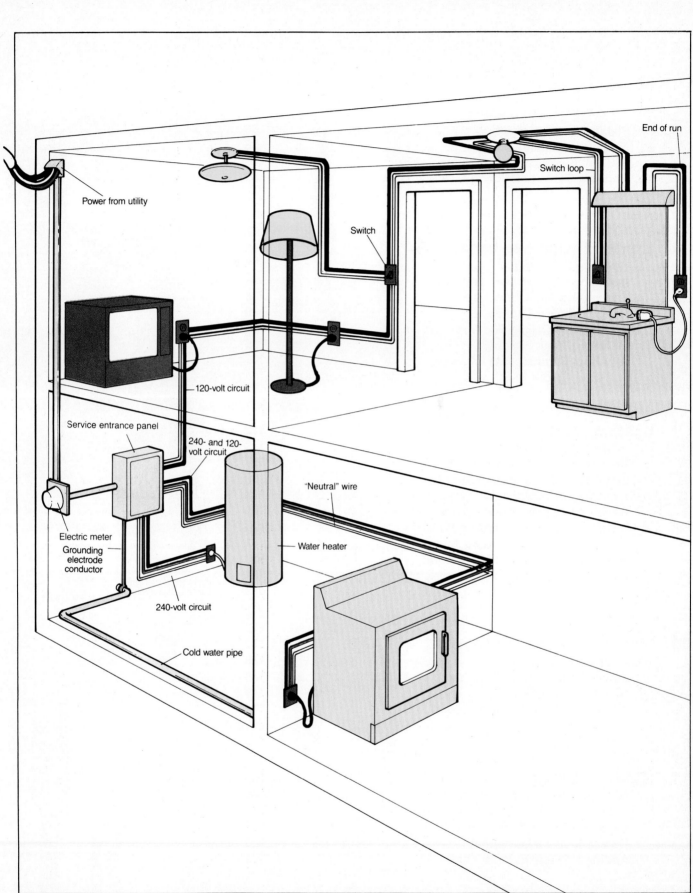

- Power from utility
- End of run
- Switch loop
- Switch
- 120-volt circuit
- Service entrance panel
- 240- and 120-volt circuit
- "Neutral" wire
- Electric meter
- Grounding electrode conductor
- Water heater
- 240-volt circuit
- Cold water pipe

This simplification of a house wiring system shows the power split into 120- and 240-volt branch circuits at the service entrance panel (SEP). Black or red wires in the branch circuits are always "hot" (power present). White wires complete the loop to the SEP. They are "neutral" (no power present) only when no current is flowing: they are hot whenever anything in the circuit is turned on. Circuit breakers or fuses in the SEP protect the branch circuits from current overloads. The grounding system for metal switch and outlet boxes is not shown; it uses bare or green wires, or metal conduit. The overall system grounding connection, from the SEP to the cold-water entrance pipe is shown.

How Electricity Works

A public (sometimes private) utility generates electricity and sends it to your home through overhead or underground wires called service conductors. At your home, the electricity goes through a meter, usually attached to the outside of the house into the main, service entrance panel.

The meter measures how much electricity your home uses during a certain period, and you are charged accordingly. At the service entrance panel, which contains a fuse or circuit breaker or fuse/breaker system, the electricity is divided into branch circuits. The fuses or breakers protect these individual circuits.

The branch circuits supply safe electrical power to the various rooms in your home: kitchen, bathrooms, living areas, bedrooms, and so on. Each circuit is protected by its own fuse or circuit breaker and is independent of the others. That's why, when something causes one circuit to fail with a blown fuse or tripped breaker, the remaining circuits are unaffected and continue to supply power to the other rooms.

Electricity, as used in your home, is the rapid flow of energy transmitted by electrons. The flow must make a complete circuit from the utility's generating station, along the lines to your home, through your household circuits, and back to the utility. The force that moves the energy is called voltage; the flow itself is called current. The direction of flow changes 60 times a second. Thus, we speak of 120- (or 240-) volt, 60-cycle alternating current (AC).

TWO- AND THREE-WIRE SYSTEMS

Most homes built before 1941 had two-conductor (two-wire) electric service. If you live in a home built during this time and the electrical service has not been remodeled, your home may have two-conductor service. In effect, one conductor carries 120-volt current and the other provides a return path. Actually, the current flow alternates in direction along both conductors.

Two-conductor service may limit the number and type of electrical appliances you can use. Even if the utility ran a third line to increase your service, your existing circuits might not let you use many of today's electrical conveniences. However, it may well be possible to add new circuits capable of handling the current demands of new appliances. Consult your power company and a qualified electrician to determine whether your present service can handle an increased demand.

Most homes have three-conductor service: two of the wires are always "hot"—power is always present. The third wire, often inaccurately called "neutral," is hot only when current is flowing—which is all the time in a modern home where appliances run day and night. There are 120 volts between each hot wire and the "neutral" conductor, and 240 volts between the two hot conductors. Thus there is power for lights and small appliances that require 120 volts, and for large appliances, which need 240 volts.

WATTAGE RATINGS

To calculate the wattage (power) available in a circuit, first determine its amperage (amp rating). It will be marked on the circuit breaker or fuse for that circuit in the service entrance panel— 15 or 20 amps for most room circuits, 30 or 50 amps for most heavy-duty circuits. Then, Watts = Volts × Amps. Thus, a 15-amp circuit with 120 volts carries (15 × 120 =) 1,800 watts: a 20-amp circuit carries 2,400 watts.

The wattage of any one appliance (see chart) should not be more than 80 percent of a circuit's total wattage capacity. Appliances with large motors, such as air conditioners or refrigerators, should not exceed 50 percent of circuit capacity. To operate properly and safely, each such appliance must have a circuit to itself.

TYPICAL WATTAGE RATINGS

Appliance	Rating
Room air conditioner	800–1500
Central air conditioner	5000
Electric blanket	150–500
Blender	200–400
Broiler (rotisserie)	1400–1500
Can opener	150
Clock	13
Clothes dryer (240-v.)	4000–5000
Clothes iron (hand)	700–1000
Coffee maker	600–750
Crock pot (2 quart)	100
Dehumidifier	500
Dishwasher	1100
Drill (hand)	200–400
Fan (attic)	400
Fan (exhaust)	75
Floor polisher	300
Food freezer	300–600
Food mixer	150–250
Fryer (deep fat)	1200–1600
Frying pan	1000–1200
Furnace (gas)	800
Furnace (oil)	600–1200
Garbage disposal	500–1000
Hair dryer	400
Heater (portable)	1000–1500
Heating pad	50–75
Hot plate	600–1000
Hot water heater	2500–5000
Microwave oven	650
Radio	10
Range (per burner)	5000
Range oven	4500
Refrigerator	150–300
Roaster	1200–1600
Sewing machine	60–90
Stereo	250–500
Sun lamp	200–400
TV (color)	200–4500
Toaster	250–1000
Toaster-oven	1500
Trash compactor	500–1000
Vacuum cleaner	300–600
Waffle iron	700–1100
Washing machine	600–900

HOW TO MAP ELECTRICAL CIRCUITS

Work with a helper. One person works at the main service panel; the other person tests switches, outlets, and appliances.

STEP 1
THE WORKING SKETCH

Draw a floor plan of each room. Mark every receptacle, switch, and light fixture. Sketch in heavy equipment that is connected to the service panel. If this equipment has its own separate circuit, so note it.

STEP 2
NUMBER THE CIRCUITS

At the main service panel, number each circuit breaker or fuse with a stick-on or glue-backed label.

STEP 3
SET UP THE TEST

Work on one room at a time. Turn on all lights and appliances in that room. Plug in any lamps. If the room has a double receptacle, plug a light into each receptacle. Do not turn on heavy equipment.

STEP 4
RECORD THE CIRCUIT

The person at the main service panel now turns off the first breaker or fuse. On the floor plan, the helper records the number of the circuit or fuse next to each affected switch, light fixture, and receptacle.

STEP 5
IDENTIFY OTHER CIRCUITS

Turn on the first circuit breaker or fuse and turn off the next one. Continue the recording procedure until every switch, light fixture, and receptacle in the room has been labeled with its circuit number. Do this in every room.

STEP 6
ADD HEAVY EQUIPMENT

When the circuits controlling all lights, switches, and receptacles have been identified, identify and label the circuits serving the heavy appliances.

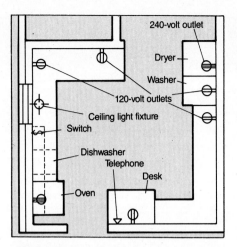

Working sketch. On graph paper, make a plan of each room, drawing in electrical components. Use sketch to compute available watts.

Number the circuits. At the main service panel, number each breaker or fuse. When circuit malfunctions, you'll know the faulty circuit.

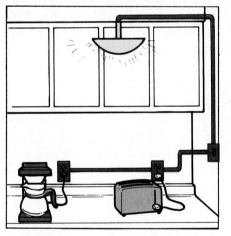

Set up the test. Turn on all lights and appliances in room being tested. Do not include heavy equipment in this test.

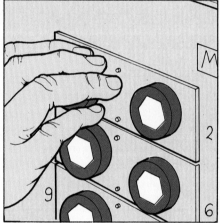

Record the circuit. Person at service panel turns off circuit. In the room, helper records number of circuit and outlet it powers.

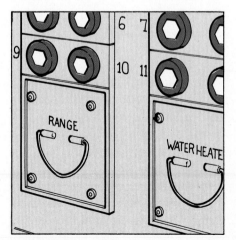

Identify other circuits. Circuit is reactivated; next one is turned off. Continue until each switch, light, outlet has been correctly labeled.

Add heavy equipment. Label circuits serving heavy appliances and equipment in all rooms. Mapping shows where power is available.

The Working Terms

Electricity has its own nomenclature or working terms. You should be familiar with these terms so you can shop for and buy the right electrical products for a project. Doing so also can save you plenty of time and money and help you better understand how electricity works. A glossary is included in the back of this book. Here you'll find complete explanations of common terms that you need to know when you go shopping.

AMPERES, AMPERAGE
Current flow is measured in amperes, or amps. The amp rating is marked on many appliances. (If wattage is given, divide by the voltage to get the amp rating.) Wires and cables are marked in AWG (American Wire Gauge) sizes.

Electrical suppliers have charts showing the amp ratings for AWG sizes.

Amp ratings are important when buying fuses or circuit breakers. The amperage of circuits, fuses/breakers, and appliances must match. Too little fuse/breaker amperage will blow immediately; too much will permit a dangerous amount of overcurrent flow.

VOLTS, VOLTAGE
A volt is a unit of measurement of the force of electrical pressure. A generator creates the pressure that keeps the electric current flowing through the conductors or wires.

In stores, you'll see electrical products marked with their voltage capacity: 120 VOLTS, or 240 VOLTS, or 110–115 VOLTS. This means that the product has been designed to operate at that voltage. For example, do not hook up an electrical device rated at 115 volts to a circuit that supplies 220–240 volts. You'll burn it out.

WATTS, WATTAGE
Wattage equals volts multiplied by amps. The wattage rating of a circuit is the amount of power the circuit can deliver safely, which is determined by the current-carrying capacity of the wires or cables. Wattage also indicates the amount of power a fixture or appliance needs to work properly.

BOXES
This is a catch-all term for several products. To buy the right box, you will have to be more specific. For example,

Light bulbs and tubes show both watts and volts. Only special-purpose lights will show amps.

Fuses are always marked with amp capacity on the face of the fuse or on the metal tip of the fuse.

Appliances are marked with amperage, voltage, and wattage. With motors, the more amps, the higher the horsepower.

switch boxes are for switches and some outlets; outlet boxes are for receptacles (outlets), and junction boxes are used to hold wires that run between switch and outlet boxes. That is, switches, outlets, and fixtures are not connected to junction boxes.

Ceiling boxes support fixtures that are installed in them. There are three types: ceiling boxes with flanges, boxes with bar hangers, and boxes with offset hangers.

The different types are illustrated in Chapter 4, Boxes and Connections.

WIRES

The correct term for the metal strand through which electricity flows is *conductor*, not *wire*. However, almost everyone, including the pros, calls conductors wires, and we will, too. There are three classifications of wires: cords (such as extension, zip, and lamp cords), single wires, which are insulated to carry electricity or left bare for grounding, and cable, which is two or more wires enclosed in insulation

(such as Romex, a trade name). Wires are rated by amps and should be specified and purchased accordingly.

The different wire specifications are charted in Chapter 2, Working with Wire.

ZIP CORD

This product is used as lamp cord. It has a thin section between the two insulated wires, so it splits down the middle. It usually is sold by the foot.

SINGLE-POLE SWITCHES

These switches have two terminals, usually located on one side (or back) of the switch. One single-pole switch is used as the only control of an outlet or fixture. The toggle is marked ON/OFF.

THREE-WAY SWITCHES

These switches have three terminals: two on one side of the switch and one on the opposite side (or back). Two

three-way switches control one outlet or fixture. The toggle is unmarked.

OTHER SWITCHES

A *four-way switch* has four terminals. Four-way switches control one outlet or fixture from three separate places; they are used in conjunction with three-way switches.

A *double-pole switch* also has four terminals; it is used to control 240-volt appliances. Only a double-pole has ON/OFF markings on the toggle.

FUSES

There are just two designs in use: plug (Edison base) and cartridge. The plug fuse has a threaded base that screws into a socket the way a light bulb screws into a lamp socket.

A cartridge fuse looks like a roll of coins; it has no threads. Some may have fins on each end.

All fuses are marked for amperage. The amperage of the fuse must match the amperage of the circuit in which it is used. Never overfuse a circuit.

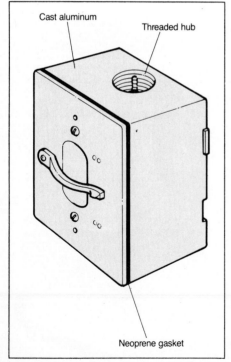

Boxes for switches, outlets, and fixtures are made of metal or plastic, and sold in many different designs.

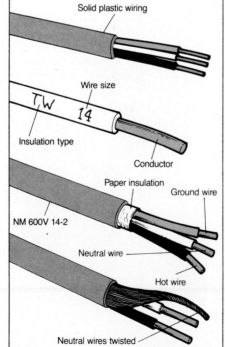

Conductors (wires) are designed for many different purposes. Some wire is stranded, e.g., lamp cord; other wire is solid, e.g., cable.

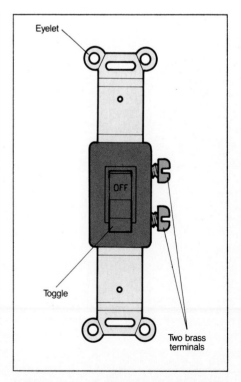

Switches have terminals—two for this single-pole switch—plus an ON/OFF toggle and mounting eyelets.

UL LISTED

The UL stands for Underwriters Laboratories. This is an independent organization—not a government agency—that tests and lists products, affirming that they meet certain specifications and perform safely as the manufacturer says they will. A manufacturer pays for UL testing and listing.

"ACCORDING TO CODE"

Salespersons frequently use this phrase. It means that a product or technique meets the standards of the National Electrical Code or the local codes. The National Electrical Code is a body of standards that define safe electrical procedures and materials. Local codes may add to or make substitutions for various NEC standards.

If you live in a different township or county from the store where you buy electrical products, you may find that certain products are not sold there. They may not meet the codes of the community where the store is located.

However, they may be perfectly legal and "according to code" in your area.

EMT

These initials stand for electrical metallic tubing, which is metal conduit through which insulated wires run. A salesperson may not speak of conduit, but of EMT. Electrical codes in some communities permit nonmetallic pipe to be used instead of metal conduit.

BX

BX is a cable wrapped in a flexible, protective metal sheathing. BX has at least two wires running through it. Local codes may not allow the use of BX, or may impose restrictions as to length and climatic conditions.

ENCLOSURES

An enclosure is a housing to prevent accidental contact between a person and an electrical part, or to protect equipment from damage. Typical enclosures include mounting boxes for switches, receptacles, and service entrance panels. Boxes are metal, or nonmetallic where permitted, and can be weather resistant or even explosion-proof.

TESTERS

Two common testing devices are used in this book. One, a continuity tester, is used to determine whether an electrical path is complete. It is used *after you turn the power off*. The tester has a battery and a built-in indicator light or buzzer.

A voltage tester is used *with the power on* to determine if power is in fact present. Touching the probes to a hot line and ground or a return line causes the indicator to light.

RHEOSTAT

This is a fancy name for a dimmer switch. When you buy a dimmer switch, be sure to get the right type. One type controls an incandescent light; another controls a fluorescent light. The difference is usually printed on the package, but always double-check.

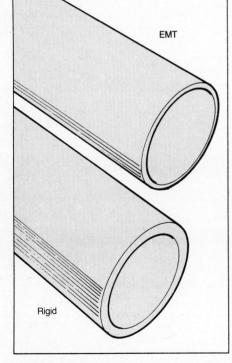

Conduit is pipe through which insulated wires run. EMT is known as thinwall. Rigid is usually heavy steel pipe.

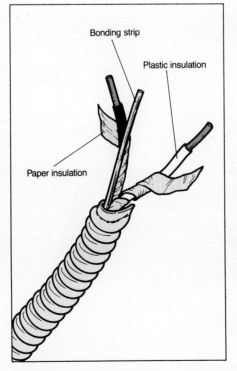

BX is an armored cable containing two or more conductors. Its use is limited by local code in some areas. Check local code first.

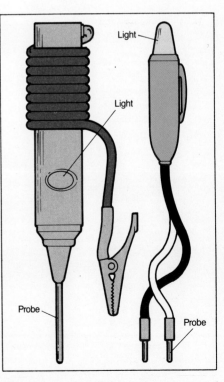

Voltage tester (right) checks for presence of power. With power turned off, continuity tester checks for a complete circuit.

The Working Tools

Electrical projects require several specialized tools. They also require several standard hand and power tools, such as hammers, chisels, squares, and portable electric drills. You may already have many of these tools. Some, especially the electrical ones, you may have to purchase on a project-to-project basis.

In order to save you time, money, and lots of frustration, we recommend that you buy the more expensive, quality electrical tools and equipment at the outset. You will pay more for quality tools, but with them you can complete quality projects in less time and with less effort than by using cheaper tools that dull easily, won't fit, and are hard to handle. Take care of quality tools, and they will last you a lifetime.

We've organized tool and equipment purchases into two categories: the basic tools needed for most repairs and simple projects, and additional tools for more ambitious projects, especially those involving carpentry skills.

You will find a selection of electrical tools and equipment at many home-center stores, hardware outlets, and retailers specializing in electrical products.

THE BASIC TOOLS

You can complete most basic electrical projects with these tools:

● Continuity tester and/or voltage tester.

● Multipurpose wire stripper. This tool removes insulation from the wire without damaging it. Some strippers also cut wire and can be used to bend wire.

● Needlenose pliers are excellent for bending tight loops in wire to go around terminals.

● Lineman's pliers. The most popular models are the 7- and 8-inch size. The pliers have flat jaws that are used to bend, pull, twist, and grip wires. Some types have wire and cable cutters; some also have moving shoulders

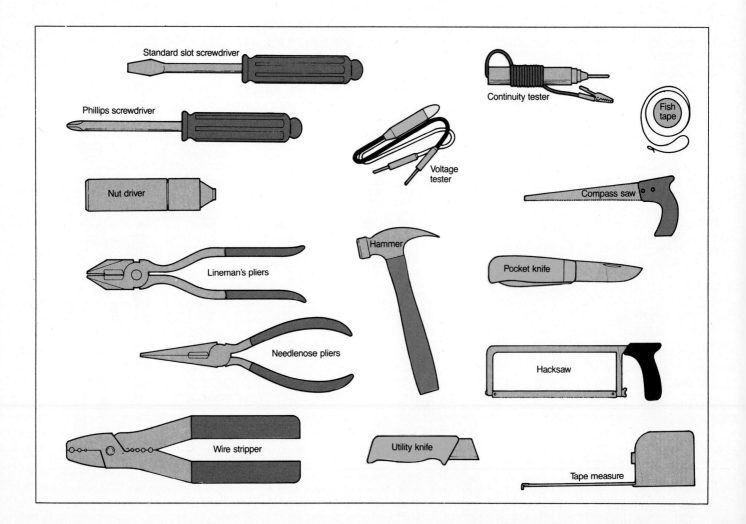

that can crush insulation and so make cutting easier.

● Fish tape. This tool is used to pull wires through finished walls and ceilings. Several lengths are available.

● Set of standard screwdrivers.
● Set of Phillips screwdrivers.
● Set of nut drivers.
● Hacksaw.
● Compass (keyhole) saw.
● Hammer.
● Tape measure.
● Pocket knife.
● Utility knife and blades.

ADDITIONAL PROJECT TOOLS

Carpentry skills often are needed when working with electricity. For example, you may have to cut into a finished wall to install a switch or outlet. In new construction, you may have to drill holes through framing members. Tools for these jobs are listed below along with several "nice-to-have" tools.

● Locking pliers are used to grip and hold wires, tighten bolts, and pull cable through conduit and holes. They also can be used to pull nails and clamp and hold wood and other building materials.

● Diagonal or cable or side cutters are used to cut wires in especially cramped quarters, such as junction, switch, and outlet boxes.

● Channel-Lock or water-pump pliers. Excellent for handling locknuts and cable connectors.

● Adjustable wrench for tightening nuts and connectors. Buy either an 8- or 9-inch wrench.

● Pipe wrench. A 10-incher is about right for gripping conduit and turning on conduit fittings.

● A ⅜-inch variable-speed portable electric drill with a hole-saw bit, masonry drill, and several wood bits.

● Cable insulation ripper. This little, inexpensive tool removes cable insulation faster than a knife.

● Wood chisel set; cold chisel.
● Portable electric saber saw.
● Carpenter's level.
● Electric solder gun.
● Volt-ohmmeter for circuit tests.
● Conduit or tubing bender (hickey).

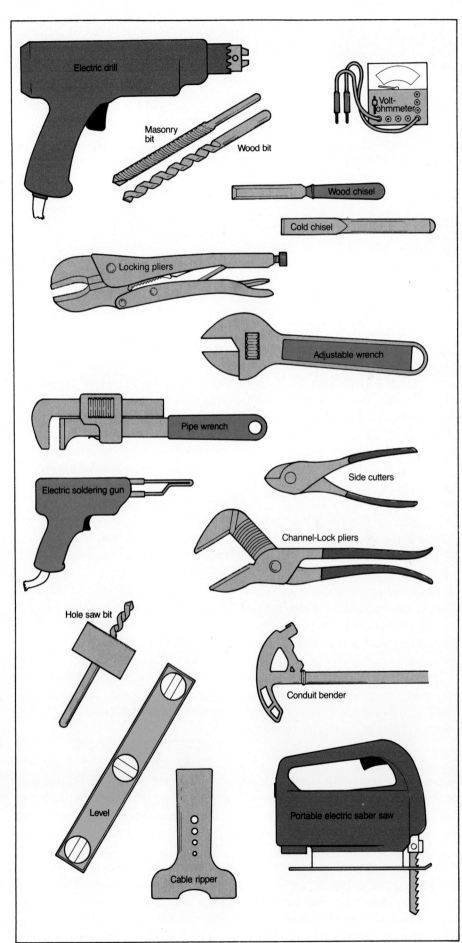

Electric drill

Masonry bit

Wood bit

Volt-ohmmeter

Wood chisel

Cold chisel

Locking pliers

Adjustable wrench

Pipe wrench

Electric soldering gun

Side cutters

Channel-Lock pliers

Hole saw bit

Conduit bender

Level

Cable ripper

Portable electric saber saw

Working Safely

Electricity can be dangerous, but if you use common sense and follow safe procedures carefully you can work with it quite safely. Below are several safety tips, plus some rules and regulations to know before starting any electrical project. None is difficult to follow.

1. Always, without fail, turn off the power at the main electrical service panel before working on a circuit.

When turning off the power, changing a fuse, or resetting a circuit breaker, stand on a short length of dry plywood or a piece of 2 × 8 or a couple of 2 × 4s side by side. Use only one hand to disconnect or reactivate the power. Keep the other hand in your hip pocket or behind your back.

Then, as you start to work, check the circuit with a voltage tester to make sure that it is powerless.

If you follow this No. 1 rule, we can assure you that you will not be injured by electrical shock.

2. Confine your electrical projects to outside the main service entrance. That is, do not go into the fuse/breaker box to add circuits or make repairs unless you have the professional knowhow.

You can wire in new circuits, repair old ones, and make countless improvements and repairs yourself. Then, when it is time to hook up the project to power at the entrance panel, call in a licensed electrician. The cost of hiring a pro for connections is not prohibitive, and the pro will also check your work.

3. Use a wooden or fiberglass ladder, never a metal one, when working with electricity. And use insulated tools.

4. Never work with electricity while standing on a damp or wet floor or earth. Don't touch any plumbing or gas pipes while working on a circuit.

5. When working outside with power equipment, make sure the electrical circuit is protected by a ground fault circuit interrupter (GFCI). You can buy a GFCI and easily wire it into the circuit, or use a GFCI extension cord.

RULES AND REGULATIONS

All electrical procedures and materials, for amateur or professional use, are governed by local building and/or electrical codes. The codes often vary from one locality to the next. Codes may prohibit the use of a certain type of electrical cable or require a particular size wiring or a minimum number of circuits, for example. The codes are for your protection, and for the protection of others residing in your community.

If the store personnel where you purchase electrical tools and supplies do not know about local codes, contact the municipal electrical inspector in your area to determine the wiring requirements that the town places on electrical installations.

You may be required to obtain a permit to do some electrical projects. Permit fees are not expensive and are usually quick and easy to obtain. You also may be required to have an official inspect your work after it has been completed to make sure that the work conforms to specifications.

THE NATIONAL CODE

Local or community codes often are based on the National Electrical Code (NEC). The code spells out safe electrical procedures for everyone—professionals and amateurs—to follow. The code, which is updated every three years, specifies as its purpose:

"The practical safeguarding of persons and property from hazards arising from the use of electricity."

The NEC does not, in itself, carry the weight of law. However, most states and municipalities conform to the specifications laid down by the code or add to the code. The NEC does not provide step-by-step instructions on how to do electrical work. Instead, it states recognized methods for doing electrical wiring and indicates the proper materials to be used.

When you undertake major and advanced electrical projects, you should become familiar with those sections of the National Electrical Code that apply to your projects. Many home-center and hardware stores sell an inexpensive booklet that contains this information. Or you can purchase a copy of the code from the National Fire Protection Association, Batterymarch Park, Quincy, MA 02269. The Canada Electrical Code serves the same purpose in Canada as the National Electrical Code in the United States.

UL RATINGS

Electrical supplies that you buy should carry the Underwriters' Laboratories (UL) symbol. The symbol is your assurance that the products meet certain safety standards.

If there is a question about whether a device that you intend to buy has been listed by UL, write or call the Public Information Office, Underwriters' Laboratories, Inc., 333 Pfingsten Road, Northbrook, IL 60062.

THE UTILITY COMPANY

Before you dig any holes or ditches outside your home to install electrical wiring or other electrical devices, contact the public utility at least three days before starting the job. In some states, this notification is required by law. It is for your protection as well as the protection of those residing around you.

Mapping Circuits

The starting point for all electrical repair and improvement projects is the main electrical service panel, usually called the fuse box or the circuit-breaker panel. Here is where all circuits start and end. When there is trouble on a circuit, such as an overload or short, the fuses or breakers shut off the power at this point. When you do any work on a circuit, you *must* first remove a fuse or trip the breaker to turn off the power at this stopping and starting location.

These two circuit protectors may not be in the main service panel:

1. A separate fuse box or circuit breaker added to the main electrical system to power a major circuit or appliance. For example, some older homes have a separate circuit to power a central air-conditioning system. You will find the location of this fuse box when you map the circuits in your home.

2. Some appliances have a built-in protective system with a fuse or circuit breaker. An example is a garbage disposer that has a power-overload device. When an overload occurs, the built-in system shuts down only the appliance. You push a reset button on the appliance to restore power to it. Appliances and devices with similar protection include ranges, clothes dryers, ground fault circuit interrupter (GFCI) outlets, and heavy-duty motors.

The built-in system protects only the appliance; the circuit to which it is connected is protected by its own fuse or circuit breaker in the main service panel—one does not substitute for the other. In general, the built-in protector is designed to trip and shut down the appliance at a lower overload level than the fuse or breaker that protects the entire circuit. This helps prevent an ap-

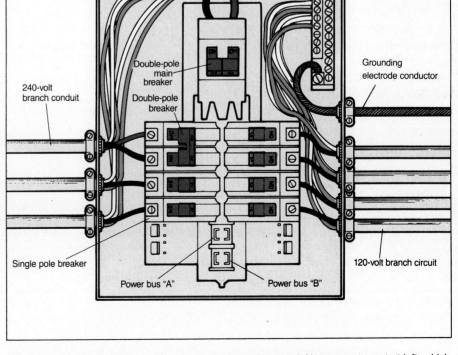

Service entrance conductors

Ground neutral bar

Grounding electrode conductor

Double-pole main breaker

Double-pole breaker

240-volt branch conduit

Single pole breaker

Power bus "A"

Power bus "B"

120-volt branch circuit

This is a typical main service entrance and circuit-breaker panel. Note arrangement at left, which provides 30 amps of power for major appliance. Empty spaces below are for future new circuits.

pliance problem from affecting the overall circuit wiring.

DIFFERENT DESIGNS

Some circuit systems use only fuses, while others use only toggle-type circuit breakers. There also are systems that combine fuses and breakers. And fuses and toggles come in somewhat different shapes and sizes.

CIRCUIT PROTECTION

Fuses and circuit breakers interrupt the current flow in situations where circuit overloading or line-to-line or line-to-ground faults have occurred.

Before you replace a fuse or reset a circuit breaker, find out what caused the power shutoff and correct this condition. Although installing a new fuse or resetting the breaker may restore power to the circuit, it will be temporary; the circuit will shut down again fairly quickly unless you correct the trouble. The problem may be an overloaded circuit, a short circuit in a damaged wire or a broken circuit in an appliance.

Sometimes, but very, very infrequently, a problem may exist in the main service panel. If, after making a thorough check, you can not find trouble on the circuit, suspect the service panel. However, don't try to repair any damage here yourself, unless you have the know-how. Call a licensed electrician for the job.

SAFETY AT THE PANEL

When replacing a fuse or resetting the toggle on a circuit breaker, work safely by standing on a completely dry piece of plywood or a short length of 2 × 6 or 2 × 8 lumber. We suggest that you cut a piece of either material, drive a nail into the edge or end of it, bend the nail over into a hook configuration, and hang the wood on a pipe or similar object near the main service panel.

Always use fuse pullers to remove or replace cartridge fuses. And wear safety goggles. Use just one hand to remove or replace plug fuses or reset circuit breakers. That will avoid creating a circuit between you and the panel.

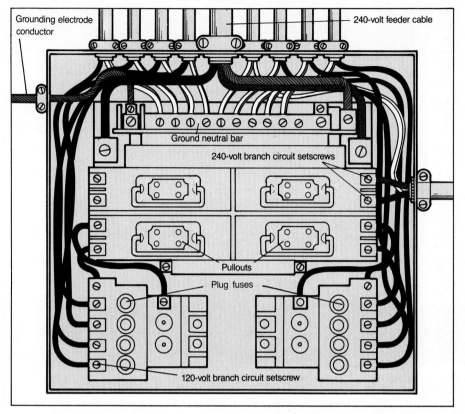

Fuse-type service entry panel is shown here. You must remove all four pull-out boxes in top section to shut off all power. Screw-in plug fuses below control the individual circuits.

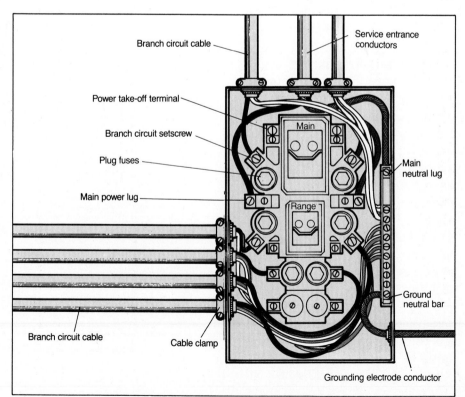

Fuses alone control this entrance panel. *Main* and *Range* fuse blocks hold cartridge-type fuses. Open terminals at ground neutral bus bar (right) can hold ground wires for new circuits.

Working with Fuses

To determine the cause of a blown plug fuse, first examine the small window of the fuse to see whether a short circuit or an overload has occurred.

Overload. An overload occurs when too many appliances and lights on a circuit demand more current than the circuit can deliver safely. In this case, the small wire in the fuse will break without heating excessively. The window will be clean, and you should be able to see the broken wire.

Short circuit. A short circuit occurs when a bare wire carrying electricity touches another bare wire carrying electricity or touches the grounded metal case of an appliance. The rate of the current flow quickly becomes excessive. This in turn produces heat, which destroys the fuse wire. The fuse wire vaporizes and sprays the fuse window with discolored material.

OPENED CIRCUIT BREAKER

Circuit breakers are protective switches that automatically flip off when there is an overload or short circuit.

You reset a circuit breaker by pushing the switch or toggle to the full OFF position, and then to the full ON or RESET position.

Since you don't have a window in a circuit breaker to help determine the cause of a short circuit or overload, make a list of the lights and appliances that were operating on the circuit when the breaker tripped and add up the total wattage you were pulling at the time of the power failure. Then divide the wattage by the voltage. If the resulting amperage figure is more than the capacity marked on the failed fuse, there was an overload.

CARTRIDGE FUSE TYPES AND HOW TO CHANGE BOTH

Two types of cartridge fuses are used in homes. The round-ended type, with a capacity of 10 to 60 amps, is used to

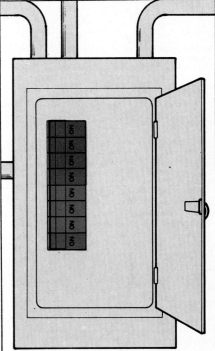

Conventional fuses. Circuits in this panel are protected by plug fuses. The fuse rating matches the size of circuit wiring.

Circuit-breaker panel. This panel's circuits are protected by circuit breakers, which snap off when a short or overload occurs in circuit.

Fuse overloads/shorts. In good fuse, window is clear. Cleanly broken strip indicates circuit overload; discolored window indicates a short.

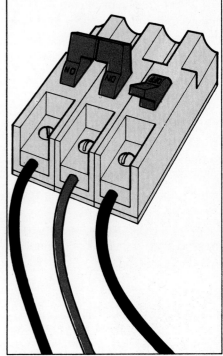

Tripped breakers. Toggles in a circuit breaker flip to OFF or to a center position for both short circuits and circuit overloads.

protect circuits that supply a major appliance.

The other type of cartridge fuse is usually used in residential installations to protect the main power circuit. This fuse has knife-blade end contacts and is rated at 70 to 600 amps. The two types cannot be interchanged.

Cartridge fuses rarely fail. Reasons for failure may include an overload on the circuit, a short circuit, or simply old age.

STEP 1
SHUTTING OFF POWER

Some service panels with cartridge fuses are controlled by a lever along the outside edge of the panel. Move the lever to the OFF position. Then open the box.

STEP 2
REMOVING THE FUSE

Using a fuse puller, grasp the middle of the fuse and pull it out of the spring clips that hold it in place. If the fuse has knife-blade ends, don't bend them.

STEP 3
FUSES IN COMPARTMENTS

Some cartridge fuses are mounted in a compartment-type housing. To remove the fuses, grasp the wire-loop handle and pull the compartment straight out of the panel.

STEP 4
TESTING THE FUSE

Touch one probe of a continuity tester to one end of the fuse and the other probe to the other end. If the tester lights, the fuse is okay. If the tester does not light, replace the fuse.

Caution: Never test a fuse while it is in the service panel. Always remove it from the service panel.

STEP 5
REPLACING THE FUSE

To install a cartridge fuse, push it into the spring clips by hand. If a new fuse fails, the problem is in the circuit wiring or there is a short circuit in an appliance.

Shutting off power. To turn off the power, pull the lever on the outside of the box. Then open the cover of the box.

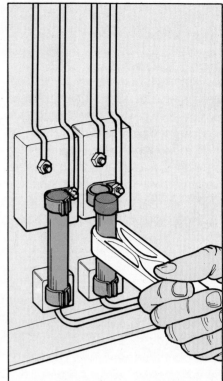

Removing the fuse. With a cartridge fuse puller, remove the fuse from the spring clips that hold it tightly in position.

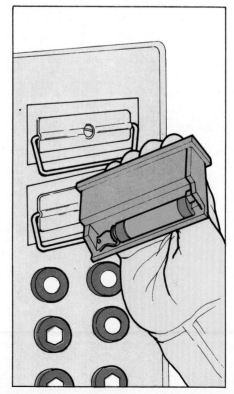

Fuses in compartments. Compartmented fuses, found in appliance circuits, are removed after compartment is pulled from panel.

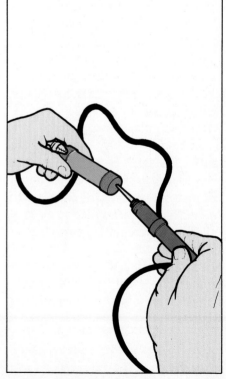

Testing the fuse. Touch continuity tester probes to fuse ends. If tester lights, fuse is okay and may be reinserted in box.

SPECIAL-PURPOSE FUSES THAT AVOID TROUBLE

There are three types of special-purpose fuses similar to standard plug fuses that provide extra safety and convenience.

TYPE S FUSES

This fuse is the same as a standard fuse, except for one notable difference. A Type S fuse has two parts: the fuse and its socket adaptor. The adaptor screws into and becomes part of the socket in the main fuse panel. The fuse then screws into the adaptor. Both parts are always used together.

Threads of a specific amperage Type S fuse are designed to be screwed into threads of the same amperage adaptor and no other. For example, you cannot screw a 15-amp Type S fuse into a 20-amp Type S adaptor.

CIRCUIT-BREAKER FUSES

These fuses have a push button that pops out from the center of the face. When the fuse blows, you simply push in on the push button to reset the fuse. It works like a toggle-type circuit breaker.

TIME-DELAY FUSES

This fuse (sometimes called a time-lag fuse) allows temporary circuit overloading. It is used in circuits that supply heavy appliances, such as air conditioners, that demand a temporary surge of power when they are turned on.

The time-delay fuse is made with a spring-loaded metal strip (link) attached to a plug of solder. When the power surges, this type of fuse doesn't blow immediately. Instead, the solder begins to melt. It must melt through completely, however, before the fuse will blow.

FUSED RECEPTACLES

A fused receptacle can save you a trip to the main service panel. If you overload the circuit and blow the fuse, only this receptacle is out of order, and the bad fuse is at your fingertips.

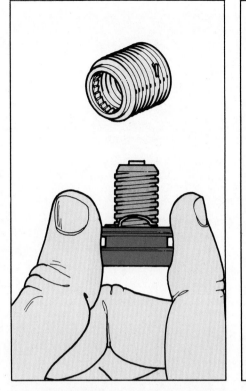

Type S fuses. Type S safety fuses have two parts: adaptor screws into a fuse-box socket; the fuse screws into the adaptor.

Circuit-breaker fuses. Circuit-breaker fuses have a push button to reset a blown fuse caused by an overload or short circuit.

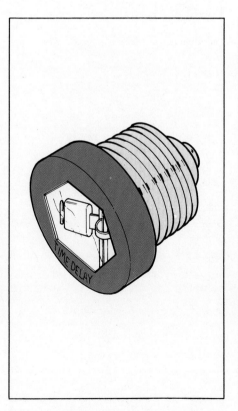

Time-delay fuses. Time-delay fuses guard appliances that require extra power for start-ups, such as heavy workshop motors.

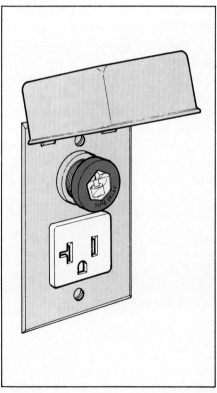

Fused receptacles. You save steps with a fused receptacle. When appliance overloads circuit, entire circuit doesn't shut down.

Working with Circuit Breakers

Replacing a damaged circuit breaker or adding a new breaker circuit to a breaker box is not difficult. There are two basic breaker unit types: snap-in and wired.

Whenever you purchase breakers, whether for a new installation or as replacements, first identify the manufacturer of the service panel and the amperage of the circuit. This information is required to get the right type of breaker, of the correct capacity, for your panel.

If you are connecting a new circuit, we strongly recommend that you rough in the wiring to the breaker box. Then call in a licensed electrician to make the necessary connections.

TO REPLACE A BREAKER

First, review the safety procedures on page 16. Then follow these steps:

1. Turn off the power at the main breaker. Stand on a dry board, wear goggles, and use just one hand to disconnect the power.

2. Remove the panel that covers the breakers.

3. Remove the damaged breaker. It pulls out of its slot in the box. It may be connected with wires, or may just snap into the opening.

4. If it is wired, loosen the terminal screws and remove the wires. A two-pole breaker will have two wires attached (red and black); a single-pole breaker will have one wire (black).

5. Connect the wires to the terminals on the new breaker and slide it in the slot. Make sure it seats firmly.

6. Replace the breaker cover and turn on the main power switch.

LOOSE BREAKERS

If you find a loose breaker that wobbles in the box, turn off the power at the main switch. Remove the breaker cover panel. Press on the loose breaker to snap it back into place. Replace the cover and turn on the power.

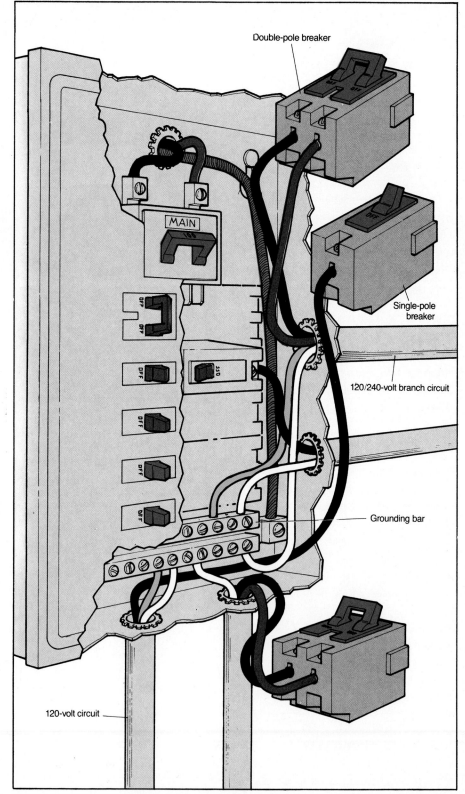

How breakers fit into a circuit-breaker box. Anatomy of typical circuit-breaker box. The breakers are connected with wires, as shown, or simply snap into the slots in the face panel. Before working, turn off power.

Double-pole breaker

Single-pole breaker

120/240-volt branch circuit

Grounding bar

120-volt circuit

ADDING A NEW CIRCUIT BREAKER

Installing a brand-new circuit breaker in a breaker box is just as easy as replacing one. However, we recommend that you have a professional electrician make the power connections—if you don't have the know-how.

IS THE POWER OFF?

The first step is to turn off the power. How can you be sure that it is really off? The very best way is to use a volt-ohmmeter or a multitester. You can buy one for under $20, or rent one. Set the meter to the range that includes 240 volts AC. Touch the probes of the meter to the terminal screws on the main power-fuse system. If the meter shows a reading, the power is still ON.

MAKE THE CONNECTIONS

Here are the installation steps:

1. Turn off the power at the main breaker and check it with a voltmeter just to make sure it is really off.

2. Remove the knockout in the breaker box for the new breaker. In the side of the box, knock out the circle of metal matching the breaker location so the cable you are using may be connected properly.

3. Strip the cable insulation to allow enough wire for the connection to the neutral bus bar and the new circuit breaker. Connect the cable to the box with the proper fitting for the box/cable.

4. Run the ground wire and the white neutral wire of the cable to the neutral bus bar. Have the licensed electrician make this connection.

5. Attach the red and/or black wire to the new circuit breaker, if the wires exist and are so labeled. Two-pole breakers are connected with a red and black wire; single-pole breakers (in most installations) are connected with just the black wire. The professional will then clip the breaker to one of the box's hot bus bars.

6. If the breaker is a two-pole unit, it will take up two spaces in the box. It is for a 240-volt circuit. Both wires are considered power wires.

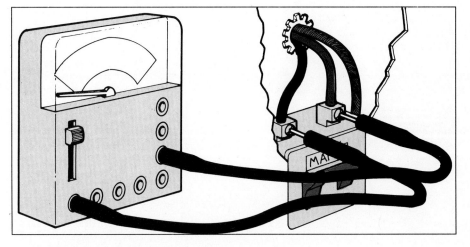

Voltmeter testing for power. Voltmeter is a sure way to test whether power is on or off. Touch probes to the terminal screws to get a power reading.

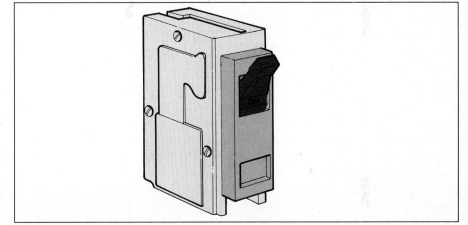

Single-pole breaker. A single-pole breaker is narrow compared with its double-pole cousin. Some types snap in; others are wired in.

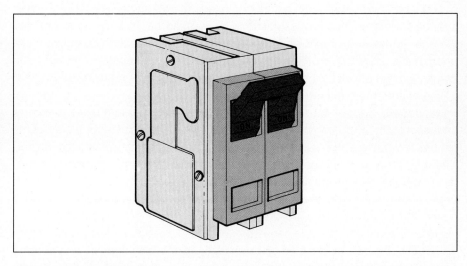

Double-pole breakers. 240-volt double-pole breakers are used for heavy equipment on straight 240-volt circuits, not 120/240 circuits.

 Working with Wire

Technically, the metal through which electricity flows is called a *conductor*. In the real world, it's called *wire*, *cord*, and *cable*. That is how it is referred to in stores that sell it. Most instructions use these simple terms, too.

For practical purposes, a *wire* is a single strand of conductive material enclosed in protective insulation. You can buy single-strand wire off a roll in any length you want. It is sometimes precut and packaged in standard lengths. A *cable* has two or more wires grouped together within a protective sheathing of plastic or metal. Cable is normally sold boxed in precut lengths of 25, 50, or 100 feet. *Cord* usually is a series of stranded wires encased in insulation. Cord is sometimes precut and packaged, but is usually sold off the roll. All conductors are priced by the lineal foot.

There are three different types of wires: *copper*, *copper-clad aluminum*, and *aluminum*. For any project, you should always use the same type of wire that is installed in your home. You can determine this by opening a switch or outlet box, pulling out the wires, and noting the information printed on the insulation. The markings (see page 26) will tell you the voltage, the type of wire or cable, the manufacturer, and the AWG wire size.

ALUMINUM WIRE

You must use special care with aluminum wire. It does not behave like copper wire. Aluminum wire tends to expand and contract, working itself loose from terminal screws. This can cause trouble—mainly electrical fires. If your home uses copper-clad aluminum wire, do not add aluminum wire to it. Use copper or copper-clad aluminum wire.

If your home has aluminum wire, check to make sure that the switches and receptacles are marked CO/ALR or CU/AL. The CO/ALR marking is used on switches and receptacles rated up to 20 amps. The CU/AL marking is used on switches and receptacles rated at more than 20 amps. If the switches and receptacles do not bear these markings, replace them with those that do.

Never use aluminum wire with any back-wired switch or receptacle that requires pushing the wire into the device. Aluminum wire must connect to terminal screws.

Since recommendations for wire sizes are generally for copper and copper-clad aluminum wires, you must readjust the designation to the next larger size when using aluminum wire. Example: If No. 14 (copper) wire is rec-ommended and you are using aluminum wire, you must use No. 12 wire instead.

WIRE SIZE NUMBERS

You will probably be concerned mostly with No. 14 and No. 12 wire sizes.

The term *wire* refers to a single conductor. In a cable containing two wires, both wires will be the same size.

Wire numbers are based on the American Wire Gauge (AWG) system, which expresses the wire diameter as a whole number. For example, No. 14 AWG wire is 0.064 inches in diameter, and No. 12 AWG is 0.081 inches. The smaller the AWG number, the greater the diameter and the greater the current-carrying capacity. The National Electric Code requires a minimum of No. 14 AWG wire for house wiring. Exceptions to this are the wiring used in lighting fixtures, furnace controls, doorbells, and other low-energy circuits.

WIRE AMPACITY

You also must consider the wire's ampacity, or the current in amperes that a wire can carry continuously under conditions of use without exceeding its temperature rating.

If a wire is too small for the job, it will present a greater-than-normal resistance to the current flowing around it. This generates heat and can destroy insulation, which can cause a fire.

No. 12 wire is rated to carry a maximum of 20 amps; No. 14 wire is rated to carry up to 15 amps.

CABLE FOR CIRCUITS

House circuits are usually wired with nonmetallic sheathed cable, with metal-armored cable, or with insulated wires running through metal or plastic pipe called conduit.

For most projects, you will be working with flexible nonmetallic sheathed cable known by its trade name Romex. It contains insulated power and neutral wires and a ground wire.

Armored cable is called BX. Inside the flexible metal sheathing are insulated power and neutral wires and a ground wire. Use of BX cable sometimes is restricted by code. Check the local codes where the material is sold. BX also is restricted to use indoors in dry locations. It sometimes is specified for use where power wires need extra sheathing protection.

Conduit, according to code, can be galvanized steel pipe or plastic pipe. Metal conduit comes in three types: rigid—often preferred for outdoor use—intermediate, and electrical metal tubing or EMT, a newer type popular for house wiring. Standard conduit diameters are ½, ¾, 1, and 1¼ inches.

There are fittings to join conduit for straight runs and at 45-degree angles. The material is bent with a tool called a hickey.

CORD

This is stranded wires encased in some type of insulation, such as plastic, rubber, and cloth.

Zip cord, for example, is two wires, usually No. 18 gauge, encased in a rubber-like insulation and held together with a thin strip between the wires. You can easily separate the wires by pulling them apart, hence the name zip cord. You zip it apart. Cord is used for lamps, small appliances, and cord sets that have plugs and/or receptacles on one or both ends of the cord.

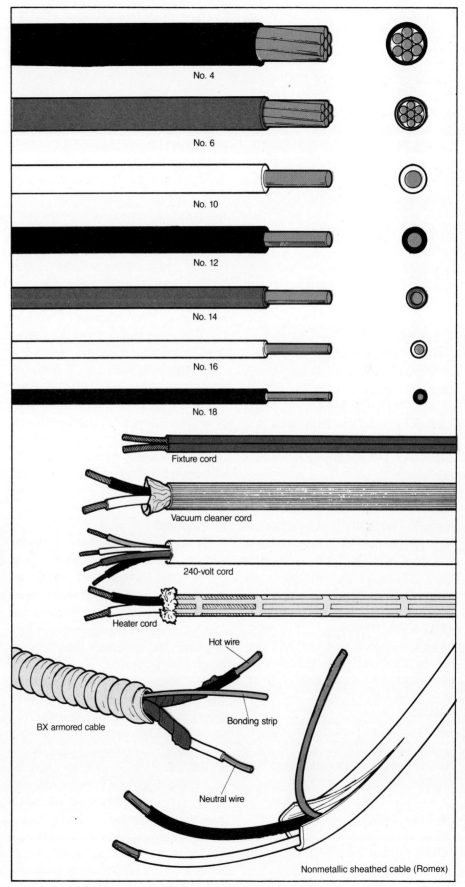

No. 4

No. 6

No. 10

No. 12

No. 14

No. 16

No. 18

Fixture cord

Vacuum cleaner cord

240-volt cord

Heater cord

BX armored cable

Hot wire

Bonding strip

Neutral wire

Nonmetallic sheathed cable (Romex)

Many kinds of wire and cable are sold to meet all project needs. Package label or wire insulation gives data on wire size or gauge, type of insulation, and power capacity.

Selecting Wire by Insulation

Wire, both solid, single strands and cable, is available with many different types of insulation. You must select the right wire for the location in which it will be used. The most commonly used types are described below.

WIRE SPECIFICATIONS
RHW
The insulation is moisture- and heat-resistant rubber. The wire may be used in either wet or dry locations.

T, TF, AND TW
The T stands for thermoplastic. You will probably use more of this type of wire than any other in household electrical projects, but it is only for dry locations. Type TF is a moisture-resistant thermoplastic insulation that may be used in place of TW in both moist and dry locations.

THHN
A flame-retardant, heat-resistant insulation specified for dry and damp locations. Because it is thin, THHN is often used in conduit to allow more wires to be installed.

THW AND THWN
A flame-retardant, moisture- and heat-resistant thermoplastic insulation for use in wet or dry locations.

XHHW
This insulation is a flame-retardant crosslinked synthetic polymer. It is specified for use in dry and damp locations as well as wet locations.

CABLE SPECIFICATIONS
The types of sheathed cable that you will use most will be NM, NMC, and UF. Specific data include:

TYPE NM
NM cable is for use only in dry locations. It is used most often in house circuits. Each wire (with the possible exception of the equipment grounding conductor) is wrapped in its own plastic insulating sheath. The three wires are then wrapped in a paper insulator, and the paper wrapping is covered with plastic.

The wire in Type NM cable is either AWG No. 12 or AWG No. 14 for normal house circuits. Larger sizes, such as No. 10 or more, are used for heavy appliances. The National Electrical Code specifies that No. 12 wire must be used for certain household circuits.

In either size, NM cable is available with two or three conductors plus an equipment grounding conductor. This ground-wire system is highly recommended. Use three-conductor NM cable for heavy-duty circuits, especially where two hot wires are needed for the hookup.

TYPE NMC
This cable may be used in both damp and dry locations. The distinguishing characteristic of this cable is that the individually insulated wires are embedded in solid plastic to provide protection against moisture. As a result, it is appropriate for basement installations where codes permit.

Type NMC is available with two or three conductors plus an equipment grounding conductor and in AWG No. 12 and AWG No. 14.

TYPE UF
This cable is for use in wet locations, including burial underground. UF cable may be used instead of conduit.

The distinguishing characteristic of this cable is that the individually insulated wires are embedded in water-resistant solid plastic that is heavier than that used in Type NMC cable. The UF cable is available in AWG No. 12 and AWG No. 14 as well as other size wires. It contains two or three conductors plus an equipment grounding conductor.

ABBREVIATIONS ON WIRE
Markings on the insulation, plastic sheathing, and on nonmetallic cable explain what is inside and identify the type of insulation covering. Consider the following designation:

14/2 WITH GROUND, TYPE NMC, 600V (UL).

The first number tells the size of the wires inside the insulation or cable, in this case No. 14 gauge. The second number tells you that there are two conductors (wires) in the cable. There also is an equipment grounding wire, as indicated. The type of cable is given; the number following indicates the maximum voltage allowed through the cable.

Finally, the UL notation assures you that the cable has been rated as safe for the uses for which it was designed. The National Electrical Code requires that wires of types NM and NMC have a rating of 90 degrees Centigrade (194 degrees Fahrenheit).

ESTIMATING WIRE NEEDS
To estimate the amount of wire or cable you will need for a project, measure the distance between the new outlet and the power source.

Add an extra foot for every connection you will make. Then, to provide a margin for error, add 20 percent to this figure.

For example, if you measure 12 feet between a new and existing receptacle, add another 2 feet for the two connections, making a total of 14 feet. Then add 20 percent (about 3 feet) to the total. To do the job, start working with 17 feet of cable. The same formula is used for wire, with the exception of lamp/appliance cord.

HOW TO STRIP OFF WIRE INSULATION

You can use a jackknife, but an inexpensive wire stripper is a better tool to remove the insulation from wires. First cut the wire to the right length. About ¾ inch of insulation should be stripped off the wire for the best terminal connection.

STEP 1
MATCH WIRE TO STRIPPER

Put the wire in the hole in the handle that matches the wire size. For lamp wire, the hole will be No. 18 or No. 16.

STEP 2
ROTATE THE STRIPPER

Lightly grip the handles of the stripper in a closed position with the wire inserted in the correct hole. Then rotate the stripper around the wire a couple of times.

STEP 3
PULL OFF INSULATION

With the handles still closed, pull the wire out of the stripper. The handles will grip the insulation and the pulling action will strip it off.

STRIPPING BY KNIFE

If you use a jackknife or utility knife to remove the insulation, be very careful to cut only the insulation and not nick the wire with the blade. Go completely around the insulation with the cut. Then pull off the insulation with your fingers.

STRIPPING CABLE INSULATION

You can buy a stripping tool to slice the insulation on cable. Once stripped, the insulation then has to be trimmed with a knife or scissors.

You can also use a jackknife or utility knife (as illustrated) to make the first stripping cut. Be extremely careful that you do not cut the insulation on the wires inside the cable as you slice the outside insulation covering.

For most connections, you will need to strip back the outer insulation about 3 to 4 inches.

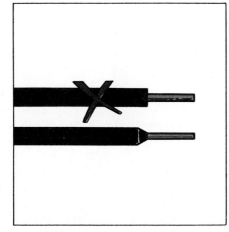

Cut insulation this way. Insulation cut should be tapered, not square, if possible. Some wire strippers provide tapered cut.

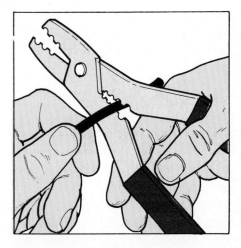

Match wire to stripper. Match the wire to the numbered hole in the handle of the wire stripper. Insert the wire in this hole; grip handles.

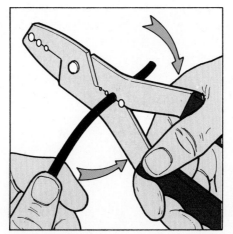

Rotate the stripper. With the wire in the right hole, lightly grip the stripper and rotate the stripper completely around the wire.

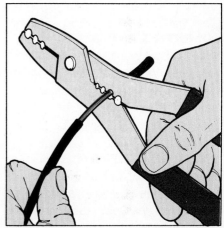

Pull off insulation. Keep the handles closed after the insulation is cut through. Then pull the wire out of the tool to strip off insulation.

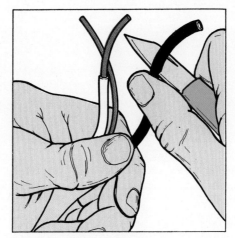

Stripping by knife. Be careful not to cut or nick the wire. A glove or thumb protector is a wise precaution against cuts.

Stripping cable. Cable stripper or knife removes outer insulation from cable. Do not cut wire insulation in cables as you strip cut it.

MAKING WIRE SPLICES

According to the code, all wire splices must be enclosed in a switch, outlet, fixture, or junction box.

STRANDED WIRES

Strip off about ¾ inch of insulation. With your fingers, twist each wire individually so the strands are tightly together. Then, with your fingers, twist the two wires together.

SOLID TO STRANDED WIRE

Strip off about ¾ inch of insulation from both wires. Twist the stranded wire tight; then wrap it around the solid wire with your fingers. Then, with pliers, bend over the solid wire to secure the stranded wire to the solid wire.

SOLID TO SOLID WIRE

Strip off about ¾ inch of insulation from both wires. With pliers, spiral one piece of solid wire around the other piece, making the twist fairly tight, but not tight enough to break the wire.

TWIST ON WIRE NUT

Pick a Wire Nut® that fits the splice. Insert the wires into the wire nut with a slight twisting motion. Don't apply too much downward pressure on stranded wire splices; if you do, the wire will buckle and flatten. Just screw the nut onto the splice.

X-RAY VIEW OF THE SPLICE

After the wire nut is in place, it should *completely* cover the splice with a tad of wire insulation seated in the opening of the wire nut.

WRAP THE SPLICE

When you're satisfied that the splice is tight and securely covered in the wire nut, wrap the wire nut and an inch or so of the projecting wires with plastic electrician's tape. The tape is a safety measure that helps to make a stronger splice. However, do not rely on the tape to hold the splice together. If the splice is not tight and covered by the wire nut, remove the splice and start again.

Stranded wires. Twist stripped stranded wire with fingers, making a tight wire. Then twist the wires together as tight as you can.

Solid to stranded wire. Wrap stranded wire around solid wire, using the solid wire as a base. Then bend over solid wire to lock the splice.

Solid to solid wire. Twist solid wires together tightly with pliers. Do not overtighten the spiraled wires or you will crack or break them.

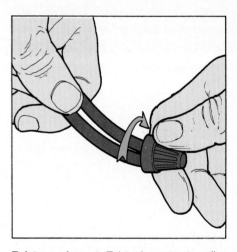

Twist on wire nut. Twist wire nut onto splice rather than twisting splice into the wire nut. If splice is too long for nut, trim the wires.

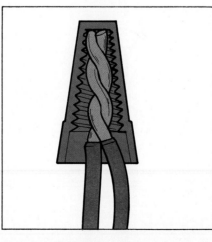

X-ray view of the splice. Here's how splice looks in wire nut. The splice should be completely covered and tight with insulation in flange of nut.

Wrap the splice. To strengthen the splice and nut, wrap the nut with plastic electrician's tape. One spiraled layer of tape is plenty.

WORKING WITH ALUMINUM WIRE

Most wire that you buy will be copper or copper-clad aluminum wire. You may discover, however, that your home has been wired with solid aluminum and, unless you decide to completely rewire with copper, you will have to work with aluminum wire.

Aluminum wire used to cause problems when it was used in switches, outlets, and fixtures that had not been designed for the characteristics of aluminum wire. The wire tends to come loose by expanding and contracting at terminals. Loose wires can cause electric arcing, which can produce electrical fires.

The industry has solved part of the problem with switches, outlets, fixtures, and equipment made especially for use with either aluminum or copper wire. The products are plainly marked with the letters CO/ALR.

WIRING PROCEDURES

Extra effort must be made when connecting aluminum wire to terminals, as described here. It's also a smart idea to apply the same rules to copper wire when connecting it.

STRIP, LOOP, AND HOOK

Remove about ¾ inch of insulation from the wire. Use wire strippers, if possible. Loop the end of the bare wire with needlenose pliers. Just grip the wire in the jaws of the pliers and wrap it around the jaws, which are rounded. This automatically forms the loop of the size that is required for terminals. Then place the loop around the terminal screw with its opening to the right.

TIGHTEN THE TERMINAL

When the loop is in place, tighten the terminal screw so the screw and contact plate make full contact with the wire.

GIVE IT ANOTHER HALF TURN

When the wire is snug under the terminal screw, give the terminal screw another half turn.

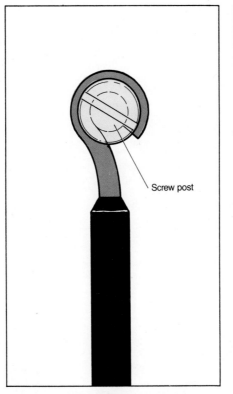

Strip, loop, and hook. Remove insulation from wire and twist end into a loop; hook the loop around the terminal with the opening to the right.

Tighten the terminal. Tighten the screw, making sure that the wire is in full contact with the screw and contact plate. Screw must be tight.

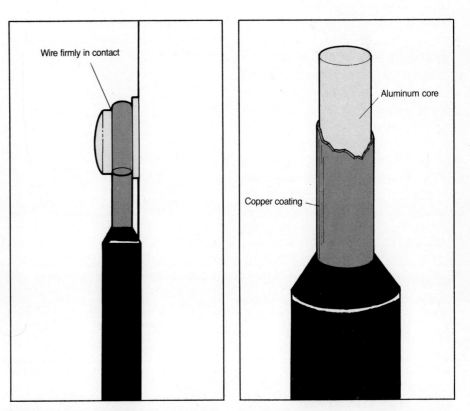

Give it another ½ turn. Give the screw another half turn after you have initially tightened it. But don't strip slot or threads with too much force.

Copper-clad aluminum. Anatomy of copper-clad aluminum wire shows how a copper plating is added to the wire to make the wire safer.

Working with Cable

WORKING WITH FLEXIBLE CLAD CABLE (BX)

Armor-clad cable, commonly called BX, a trade name, has an outer wrapper of galvanized steel; the cable contains two or three wires. Each wire is individually wrapped in insulation and then with paper. The cable must contain an internal bonding strip that is in intimate contact with the armor for its entire length. Your local code may limit or prohibit the use of BX cable. BX is specified for use in dry locations only.

CUTTING THE ARMOR

Use a hacksaw to cut the flexible steel wrapper about 8 inches from the end.

Make the cut diagonally across one of the metal ribs, and stop sawing just as soon as the blade cuts through the metal. Do not cut any deeper or you will damage the wires inside the wrapper.

Then, with your fingers, bend the cable back and forth until the metal snaps apart. Slide the armor off the cable.

REMOVE THE INSULATION

Unwind the paper insulation around the wires inside the cable and cut the paper with a knife or scissors. Then remove the plastic insulation. The amount of insulation to be removed depends on what you plan to do with the ends of the wires. For terminals, strip off about ½ to ¾ inch. For splicing, strip ¾ inch. For push-in terminals, use the stripping gauge on the back of the switch or receptacle.

INSERT THE BUSHING

Slip a plastic bushing made for this cable around the wires and into the cut cable opening. The bonding strip goes outside the bushing, between the bushing and cable.

CONNECT THE STRIP

The bonding strip is sometimes fastened to the cable connector screw.

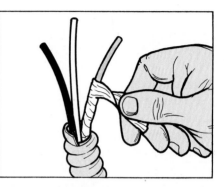

Cutting the armor. Saw diagonally across the cable using a hacksaw. When blade has almost cut through steel, bend cable over to break it.

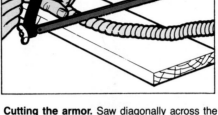

Removing the insulation. Remove the paper wrapping to expose wires inside cable. Then strip wire insulation for connections you'll make.

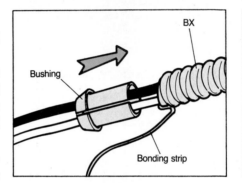

Inserting the bushing. Insert plastic bushing in end of cable around wires with bonding strip positioned between bushing and armored cable.

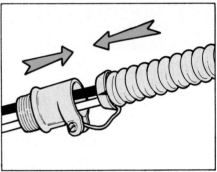

Connecting the strip. Bonding strip is connected to screw tightener on cable connector. Strip is a grounding device for the cable circuit.

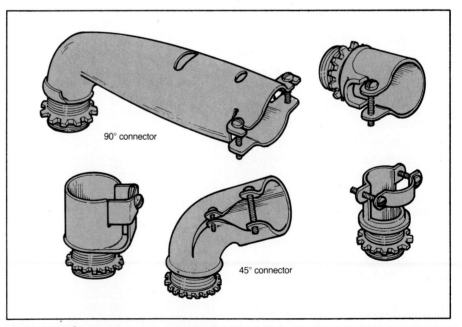

Types of flexible armored cable connectors. Different types of armored cable connectors are shown here. Some connectors have tiny view slots so electrical inspectors can see that bushings have been installed without disassembling entire connection. You can buy 90- and 45-degree connectors.

WORKING WITH CONDUIT

Codes specify the use of conduit and the kind of wiring method that may be used. Conduit is easiest to use if the wall surface is removed and the studs or framing exposed. The conduit is then fitted and fastened into or onto the framing members.

There are three types of metal conduit: rigid, intermediate, and EMT (electrical metal tubing) or thinwall. Some codes also permit plastic conduit. You buy conduit usually in 10-foot lengths and cut it to size. The wires are pulled through during installation; conduit is not sold with wires installed.

CONNECTORS

You can buy a selection of conduit connectors: straight, elbows, right- and left-handed elbows; LB fittings, C Body, T Body, and corner elbows are for outdoor use.

CUTTING WITH PIPE CUTTER

Metal (and plastic) conduit is best cut with a pipe or tubing cutter. The shoulders of the cutter keep the pipe square in the device and ensure a square cut across the conduit. Deburring is minimized.

CUTTING WITH A HACKSAW

Conduit also can be cut to size with a hacksaw. Keep the cut as square as possible. To reduce burring, wrap the cut-line with masking tape; run the saw through it.

DEBURR THE CUT

If the pipe cutter or hacksaw leaves burrs on the metal conduit, remove the burrs with a fine-toothed metal file. Use sandpaper to deburr plastic.

BENDING CONDUIT

Plastic conduit is flexible enough to be bent slightly. Metal conduit has to be shaped with a conduit bender, known as a hickey. Slip the conduit through the hickey clamp attachment. Put the conduit on the ground and your foot on the conduit. Pull the handle of the hickey toward you.

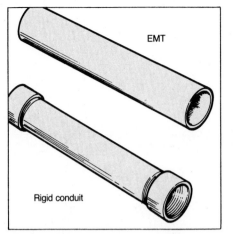

Metal conduit. Rigid conduit commonly has threaded ends. EMT and intermediate (not shown) are smooth for slip-on fittings.

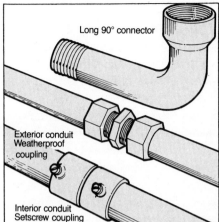

Connectors. Connections for conduit include straight couplings and elbow joints. There also is a big selection of outdoor connectors.

Cutting with pipe cutter. Pipe cutter is best tool for cutting metal and plastic conduit to length. Lock conduit into cutter and then twist cutter.

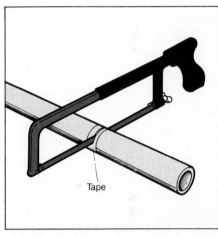

Cutting with hacksaw. You can use a hacksaw to cut conduit. Saw leaves burrs on metal or plastic. Reduce burring by sawing through tape.

Deburr with metal file. Deburr metal with a fine-tooth metal file. Use the file lightly. Use medium-grit abrasive paper for any burrs on plastic.

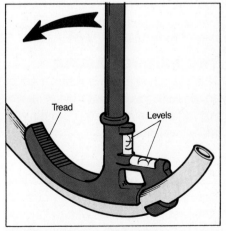

Bending conduit. Conduit bender or hickey is used to bend metal conduit. Put conduit in hickey and pull the handle toward you.

WORKING WITH NONMETALLIC CABLE

You probably will buy and work with nonmetallic plastic-sheathed cable more than any other conductor or wire. It is often called by its trade name, Romex, which has almost become synonymous with any nonmetallic electrical cable. Local codes may allow nonmetallic cable only in certain locations, or may specify that you use another type, such as metallic armored cable, or wires running in conduit.

The outer sheath of nonmetallic cable is usually a moisture-resistant, flame-retardant material. Inside, there are two or three insulated power wires, and perhaps a grounding wire.

For most residential wiring, two types of nonmetallic cable are often used. They will be labeled Type NM or Type NMC on the package or the cable.

Type NM may be used in dry locations and be either concealed or exposed. Type NMC meets the same requirements as NM, but it also is fungus- and corrosion-resistant. It may be used in moist, damp, and corrosive locations; it may be used in hollows of brick and concrete blocks used in building.

Both types contain either copper wire in gauges 14 through 2, or aluminum or copper-clad aluminum in gauges 12 through 2.

TWO-WIRE/BARE GROUND

The cable has a hot wire in black insulation, a neutral wire in white insulation, and a grounding wire, which is bare—no insulation.

TWO-WIRE/NO GROUND

This cable has just two wires: a hot or power wire covered with black insulation and a neutral wire covered with white insulation.

THREE-WIRE/NO GROUND

This old-style cable has one hot wire covered with black insulation and another hot wire covered with red insulation; the neutral wire has white insulation. A three-wire cable is used to connect three-way switches.

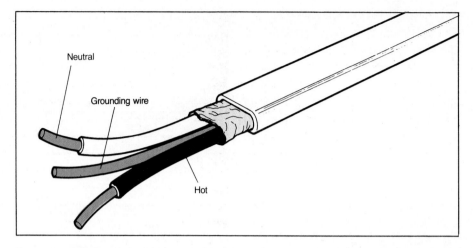

Two-wire cable with bare-wire ground. Two-wire nonmetallic cable with bare grounding wire has a hot or power wire encased in black insulation. The so-called neutral wire has white insulation; the grounding wire is uninsulated. This cable is commonly specified for residential wiring.

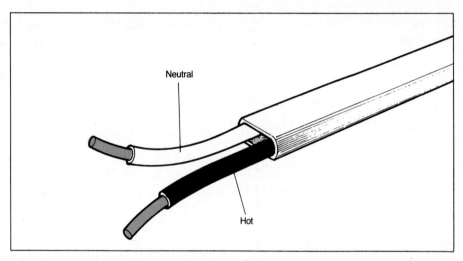

Two-wire cable with no grounding wire. Two-wire nonmetallic cable with no grounding wire has a hot wire in black insulation and a neutral wire in white insulation. Wires in cable are color-coded so they are not mixed when hooking up fixtures along a circuit's entire run. Color matches terminals.

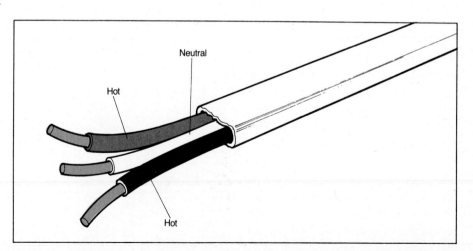

Three-wire cable with no grounding wire. Three-wire nonmetallic cable without a grounding wire has a black-insulated hot wire, a white-insulated neutral wire, and a red-insulated wire that is considered a hot wire. In three-way switch hookups, the red wire becomes the hot switch wire.

TWO-WIRE/CODED GROUND

In this cable, the grounding wire is insulated and often color-coded green or green and yellow stripes. The other color codes are the same: black for hot wires, white for neutral.

THREE-WIRE/GROUND

This cable is commonly used for house circuits in which a grounding wire runs through the complete circuit. The grounding wire may be hooked to a clip or terminal in an outlet box, or it may be connected by a pigtail—a short length of wire—to a grounding terminal in the box or on a receptacle.

TYPE UF CABLE

Type UF cable can be used for interior wiring in wet or corrosive locations where type NM cannot be used. It looks the same as other types of nonmetallic cables but is marked with the letters UF on the package or insulation.

Like type UF, type USE cable may be buried underground. It is often used for underground service entrances to buildings.

CABLE WIRE SIZES

It is recommended that all new residential circuits use No. 12 gauge wire. No. 14 gauge wire may be added to an existing circuit of No. 14 wire.

In the store, you will find cable packages and the cable itself marked with the wire size, followed by the number of wires inside the cable sheath. Check the markings carefully so you buy exactly what you need.

For example, a cable with two No. 12 wires will be marked "12/2." If there is also a grounding wire, it will be marked "12/2 with Ground." The first cable has two insulated wires, black and another color. The second has those wires and the ground wire either bare, or insulated in green or green and yellow.

Wire gauge Nos. 8–14 designate single wires. Nos. 6–2 are multiple wires held together by the insulation. Nos. 16 and 18 contain multiple strands twisted or braided together.

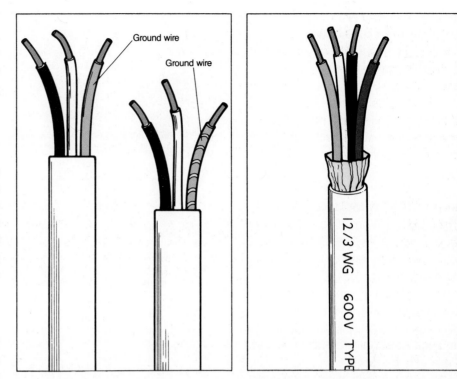

Two-wire/coded ground. Two-wire cable with insulated ground wires may be color-coded with solid green or green and yellow stripes.

Three-wire/ground. Cable for three-way switches has a black-insulated power wire, white neutral wire, red switch wire, bare or green ground wire.

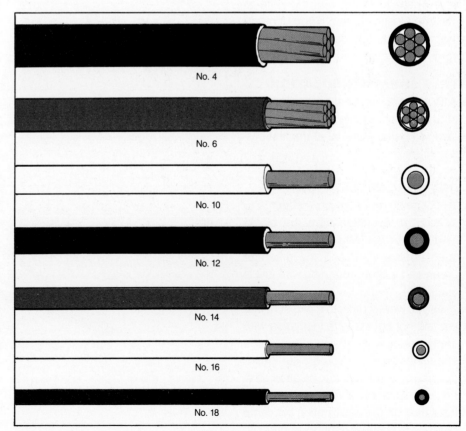

Cable wire sizes. Wire gauge numbers indicate conductor sizes; the smaller the number, the larger the wire. Nos. 4 through 8 have multiple wires and use special connectors (see page 35). No. 16 and 18 wires are used only on fixtures or as extension cords, never for installed circuit wiring.

WORKING WITH NONMETALLIC CABLE

To prepare nonmetallic or plastic-sheathed cable for installation, you need a sharp utility knife, a wire stripper, and a cable ripper. You can cut the cable with a knife, but a ripper is better in many cases because it protects the insulated wires within the cable sheathing.

CUT SHEATH INSULATION

Place the cable on a flat surface, such as a workbench. Measure about 8 inches from the end of the cable and make a mark.

Then insert the cable in a cable ripper at the marked point. Press the cable ripper together with your fingers and pull the cable through the ripper to the end of the cable.

If you use a knife instead of a ripper, start cutting the sheath at the mark. Run the knife down the sheath, being extremely careful not to cut the insulated wires inside the cable. It may take several shallow cuts with the knife to part the plastic sheath. If you damage the wire, cut that part off and start again.

TRIM SHEATH INSULATION

With your fingers, peel back the sheath and then use a knife to trim away the excess sheath material at the first cutting mark.

CUT WIRE INSULATION

With wire strippers, remove about ½ to ¾ inch of insulation from the black-insulated power wire, the white-insulated neutral wire, and the green or green and yellow grounding wire (if it is insulated).

As you work, check to make sure that you did not cut the wire insulation with the ripper or knife as you removed the sheath insulation. If you did cut the insulation on the wires, trim off all wires at the cutting mark and start over. The insulation on the wires inside the cable must be completely sound in order to prevent hazards, such as an electrical short circuit or, worse, an electrical fire.

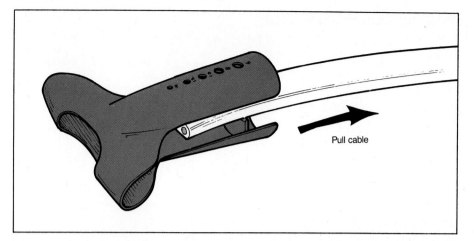

Pull cable

Cut the sheath insulation. Cable ripper makes a clean cut in the outer sheath of nonmetallic electrical cable. Slip the wire into the ripper at the cut-off mark—about 8 inches from the end—and grip the ripper firmly. Then pull the cable through the ripper to make the proper cut.

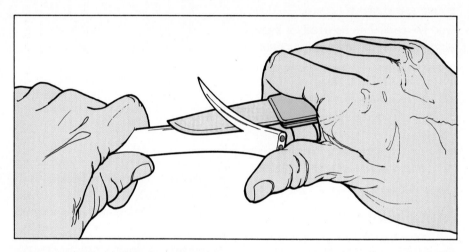

Trim and remove the sheath insulation. Remove excess sheath insulation with a sharp utility knife or jackknife. Trim it flush with the cutoff mark that you made on the cable. Don't nick the inside wire insulation. With a knife, it is wise to wear a glove or thumb protector to avoid cuts.

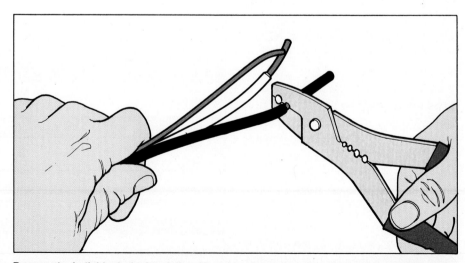

Remove the individual wire insulation. Use wire strippers to remove the insulation from the wires inside the cable. If you have accidently cut this insulation with the ripper or knife, trim the wire at the cut-off mark and start the process over again. Damaged insulation can cause electrical hazards.

WIRE (CABLE) CONNECTORS

Cable, or more specifically the wires inside the cable sheathing, may be connected in several ways: with wire nuts, crimped connectors, split-bolt connectors, and solder.

The code specifies that all connections (splices) must be made inside a box.

WIRE-NUT CONNECTORS

Wire nuts or solderless connectors (discussed on page 28) are sized according to the size of the wires to be spliced. They are widely used and are code-approved.

CRIMPED CONNECTORS

These fasteners are similar to wire nuts, but they sometimes are not permitted by code in local areas. Check your local code.

To use crimped connectors, strip about ½ to ¾ inch of insulation off the wires to be connected. Twist the wires together with pliers so the joint is well wrapped and tight. Then insert the wire ends in the connector and crimp the end of the connector with a tool made especially for this job.

SPLIT-BOLT CONNECTORS

Split-bolt connectors are available in assorted sizes to correspond with wire sizes. Split-bolt connectors are basically designed to be used with the larger wire sizes—from No. 6 gauge and larger.

Strip about ½ to ¾ inch insulation off the wires to be joined. Thread the wires into the connector loop and tighten the nut with pliers or an adjustable wrench or nut driver. Then wrap the splice with several layers of plastic electrician's tape.

SOLDER CONNECTIONS

You may solder wires together for a strong, tight splice. It is time-consuming to do so, however.

Use only *rosin-core* solder to create the soldered splice. Wrap the splice with electrician's tape to match wire insulation.

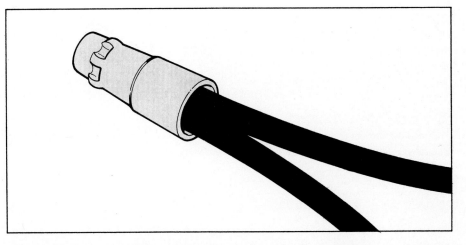

Crimped connectors are similar to wire nuts. Crimped connectors work like wire nuts, except that the connector ends are crimped with a special tool after the wires are inserted into the connector. This connector may be prohibited by code in your area. Check codes before use.

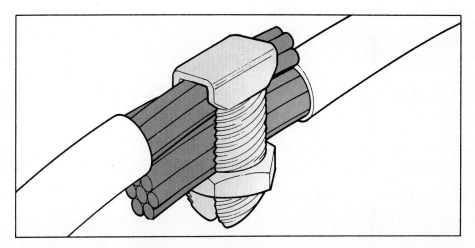

Split-bolt connectors are used for large wires. Split-bolt connectors are used mainly for large wires. The wire ends are stripped and then slipped into the connector. A nut on the connector compresses the wires, making a very strong splice. Wrap the splice with plastic electrician's tape.

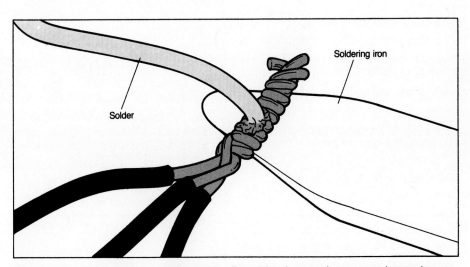

Solder

Soldering iron

Solder connections using rosin-core solder. For soldered connections, use rosin-core (noncorrosive) solder. Lay the wires on the soldering gun (iron), let the wires heat, and then apply the solder to the splice. Wrap the splice with plastic electrician's tape to the thickness of the wire insulation.

3 Switches and Outlets

A switch controls the flow of power in an electrical circuit. When the switch is on, electricity flows through the circuit from its source to a point of use.

TYPES OF SWITCHES

Most residential switches are toggle types, also called *snap switches*. Others include dimmer, pilot-light, time-clock, and silent switches.

SINGLE-POLE SWITCHES

A switch with two terminals is called a single-pole switch; it alone controls the circuit. The incoming hot wire is hooked to one terminal screw, and the outgoing hot wire is connected to the other screw.

THREE-WAY SWITCHES

A switch with three terminal screws is called a three-way switch. One terminal is marked COM, or "common"; the hot wire is connected to this terminal. The other terminals are switch leads. Two three-way switches are used to control a circuit from two places.

DOUBLE-POLE SWITCHES

A double-pole switch has four terminals. It is normally used to control 240-volt appliances. A four-way switch also has four terminals. Three four-way switches are used in a circuit to control one outlet or fixture from three separate places. Both switches look the same,

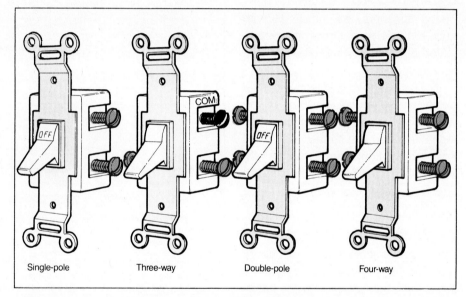

Single-pole   Three-way   Double-pole   Four-way

Common types of switches include this basic selection for residential housing. Note the difference between four-way and double-pole, which has OFF/ON stamped on the toggle.

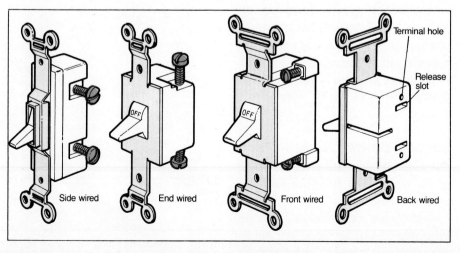

Side wired   End wired   Front wired   Back wired

Switches come with different terminal positions for wiring convenience. All those shown here are single-pole. Back-wired switches have terminal holes instead of screws.

but only a double-pole switch has ON-OFF markings.

HOW TO READ SWITCHES BEFORE YOU BUY THEM

Switches are stamped with code letters and numbers. Learn how to read these codes so you buy the right products. Here's what the codes on the switch at right mean:

UL means that the switch is listed by Underwriters Laboratories, a testing organization (see UL Listed, page 13). AC ONLY means that the switch will handle only alternating current. CO/ALR is a wire code indicating that the switch will handle copper, copper-clad, and aluminum wire. 15A–120V means that the switch will handle 15 amperes and 120 volts of power. A new switch must have the same amp and volt rating as the switch it replaces.

REMOVING SWITCH PLATES

If you have trouble removing an old switch or outlet cover plate, try cutting around the edge of the cover with the tip of a utility knife.

HOW TO TEST A SWITCH

When you flip a switch and the circuit doesn't work, the fault may not be in the switch. It could be in the fixture or a fuse. After checking the fuse (see page 20), test the switch, using this procedure:

1. Remove the fuse or set the breaker in the switch circuit to OFF.

2. Remove switch plate. Touch voltage tester probes to black and white wire terminals to check power is off.

3. Turn switch ON. Touch continuity tester probe and clip to the terminals. Tester should light with good switch.

4. Turn switch OFF. Touch terminals with probe and clip. Continuity tester should *not* light with good switch.

5. Fasten tester clip to switch mounting strap. Touch probe to one terminal, then the other, and flip switch ON and OFF each time. Tester should not light in any position. If the switch fails any of the tests, replace it as explained on the next pages.

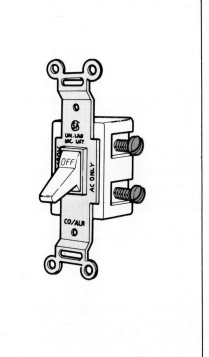

Reading the switch. Codes are stamped on switches so you know which one to buy for a project. How to read code is explained at the left.

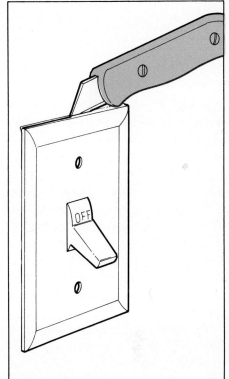

Removing switch plates. Paint-sealed switch/outlet plates are easy to remove. Slice the paint seal with the point of a utility knife; then remove the screws.

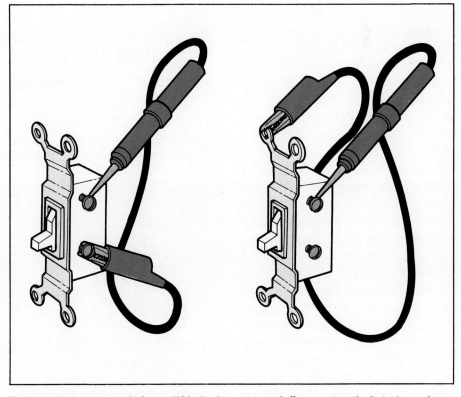

Testing switches: two techniques. With circuit power turned off, connect continuity tester as shown at left. Tester should light with switch ON, not light with switch OFF. When connected as at right, tester should not light with switch either ON or OFF with probe at either terminal.

Working with Single-Pole Switches

It is not difficult to replace or add a single-pole switch. The process may vary slightly, depending on your house wiring and whether the switch is grounded or not. A grounded switch has an extra terminal screw at the base that is green or shows the letters GR. This redundant grounding system is more reliable than systems that don't connect the ground to the switch. If wires are encased in metal conduit, the conduit is usually grounded, but not always.

When replacing a switch or adding a new one, buy switches with a ground-terminal screw, even though it may be necessary to modify your wiring, as explained in this section. Detach only those wires that are connected to the switch itself.

CONNECTING WIRES

Connect wires to terminals by looping the end around the terminal screw in the direction the screw tightens. This is usually clockwise.

The best way to form a loop in the wire for terminal screws is with needlenose pliers. Strip about ½ to ¾ inch of insulation off the wire end of the wire and bend the bare wire around the jaws of the pliers, forming a perfect loop. Then hook the loop onto the terminals in the direction the screws turn down, and tighten the screws. As the terminals are tightened, the wire is forced under the screw heads and clamped.

REMOVING OUTLET TABS

To install a receptacle with the lower outlet functioning as an "always on" outlet but the upper outlet controlled by a switch, you must break off the metal link between the terminal screws. Use a screwdriver to pry the link up, then break it off with pliers.

Connect the incoming hot (black) power wire and one switch wire to the

lower outlet terminal. Connect the white wire and the other switch wire to the upper outlet terminal.

SINGLE-POLE TO LIGHT

The easiest switch/light wiring hookup is probably a single-pole switch controlling a light fixture. Follow these procedures:

1. Turn off the power at the main service entrance when you work. If the circuit is a new one, run the wire from the service panel to the switch and light, but do not connect it to the panel. Have a licensed electrician do this.

2. Cut the wire at the switch.

3. Strip off about ½ to ¾ inch of wire insulation on each end of the wire. Use wire strippers to avoid cutting the wire itself.

4. Connect the black wires to the terminals, hooking the wire loops around the terminals in the direction the screw tightens.

5. The white wire bypasses the switch completely.

6. Connect the grounding wires in the cable from the light and in the power cable to a pigtail (a short piece of wire of the same gauge) that is attached to the grounding terminal in the box. Use a wire nut.

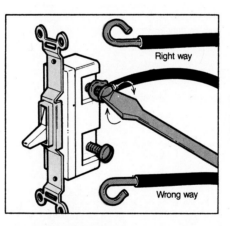

Connecting wires. Wire is looped around the terminal screws in the direction the screws turn downward.

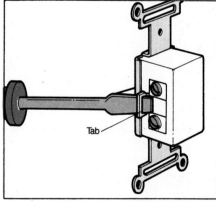

Removing outlet tabs. To make one half of a receptacle switch-operated, remove the side link. Text explains wiring.

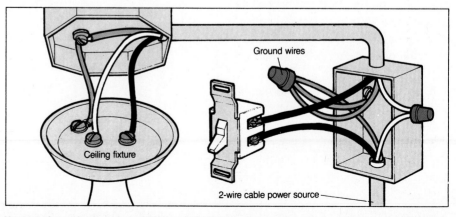

How to wire a single-pole switch to a light fixture. Single-pole switch controlling one light fixture with power coming from the switch is wired this way. White wire bypasses switch; ground connects to both metal boxes.

SINGLE-POLE SWITCH CONTROLS LIGHT, CONSTANT POWER TO OUTLET

In this single-pole connection the power is supplied by a two-wire cable with ground. A three-wire cable with ground goes to the light and a two-wire with cable ground to the outlet.

STEP 1
WIRING THE SWITCH

With a length of black-insulated wire pigtail (same gauge wire), connect the black power wire to the switch and then to the black wire in the three-wire with ground cable. Wrap the wire nut with electrician's tape. Now connect the white wire from the power source to the white wire in the three-wire cable. Use a wire nut and tape it. Connect the red wire in the three-wire cable to the open switch terminal. Finally, connect the cable grounding wires (green or bare) to a pigtail that is attached to the box ground terminal.

STEP 2
WIRING THE OUTLET

Connect the black wire to the brass terminal and the white wire to the silver terminal of the outlet, using the two-wire with ground cable. With a pigtail, splice the ground and connect it to the box and the outlet ground terminal.

STEP 3
WIRING THE CEILING BOX

Connect the black wire from the switch to the black wire from the outlet. Add a wire nut; tape. Connect the grounding from the switch box cable to pigtails from the receptacle ground terminal and the box ground terminal.

STEP 4
WIRING THE LIGHT FIXTURE

Connect the red wire from the switch to the black light wire, if the light is pre-wired. If it is not, then connect the red wire to the brass-colored light terminal. The white wire is spliced to the light's white wire or connected to the light-colored terminal on the light.

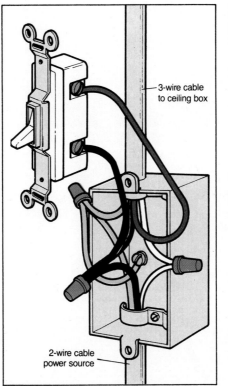

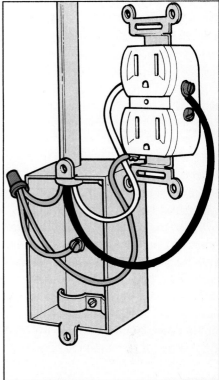

Wiring the switch. Connect black power wire to black wire in three-wire cable; white wire to white wire, red wire to the brass switch terminal.

Wiring the outlet. Black wire goes to brass terminal on outlet; white wire goes to silver terminal. Ground goes to terminal and box.

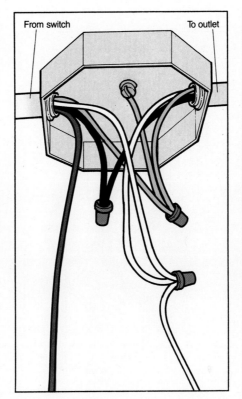

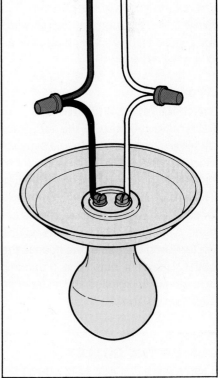

Wiring the ceiling box. Splice red wire to black wire of lamp or to brass terminal. Black wire goes through box to outlet; white to light/outlet.

Wiring the light fixture. Red wire to black light wire, if prewired; if not, to brass light terminal. White to white. Wire nut, tape any splices.

SINGLE-POLE SWITCH CONTROLS LIGHT, OUTLET; POWER THROUGH FIXTURE

In this hookup, power runs through the light fixture to a switch and then to an outlet. This circuit requires three-wire cable with ground and two-wire cable with ground, plus pigtail wire.

STEP 1
WIRING THE CEILING BOX

Power is supplied by a two-wire cable with ground into the box at the light.

Splice the black wire from the power source to the red wire of the three-wire cable. Splice the white wire to the white wire of the three-wire cable, and hook the black wire to the black wire of the light fixture. Also splice the white wire of the power source cable to the light. Use wire nuts and tape the nuts.

STEP 2
WIRING THE LIGHT FIXTURE

The black wire connected to the red wire of the three-wire cable is fastened to the brass terminal of the light. The white wire, connected to the power source and the white wire of the three-wire cable, is fastened to the silver terminal of the light fixture. Or the wires are spliced to the white and black wires of a prewired light.

STEP 3
WIRING THE SWITCH

Fasten the red wire to the top brass terminal of the switch. Make a pigtail of black-insulated wire and connect it to the bottom brass terminal of the switch. Then connect the pigtail to the black wires in the fixture and receptacle cables. Connect the white wire to the white wire in the cable that goes to the outlet. Use wire nuts. The grounding wire (green) is pigtailed and fastened to each box as shown.

STEP 4
WIRING THE OUTLET

Fasten the black wire to the brass terminal and the white wire to the silver terminal. Break the tab if half of the outlet will be switch-operated. Connect the ground with a pigtail to the box.

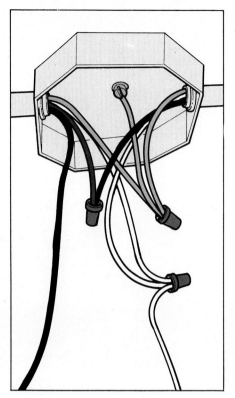

Wiring the ceiling box. The two-wire power cable connects to the three-wire cable from the light to switch. Splice black to red; pigtail the ground wire.

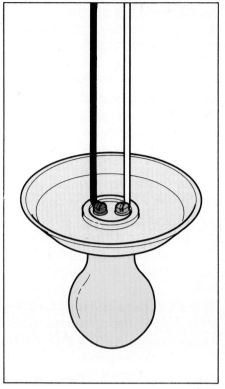

Wiring the light fixture. Connect the black wire to the brass light terminal and the white wire to the silver or light-colored light terminal.

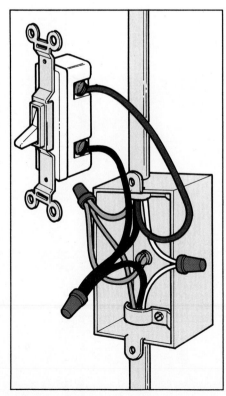

Wiring the switch. At switch, red hooks to top terminal and black to bottom terminal. White bypasses switch; ground is connected.

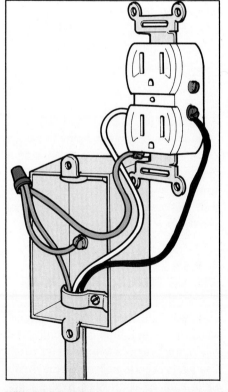

Wiring the outlet. Black to brass terminal; white to silver at the outlet. Break metal tab on outlet if half will be switch-operated.

SINGLE-POLE SWITCH CONTROLS OUTLET ONLY

If you're operating a light or other device from an outlet and want to control it with a switch, here is how to wire it.

Use two-wire cable with ground throughout. *Turn off the power before starting to work.*

STEP 1
AT THE OUTLET

Connect the incoming white wire from the power source to the silver terminal on the outlet. Connect the outgoing black wire to the bottom brass-colored terminal on the outlet. Then connect the incoming black wire to the outgoing white wire. Mark the white wire HOT by taping the insulation with a few wraps of black electrician's tape. The ground wire is pigtailed to the metal box, to the outlet grounding screw, and to the outgoing ground valve. Twist wire nuts around all splices and wrap the joints with electrician's tape.

STEP 2
AT THE SWITCH

Connect the white wire to the top brass-colored terminal. Then wrap this white wire with electrician's tape to indicate a hot wire. Connect the black wire to the other switch terminal. Fasten the ground wire to the junction box. If the switch has a ground terminal, pigtail the ground wire and connect it both at the box and the switch grounding terminal.

GENERAL PROCEDURE

To make terminal connections, you will need approximately 6 inches of wire in the box to make the connections easily. Strip about ½ to ¾ inch of insulation from the ends of the wires without nicking the metal conductor. Use a pair of needlenose pliers to bend each wire end into a hook that goes around the terminal screw with the opening to the right. Tighten each screw firmly to secure its wire. Fold the extra wire accordionwise as you place the switch or receptacle in its box. The wire is stiff, but use your fingers, not pliers, to avoid damaging it.

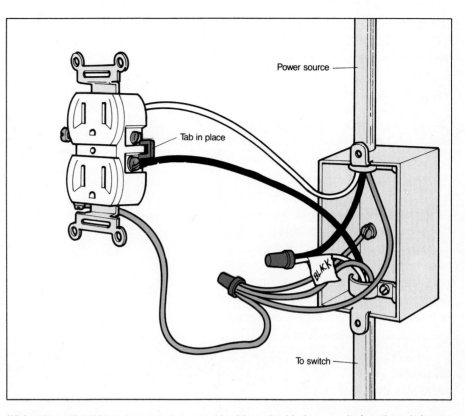

Wiring the outlet. White wire connects to one side of the outlet; black power wire from the switch goes to the other side of the outlet.

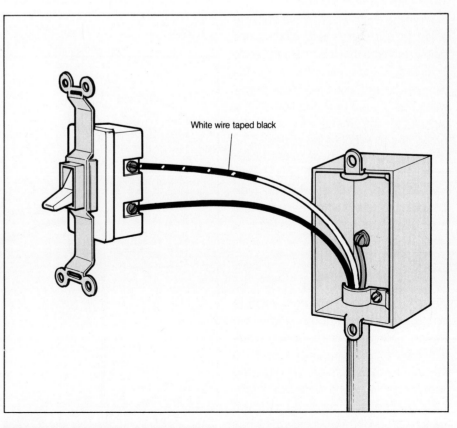

Wiring the switch. White wire taped black is power wire. Black wire also is power wire. Power bypasses outlet to the switch control.

SINGLE-POLE SWITCH CONTROLLING SPLIT OUTLET WITH POWER THROUGH OUTLET

Use this hookup when you want a single-pole switch to control half of an outlet with the other half of the outlet (bottom) hot at all times. This installation might be in a living or family room where you want to control table lamps along a circuit with a switch, but want other outlets hot at all times.

A two-wire with ground cable is used throughout this circuit with the power coming through the outlet. If this project involves a new circuit, make all the wiring/outlet/switch hookups and then let a professional electrician connect the circuit to the power supply.

STEP 1
WIRING THE OUTLET

Turn off the power before doing any work on the circuit.

The black wire, using a pigtail, is connected from the power source to the bottom brass terminal of the outlet. The white wire is connected to the upper silver terminal of the outlet.

Wrap the white wire running from the outlet to the switch with electrician's tape to indicate that it is now a hot wire. This wire is then spliced to the black wire pigtail and incoming black power wire. The ground is connected, with a pigtail, to the metal box and the grounding terminal of the outlet.

Use a screwdriver or pliers to remove the tab between the brass terminals of the outlet. The switch will then control the upper half of the outlet and the bottom half will always be hot.

STEP 2
WIRING THE SWITCH

The black power wire is connected to one brass terminal of the single-pole switch. The white wire, coded black with electrician's tape, is connected to the other brass terminal. The ground wire is screwed to the metal box. It may be pigtailed and connected to the switch ground terminal if the switch has a ground terminal.

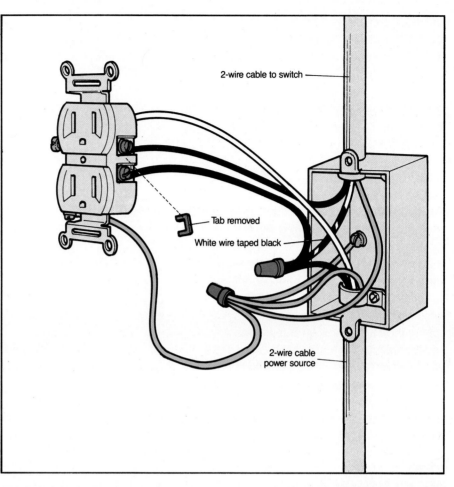

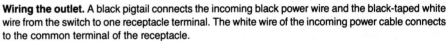
Wiring the outlet. A black pigtail connects the incoming black power wire and the black-taped white wire from the switch to one receptacle terminal. The white wire of the incoming power cable connects to the common terminal of the receptacle.

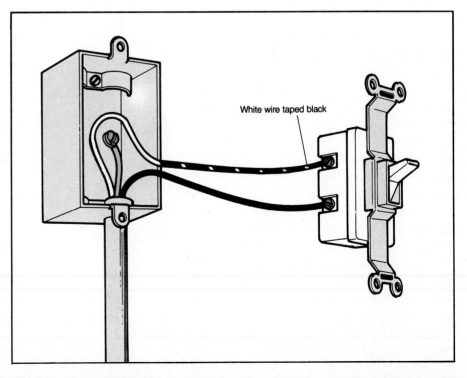
Wiring the switch. Black wire to switch; white wire wrapped black to switch. Ground wire to box and switch if it has a ground terminal.

Adding or Replacing Three-Way Switches

Three-way switches control the power to a light or other electrical device from two separate points. An example is a light in a hallway that can be operated from both the first floor and the second floor. Another example is a light in a garage that can be turned on/off from the garage and also from the kitchen or living room.

Three-way switches require a three-wire system: a power wire and two interconnecting wires called travellers. A fourth, grounding, wire is also required except with metal conduit. The proper cable is marked 12/3 WITH GROUND or 14/3 WITH GROUND.

Two three-way switches are also required. Each switch has three terminal screws on the side or back: two on one side, one on the other side. One terminal will be a distinctive color—often black—or will be marked COM, for common. This terminal is for the prime power wire, the black wire in a cable. The other two terminals are for so-called traveller wires that interconnect the switches. When a white wire is used as a traveller in a three-way switch hookup it must be marked with black tape because it too carries power.

CODE REQUIREMENTS

The NEC specifies that all wire must be spliced inside a switch, outlet, or junction box. If you splice wire outside the box and there is an electrical fire at this point, your fire insurance coverage could be void.

If you're simply replacing a switch—removing the old switch and installing a new switch—additional wire will not be necessary. In this situation, just connect the new switch to the same wires as the old switch.

You cannot add a three-way switch circuit using two-wire with ground cable.

To add a three-way switch circuit, you will need either (1) three-wire with ground nonmetallic or BX armored ca-ble, or (2) three wires (black, red, white) to pull through metal conduit. The conduit itself can act as a grounding wire.

HOW MUCH WIRE?

To figure how much wire you need, measure the distance between the new outlet and the power source. Add an extra foot for every connection you will make along the line. Then, to provide a margin for error, add 20 percent more. For example, if you measure 12 feet of cable between a new and existing receptacle, add another 2 feet for the two connections, making the total 14 feet. Then add 20 percent, about 3 feet to the total. To do this job you should buy 17 feet of cable.

As mentioned above, wire may not be spliced outside a box. Inside a box, the wire must be spliced together using a twisted wire splice covered by a wire nut and electrician's wire tape.

The wire may be attached to a fixture, switch, and outlet terminals. To make connections, pull the wire through boxes about 6 inches. Then cut the wire and strip the insulation from the end. This procedure is shown on page 27.

WIRING THREE-WAY SWITCHES

On the following pages, you will find wiring diagrams for three-way switches. By following the paths of individual wires carefully, you can make the connections properly.

Whether you are installing a new circuit or are adding three-way switches to an existing circuit, be sure to identify which wire brings the power into each switch box. It must go to the common terminal of the switch. This is the key to wiring the switches correctly.

When adding new circuits with three-way switches, you should install the wiring for the project and then have a professional electrician connect the circuit to the main service panel.

SOLVING THE PUZZLE

In wiring three-way switches you will use two-wire (black and white) and three-wire (black, white, red) cables with ground to make connections between two switches and one or more fixtures, all in individual boxes. Electricians use the procedure described here to make the work go faster:

1. Run lengths of cable from box to box in the circuit. Add enough to make the connections, as explained above.

2. If the power source cable comes into a switch box, connect its black wire to the common (COM) terminal of the switch there. If the power cable comes into the fixture box, connect its black wire to the black wire running to one of the switches, and connect that to the COM terminal.

3. The power cable white wire must connect to the silver terminal of the fixture. If the power comes into the fixture box, connect it directly. If it comes into a switch box, connect it to the white wire of the other cable there. Depending on the hookup, that may go to the fixture box, where you can connect it. If it goes to the other switch box, connect it to the white wire there that goes to the fixture.

4. Connect the COM terminal of the second switch to the black wire that goes to the fixture box, and there connect to the brass fixture terminal.

5. Two unconnected wires remain at each switch, red and black or red and white, depending on the layout. Connect these traveller wires to the two open terminals on each switch. If one wire is white, tape both ends black to mark it as a hot wire. If the travellers pass through the fixture box, connect them there: red to red, and black to black (or taped whites together).

6. Where there are two or more grounding wires, connect them with a pigtail to the ground terminal in the box. Where there is only one grounding wire, connect it to the box terminal.

ONE FIXTURE CONTROLLED BY TWO SWITCHES, POWER THROUGH A SWITCH BOX

In this circuit, the power cable comes into the first switch box. The path goes through the second switch, and on to the fixture.

To install this circuit, you will need three-wire cable with ground between the two switches, and two-wire cable with ground between the second switch and the fixture. Local codes may require the use of conduit, especially for an outdoor light.

Turn off the power to this circuit at the service panel before starting work.

STEP 1
WIRING NO. 1 SWITCH

Power enters the first switch box on a two-wire cable with ground. Hook the black or power wire to the common terminal on the switch. Connect the white wire to the white wire of the three-wire cable going to switch No. 2. Connect the red and black wires in the three-wire cable to the two lower terminals on switch No. 1. Connect the grounding wires in both cables to a pigtail connected to the box ground terminal.

STEP 2
WIRING SWITCH NO. 2

Connect the black and red wires in the three-wire cable from switch No. 1 to the two lower terminals of the switch. Connect the white wire to the white wire of the two-wire cable that goes to the light. Connect the black wire in the light cable to the common terminal of switch No. 2. Connect the cable grounding wires to a pigtail attached to the box.

STEP 3
WIRING THE FIXTURE

Connect the black wire in the two-wire cable from switch No. 2 to the black lead or brass terminal of the fixture. Connect the cable white wire to the white fixture lead or silver terminal. Connect the cable grounding wire to the box grounding terminal.

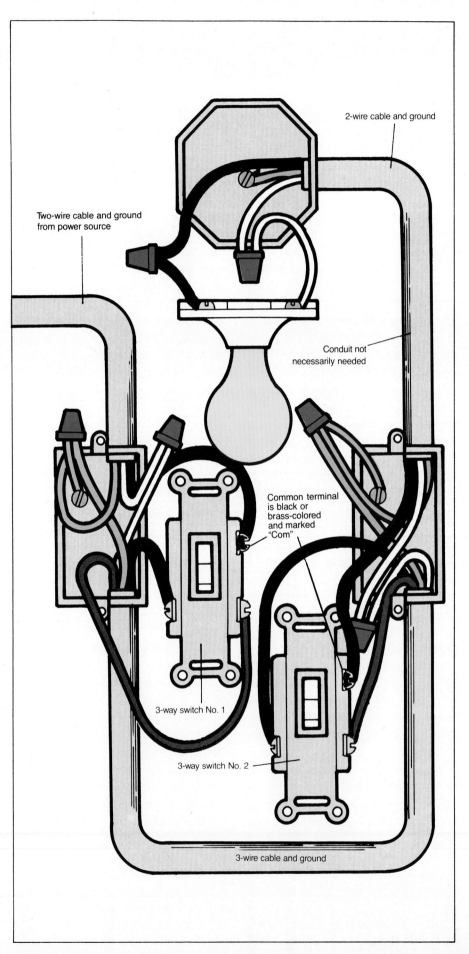

2-wire cable and ground

Two-wire cable and ground from power source

Conduit not necessarily needed

Common terminal is black or brass-colored and marked "Com"

3-way switch No. 1

3-way switch No. 2

3-wire cable and ground

FIXTURE CONTROLLED BY TWO SWITCHES, POWER THROUGH FIXTURE BOX

In this setup, the power comes into the light fixture on a two-wire cable with ground. The power is wired to pass through the fixture box to the two switches and then return to the fixture. A two-wire cable with ground is used between the fixture and one switch, and a three-wire cable with ground between the two switches. In this circuit the white wire in both cables becomes a hot wire. Therefore it must be marked with black tape.

Turn off the power at the service panel before starting work.

STEP 1
WIRING NO. 1 SWITCH

Connect the black wire from the cable between switches to the common terminal. Tape the white wire black and connect it to one lower terminal. Connect the red wire to the other terminal. Connect the grounding wire to the box terminal.

STEP 2
WIRING NO. 2 SWITCH

Connect the red wire from the cable between switches to one lower terminal. Tape the white wire in this cable black and connect it to the other lower terminal. Tape the white wire in the fixture cable black and connect it to the black wire in the switch cable. Connect the black wire in the fixture cable to the common switch terminal. Connect the cable grounding wires to a pigtail to the box ground terminal.

STEP 3
WIRING THE FIXTURE

Connect the black wire in the cable from switch No. 2 to the black power wire. Tape the white wire in the switch cable black and connect it to the black fixture wire or brass terminal. Connect the white wire in the power cable to the white fixture wire or silver terminal. Connect the cable grounding wires to a pigtail to the box terminal.

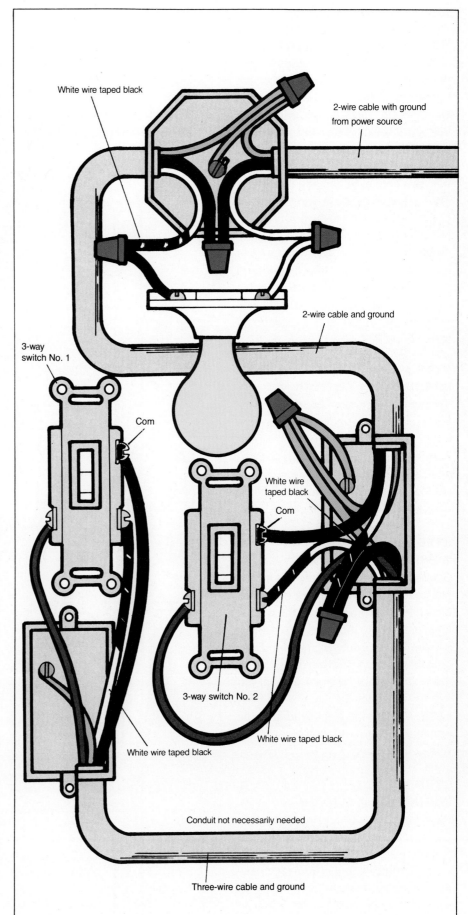

White wire taped black

2-wire cable with ground from power source

2-wire cable and ground

3-way switch No. 1

Com

White wire taped black

Com

White wire taped black

3-way switch No. 2

White wire taped black

White wire taped black

Conduit not necessarily needed

Three-wire cable and ground

FIXTURE BETWEEN TWO THREE-WAY SWITCHES, POWER THROUGH SWITCH

Here, a light fixture is between two three-way switches with power coming to the first switch on a two-wire cable with ground. The power passes on through the fixture box to the second switch, and returns to the fixture. Three-wire cable with ground is used between both switches and the fixture. The cable grounding wire (bare or green) is connected to the box of switch No. 2, and to pigtails in the fixture and switch No. 1 boxes. The white wire in the cable between the fixture and switch No. 2 becomes a hot wire in this circuit, so it must be marked with black tape as illustrated and explained in steps 2 and 3.

STEP 1
WIRING NO. 1 SWITCH

Connect the incoming black power wire to the common terminal of the switch. Connect the white wire to white wire of the three-wire cable to fixture box. Connect the red and black wires of that cable to the other two switch terminals. Check ground wire connections.

STEP 2
WIRING THE FIXTURE

Connect the red wires of the two switch cables together. Wrap black tape onto the white wire coming from switch No. 2 and connect it to the black wire coming into the fixture from switch No. 1. Connect the white wire from switch No. 1 to the white lead or silver terminal of the fixture. Connect the black wire from switch No. 2 to the black lead or brass terminal of the fixture. Check ground wire connections.

STEP 3
WIRING NO. 2 SWITCH

Wrap black tape around the white wire. Connect the incoming black wire to the common terminal. Connect the white wire taped black to the terminal below the common terminal. Connect the red wire to the terminal on the opposite side. Check ground wire connections.

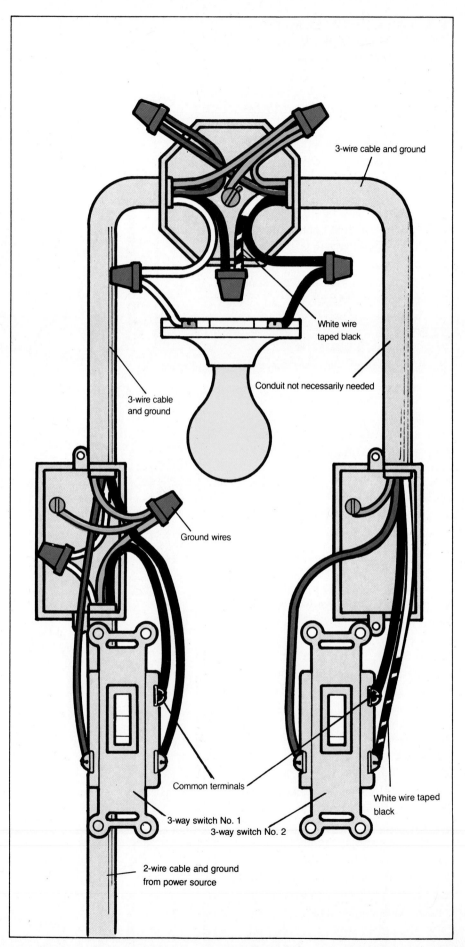

3-wire cable and ground

White wire taped black

Conduit not necessarily needed

3-wire cable and ground

Ground wires

Common terminals

3-way switch No. 1

3-way switch No. 2

White wire taped black

2-wire cable and ground from power source

FIXTURE BETWEEN THREE-WAY SWITCHES WITH POWER SOURCE AT THE LIGHT

In this hookup you can use three-wire cable with ground very easily. The power comes through the light ceiling box. Then you connect it to the switches, which are powered on separate lines from opposite sides of the fixture.

Note that the white wire in the power source cable connects directly to the silver terminal of the fixture. The black power wire is connected to the common terminal on switch No. 2. Power is fed back and across to switch No. 1 by white wires coded black with tape to indicate that they are hot between the switches.

STEP 1
WIRING NO. 1 SWITCH

The black wire in the cable from the fixture box connects to the common terminal. The white wire is taped black. It and the red wire connect to the other two switch terminals. The grounding wire connects directly to the switch box.

STEP 2
WIRING THE FIXTURE

The white wire of the power source cable connects to the white lead or silver terminal of the fixture. The black power wire connects to the black wire of the cable to switch No. 2. The red wires of the switch cables connect together, and the white wires of these cables, taped black, connect together. The black wire from switch No. 1 connects to the black lead or brass terminal of the fixture. The grounding wires all connect to a pigtail attached to the box.

STEP 3
WIRING NO. 2 SWITCH

The connections are the same as at switch No. 1. The black power wire goes to the common switch terminal. The white wire is taped black. It and the red wire go to the other two terminals. The grounding wire connects directly to the box.

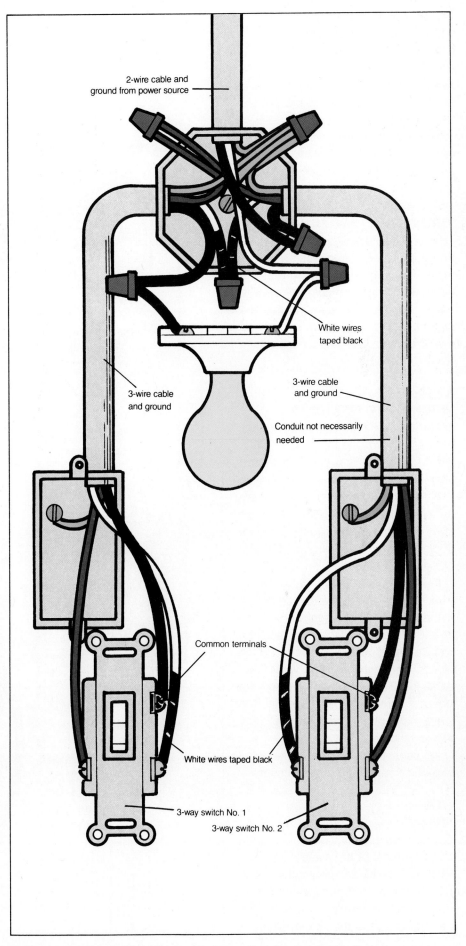

2-wire cable and ground from power source

White wires taped black

3-wire cable and ground

3-wire cable and ground

Conduit not necessarily needed

Common terminals

White wires taped black

3-way switch No. 1

3-way switch No. 2

TWO LIGHTS BETWEEN TWO THREE-WAY SWITCHES WITH POWER THROUGH SWITCH

Power comes into switch No. 1 on a two-wire cable with ground. Three-wire and two-wire cables with ground are used between the four boxes.

Note that two white wires specified below must be taped black because they become power-carrying wires.

STEP 1
WIRING NO. 1 SWITCH

Connect the black wire in the incoming power cable to the common switch terminal. Connect the white wire to the white wire of the outgoing three-wire cable. Connect the outgoing red and black traveller wires to the other two switch terminals. Pigtail the grounding wires to the box.

STEP 2
WIRING THE FIXTURES

In No. 1 fixture box, connect the black from switch No. 1 to the black in cable No. 1 to the next box. Connect the red traveller to the white—taped black—in cable No. 1. Connect the whites from switch No. 1 and cable No. 2 to the silver terminal of the fixture. Connect the black wire of cable No. 2 to the brass fixture terminal.

In No. 2 fixture box, tape the white wire in cable No. 1 black and connect it to the red traveller to switch No. 2. Connect the black in cable No. 1 to the white—taped black—going to switch No. 2. Connect the black wires from cable No. 2 and the switch cable to the brass fixture terminal. Connect the white wire in cable No. 2 to the silver fixture terminal.

In both fixture boxes, pigtail all grounding wires to the box terminals.

STEP 3
WIRING NO. 2 SWITCH

Connect the incoming black wire to the COM terminal of the switch. Tape the white wire black and connect it to one open terminal; connect the red wire to the remaining terminal. Connect the grounding wire to the box terminal.

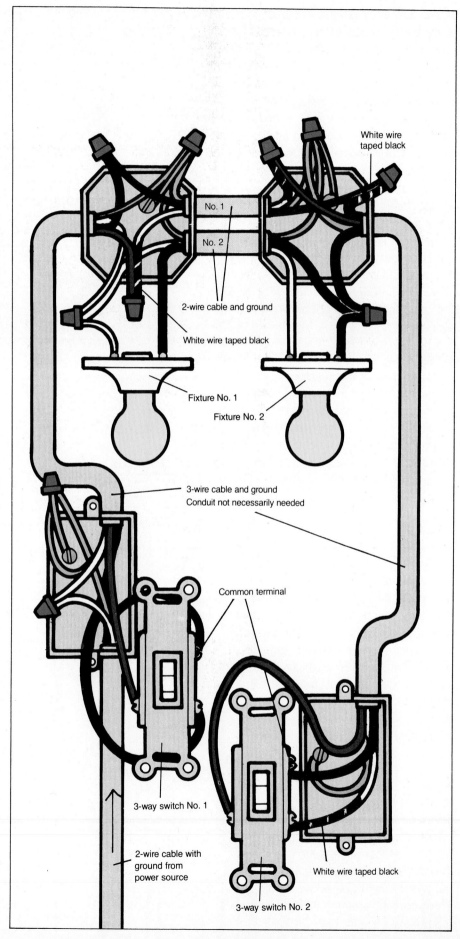

White wire taped black

No. 1

No. 2

2-wire cable and ground

White wire taped black

Fixture No. 1

Fixture No. 2

3-wire cable and ground
Conduit not necessarily needed

Common terminal

3-way switch No. 1

2-wire cable with ground from power source

White wire taped black

3-way switch No. 2

TWO THREE-WAY SWITCHES CONTROLLING TWO LIGHTS, POWER THROUGH LIGHT

In this arrangement, power comes into one fixture box on a two-wire with ground cable. The two fixture boxes have a three-wire leg between them, as do the switch boxes, but the leg between switch box and fixture box requires only a two-wire cable. The (green) grounding wires are connected to the metal boxes throughout the run.

STEP 1
WIRING NO. 1 FIXTURE

Connect the black wire of the power source cable to the black wire in the three-wire leg to the next box. Connect the white power cable wire to the white wire in the ongoing leg and to the silver fixture terminal. Connect the red wire in the ongoing cable to the brass fixture terminal.

STEP 2
WIRING NO. 2 FIXTURE

Connect the black wire from the first fixture box to the black wire in the cable to switch No. 1. Connect the white wire from the first box to the silver fixture terminal. Connect the red wire to the white wire—taped black—to the switch, and with a pigtail to the brass fixture terminal.

STEP 3
WIRING NO. 1 SWITCH

Connect the black wire coming from the fixture box to the common terminal. Tape the white wire of that cable black and connect it to the black in the three-wire cable that goes to switch No. 2. Tape the white traveller in the cable to switch No. 2 black. Connect it to one open switch terminal and connect the red traveller to the other terminal.

STEP 4
WIRING NO. 2 SWITCH

Connect the incoming black wire to the common switch terminal. Tape the white wire black and connect it to one open switch terminal. Connect the red to the other terminal.

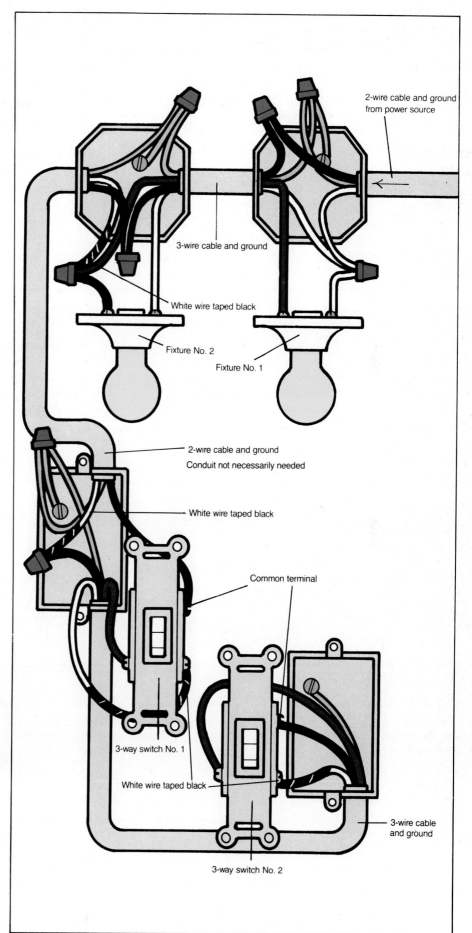

2-wire cable and ground from power source

3-wire cable and ground

White wire taped black

Fixture No. 2

Fixture No. 1

2-wire cable and ground
Conduit not necessarily needed

White wire taped black

Common terminal

3-way switch No. 1

White wire taped black

3-wire cable and ground

3-way switch No. 2

END-OF-RUN LIGHTS CONTROLLED BY TWO THREE-WAY SWITCHES

In this hookup, the two lights are at the end of the circuit with the power coming through the first switch, running to a second switch, and then on to the light fixtures.

Since only two-wire cable is needed for the fixture–fixture and fixture–switch wiring, you will save money if either or both of these legs in the run is long. Note that in this circuit the red and black wires in the three-wire cable between the switches are the traveller wires.

Throughout the circuit, the grounding wires connect to each other and to pigtails to the metal boxes.

STEP 1
WIRING NO. 1 SWITCH

Connect the incoming black power wire to the common terminal. Connect the power cable white wire to the outgoing white wire. Connect the outgoing red and black traveller wires to the open switch terminals.

STEP 2
WIRING NO. 2 SWITCH

Connect the incoming red and black to the two lower switch terminals. Connect the incoming and outgoing whites together. Connect the outgoing black to the common terminal.

STEP 3
WIRING NO. 1 FIXTURE

Connect the incoming and outgoing black wires together and to the brass fixture terminal. Connect the two white wires together and to the silver fixture terminal.

STEP 4
WIRING NO. 2 FIXTURE

Connect the incoming black wire to the brass fixture terminal and connect the white wire to the silver terminal. Connect the grounding wire to the box terminal and check that the grounding connections are correct and secure in the other three boxes.

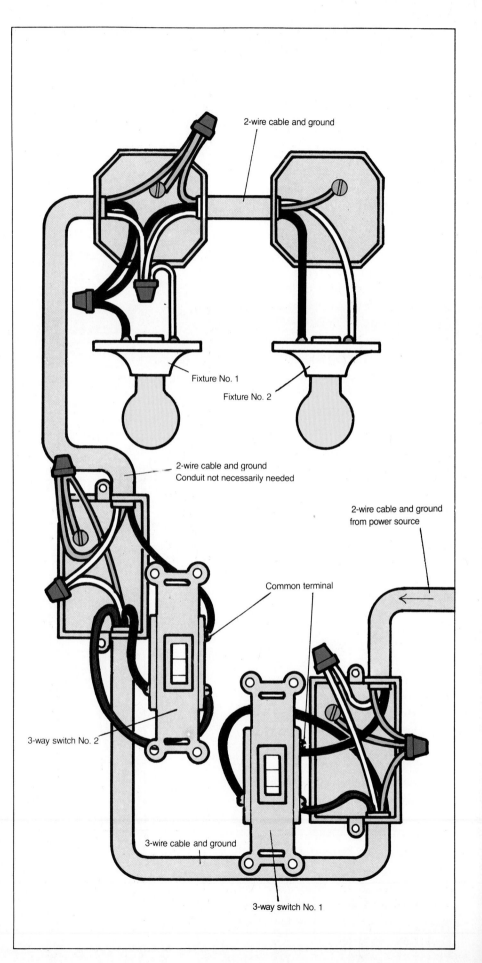

2-wire cable and ground

Fixture No. 1

Fixture No. 2

2-wire cable and ground
Conduit not necessarily needed

2-wire cable and ground
from power source

Common terminal

3-way switch No. 2

3-wire cable and ground

3-way switch No. 1

END-WIRED SWITCHES WITH POWER THROUGH A FIXTURE BOX

Power is furnished by a two-wire cable with ground coming into the first fixture box. It is routed to the first switch, then by the traveller wires to the second switch, and finally back to the lights. One traveller is red, the other a white wire marked with black tape. The grounding wires are pigtailed to the metal fixture boxes, and connected directly to the switch box terminals.

As in the previous two-light hookups, the switches operate both lights, but the wiring arrangement ensures that even if one bulb should burn out, the other will still work.

STEP 1
WIRING NO. 1 FIXTURE

Connect the incoming power cable black wire to the black wire going to switch No. 1. Connect the power cable white wire to the white in leg No. 2 to the other fixture and to the silver terminal of the fixture in this box. Connect the black wire in leg No. 2 between fixtures to the brass fixture terminal.

Connect the red wire from switch No. 1 to the black in leg No. 1 to the other fixture. Tape the white from switch No. 1 black and connect it to the black in leg No. 1.

STEP 2
WIRING NO. 2 FIXTURE

Connect the white in leg No. 2 to the silver fixture terminal. Connect the black in leg No. 2 to the black to switch No. 2 and to the brass fixture terminal. Connect the black in leg No. 1 to the red going to switch No. 2. Tape the whites in the leg No. 1 and switch No. 2 cables black and connect them together.

STEP 3
WIRING THE SWITCHES

Both switches are wired the same way. Connect the incoming black wire to the common terminal. Tape the white wire black and connect it to one lower terminal. Connect the red wire to the other terminal.

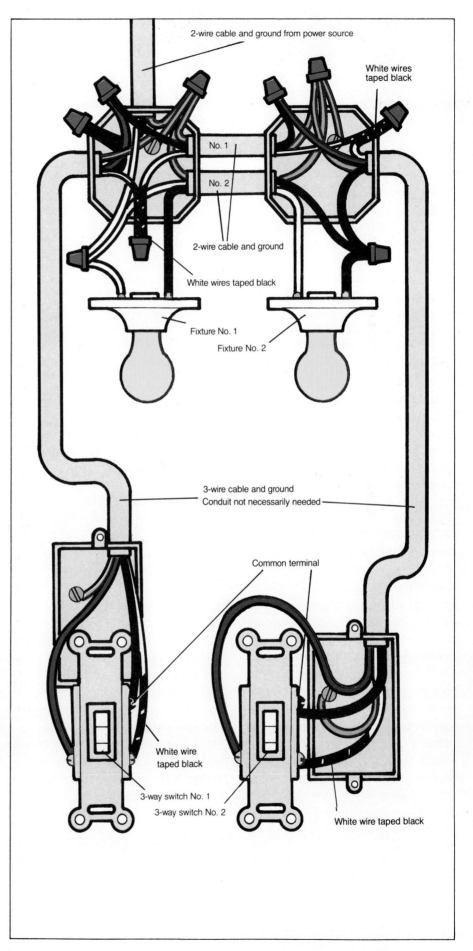

2-wire cable and ground from power source

White wires taped black

No. 1

No. 2

2-wire cable and ground

White wires taped black

Fixture No. 1

Fixture No. 2

3-wire cable and ground
Conduit not necessarily needed

Common terminal

White wire taped black

3-way switch No. 1

3-way switch No. 2

White wire taped black

Working with Receptacles (Outlets)

Before you replace a receptacle (outlet), or even remove the faceplate covering it, *turn off the power* to the outlet circuit. You can check to see if the power is off by plugging in a lamp. Or you can use a tester as described on page 53.

Receptacles are housed in metal or plastic boxes similar to switch boxes. The boxes are covered with a faceplate usually held by a single screw. Behind the faceplate, the receptacles are held by two mounting screws to a metal mounting strap and the box. When these screws are removed, the receptacle may be pulled gently from the box.

To replace a receptacle, you do not have to do anything to the box or replace any wiring. You replace only the receptacle.

If the box is tilted a bit left or right in the wall, do not try to straighten it. The wide slots in the receptacle mounting strap will let you shift the receptacle to get it aligned vertically. Then tighten the mounting screws.

THE WIRING LAYOUT

Although you don't replace any wires, consider the position of the receptacle in the circuit. This affects the way the receptacle is wired. The box falls either at the middle or at the end of a circuit. Determine the position by the number of cables, or sets of wires, that enter the box through openings in the back or sides.

Each set of wires includes one or two *hot wires* covered with black or red insulation, which carry live current. If you spot a wire taped with black electrician's tape, consider this wire a hot wire.

Each set of wires also includes one with white insulation. Often miscalled "neutral" from earlier wiring practice, the white wire carries power whenever any device in a circuit is operating. It

completes the path that must run from service entrance panel to device, back to panel.

If there is an equipment-grounding wire, it will be bare or in green insulation. This wire provides a path to quickly trip the branch circuit breaker in case a hot wire in a piece of grounded equipment comes in contact with the metal equipment case.

End-of-the-run wiring has only one set of two or three wires entering the box. The black and white wires attach to the terminal screws. The bare or green wire, the grounding wire, loops around a screw attached to the metal box.

Middle-of-the-run wiring has two sets of wires entering the box. The hookup varies according to the type of receptacle and the type of ground system used.

REPLACEMENT DATA

When you buy a replacement (or new) receptacle, be sure you get the one that matches the circuit. The markings and ratings on old and new equipment must match. The markings below are those found on receptacles.

● Underwriters' Laboratories (UL) and Canadian Standards Association (CSA) monograms indicate that the receptacles have been tested and listed by these organizations. The associations are not connected with the government or special code groups.

● Amperage and voltage ratings are figures that indicate the maximum amperage and voltage a receptacle can handle. For instance, a rating of 15A-125V means that the receptacle can carry a maximum of 15 amperes of current at no more than 125 volts.

● The type of current indicated on the receptacle is the only one that the receptacle can use. Receptacles that are used in houses and condominiums in the United States and Canada are

marked AC ONLY, which means they are designed for use only with alternating current.

● Check the types of wire that the receptacle can handle. The wire in your home must match it. The wire in your home will be copper (CO or CU), copper-clad aluminum (CO/ALR), or solid aluminum (ALR). Make sure that the receptacle design can use that wiring.

RECEPTACLE TYPES

The types of receptacles vary. There are some designed exclusively for use outside; some are made to handle heavy-duty equipment such as major appliances; some are integrated into light fixtures, and some are combined with switches.

The most common home receptacle is the duplex receptacle that is rated at 15 amperes and 125 volts. A duplex receptacle has two outlets and accommodates two pieces of equipment.

RECEPTACLE WIRING

Side-wired receptacles, the most common, have two terminal screws on each side. One pair is brass or black in color, the other is silver. A brass terminal always connects to a hot (red or black) wire, a silver terminal only to a white wire. When the break-off link between brass terminals is removed, each terminal will bring power to just one of the two outlets in the receptacle.

Back-wired receptacles have openings at the rear in which circuit wires are inserted. Some receptacles have both side- and back-wire terminals.

New receptacles also have a green terminal at the bottom to which the equipment grounding wire connects. Each half of such a receptacle has three openings on the front: two slots for plug blades, a half-round hole for a grounding prong. In polarized outlets the left slot is wider than the "hot" slot on the right, brass terminal side.

MODERN OUTLETS

Standard duplex receptacles have two outlets for plugs, as shown at right. Both outlets will be on the same circuit unless the break-off links between terminals on both sides (not shown) are removed—for instance to control one outlet with a switch.

Receptacles are sturdy devices but they can wear out or fail, usually from damage caused by inserting plugs carelessly, with excessive force, and disconnecting devices by yanking on the cord. If plugs fit loosely or fall out, replace the receptacle.

IS THE RECEPTACLE WORKING? TWO TESTS

The best outlet-testing procedure is to use an inexpensive voltage tester. It has no power, and the test light glows only if the probes connect points where voltage is present.

Another way to test an outlet is with a table lamp. Simply plug the lamp into the outlet and turn the lamp on. If the outlet works, don't fix it. The voltage tester, however, will provide you with a better reading on the outlet and circuit.

STEP 1
TESTING POWER PATH

Using a voltage tester, insert a probe into each slot of an outlet. If the wiring is correct and the outlet is working, the bulb will glow.

STEP 2
TESTING THE GROUND

To see if the grounding system is working properly, insert one probe in the left outlet slot and the other in the ground-prong hole. The tester should *not* light. Next check between the ground-prong hole and the right, hot, outlet slot. Now the tester *should* light. If the outlet fails any test, turn off the power, check the circuit, and replace the receptacle if necessary.

You can also check outlets with an inexpensive three-prong circuit tester that tests for power, grounding, and faults such as reversed black and white wire connections.

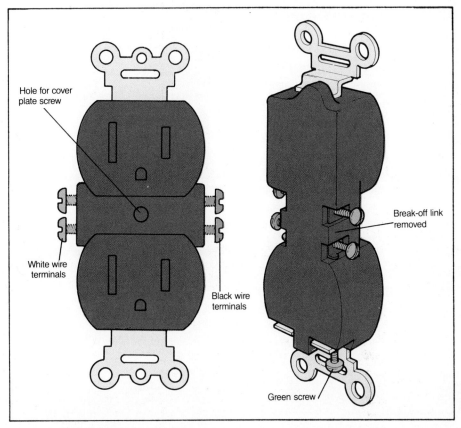

Modern outlet. A polarized, grounded duplex receptacle has wide and narrow plug blade slots, half-round ground prong holes, and a green terminal for connection to an equipment grounding wire. Usually both outlets are on the same circuit; removing break-off links on each side separates them.

Testing power path. Insert one probe of tester in each slot of an outlet. With circuit breaker on, tester bulb should light.

Testing the ground. With probes as shown tester bulb should not light. Between right slot and ground it should light.

REPLACING A SIDE-WIRED RECEPTACLE

To get to the receptacle to change it, first *turn off the power at the main service panel*. Then remove the faceplate, which is held by a screw.

STEP 1
REMOVE THE OUTLET

Back out the two screws holding the outlet in the mounting bracket using a standard slot screwdriver. Then gently pull the outlet from the box far enough to expose the terminals.

STEP 2
NOTE THE HOOKUP

You will see one or two sets of wires in the box that are connected to the receptacle. Black power wires go to the brass terminals; white wires go to the silver terminals; bare or green wires to the ground terminal. Connect a new receptacle that way.

STEP 3
DISCONNECT/RECONNECT

Remove the wires from the terminals, remove the old receptacle, and reconnect the new receptacle. The wires go around the terminals in a clockwise direction. Then reinstall the outlet in the box.

END-OF-RUN-OUTLETS

Only one brass and one silver terminal are connected at the end of a run. Pigtails will probably connect box and green terminal to grounding wire.

MIDDLE-OF-RUN OUTLETS

Wires go to all terminals on middle-of-the-run outlets. All grounding wires are spliced together and connected by pigtail to the box ground terminal.

REPLACEMENT OUTLETS

Make sure that the replacement outlet matches the old one as to volts, amps, and prong configuration. Typical household outlets are illustrated at the right.

Remove the outlet. Remove the faceplate and then the mounting bracket screws. Pull out the outlet so the terminals will be exposed.

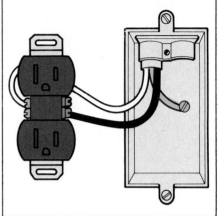

Note the hookup. You will see two or more wires connecting the outlet terminals. Make a note of these connections or tag wires.

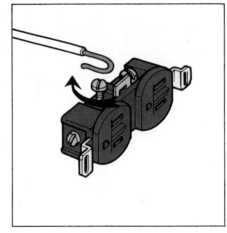

Disconnect/reconnect. The wires go around the terminals in a clockwise configuration. As you tighten terminals, you lock the wires.

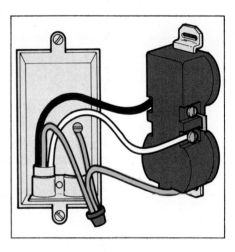

End-of-run outlets. End-of-run outlets are the last outlets on a circuit. Only two terminals are connected, along with a grounding wire.

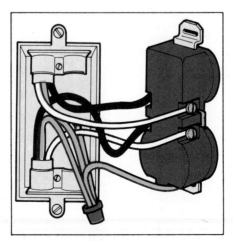

Middle-of-run outlets. Middle-of-run outlets are connected to all wires coming from both directions. If needed, tag wires for reconnection.

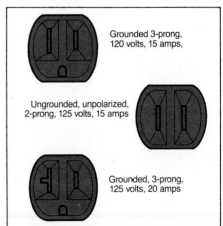

Grounded 3-prong, 120 volts, 15 amps,

Ungrounded, unpolarized, 2-prong, 125 volts, 15 amps

Grounded, 3-prong, 125 volts, 20 amps

Buy the right replacement receptacle. Replacement outlets should have the same voltage and amperage ratings as the original outlet.

SPECIAL RECEPTACLES

Several specialized outlets complement the standard duplex models. New
wiring of two widely used devices is
shown here: a combined switch/outlet,
and a combined light/outlet. Be sure to
make the grounding wire (green) connections also shown. To make a replacement, follow the old wiring.

SWITCH/OUTLET

Units may differ a bit from the illustration. There will be two linked brass terminals on one side; on the other side, a
brass terminal for the switch, and a
silver terminal for the outlet.

SWITCH CONTROLS OUTLET

In this hookup, the switch controls
power to both the outlet and a light
farther along in the circuit.

Connect the black power wire to the
switch single brass terminal, and the
black wire from the switch to the linked
brass terminals. Connect the two white
wires together with a pigtail to the outlet
silver terminal.

OUTLET ALWAYS HOT

To have constant power to the outlet,
with the switch controlling only a light,
connect the black power wire to the
linked brass terminals. Connect the
black wire from the light to the switch
single brass terminal. Connect the
white wires with a pigtail to the outlet
silver terminal.

END-OF-RUN LIGHT/OUTLET

This kind of unit has four prewired
leads, a black–white pair to the light,
and a pair to the outlet. At the end of a
run, connect both black leads to black
wire from the switch, and connect both
white leads to the white wire.

MID-RUN LIGHT/OUTLET

Connect the power line white wire to
both white fixture leads. Connect the
black power wire to both the black outlet lead and the white wire—taped
black—from the switch. Connect the
black wire from the switch to the black
light lead.

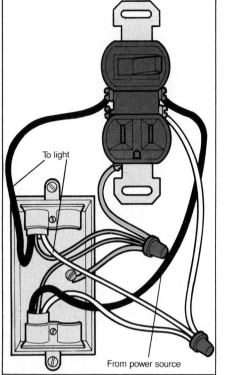

Switch controls outlet. Power wires go to brass switch terminals. Pigtail from joined white wires goes to silver outlet terminal.

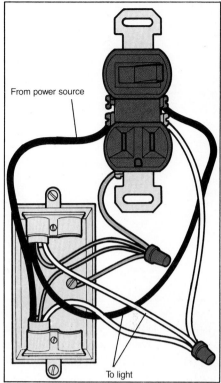

Outlet always hot. Black power wire goes to linked brass terminals; black wire from light goes to switch single brass terminal.

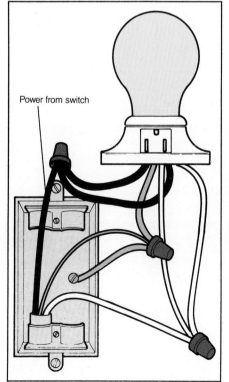

End-of-run light/outlet. Fixture leads are paired by color and connected to wires of the same color in the incoming cable.

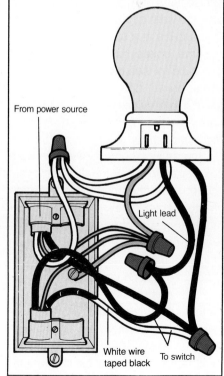

Mid-run light/outlet. Black power wire connects to outlet lead and one switch wire. Light connects to other switch wire.

4 Boxes and Connections

Switches, outlets, and fixtures are mounted in electrical boxes. All wires are terminated, spliced, and stored in electrical boxes. Boxes are designed to serve specific purposes. For example, paneling switch and outlet boxes are extraslim so that they fit between ¾-inch furring strips and the back surface of the paneling material. A standard switch box is too deep for this application. You must specify which box you want by name when purchasing supplies at a store.

Some boxes have special clamps and clips for securing wire and cable; some boxes have special fastening and nailing devices, such as adjustable hangers that go between framing members: studs, joists, and rafters.

Other buying considerations include box capacity—how many wires it can accept—and the number and position of cable entry holes. These are commonly knockout or pryout plugs in general-purpose boxes, but threaded plugs are used in weatherproof boxes.

You can also choose between metallic and nonmetallic (plastic) boxes. Metal boxes may be a bit more expensive, but they are more adaptable. Nonmetallic boxes are not permitted in most large cities, or even in many localities where nonmetallic cable is permitted. Check your local electrical code carefully on this point.

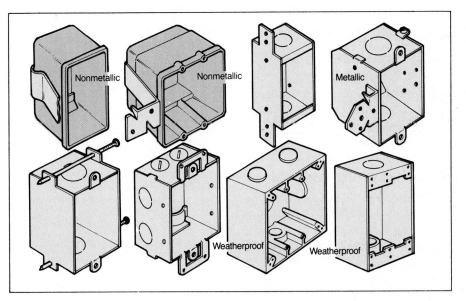

Switch and receptacle boxes. Typical switch and receptacle boxes available in metal and plastic are shown here. Note the different nailing and fastening devices designed to save you time and money.

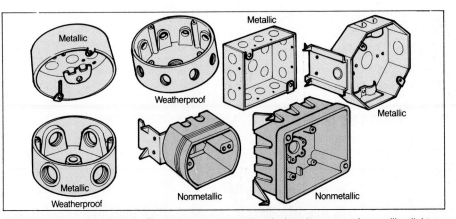

Fixture and junction boxes. Fixture boxes support electrical equipment, such as ceiling lights. Junction boxes are used to splice wires and redirect wiring in long household circuit runs.

JUDGING BOX CAPACITY

A box can hold only a certain number of connections or wires, depending on both physical space and the regulations set down in the National Electrical Code.

If you are adding a new circuit or wires to a box, you must install a proper-size box. Too many wires in a box can cause electrical hazards. The chart below will help you make the right selections.

REMOVING KNOCKOUTS AND PRYOUTS FOR WIRES

To insert wires into boxes, knockout or pryout plugs must be removed from appropriate holes. To open a hole, tap the knockout with a punch and hammer to break one side free, then twist it off with pliers. Knockouts usually open round holes for cable connectors.

Pryouts are common at the U-shaped holes for interior box cable clamps. Insert the tip of a screwdriver in the slot and twist the pryout free.

Do not remove pryouts or knockouts from any holes that will not be used. Do unscrew and remove unused cable clamps in a box to provide more room for a device and wires.

CABLE CONNECTORS

Cables are anchored to boxes either by interior clamps or by connectors. A cable connector is a threaded collar that clamps around the outer insulation and extends into the box, where a locknut secures it. Be sure to get the right connector for the kind of cable or conduit you are using.

NONMETALLIC BOXES

Plastic boxes may be used only with nonmetallic cable. They also have knockouts for wire or cable entry. You remove the knockouts with a punch and hammer. Be careful: don't crack the plastic by hammering too hard.

In a single-device nonmetallic box, cable clamping is not required if the cable is held by a fastener within 8 inches of the box. The cable sheath must go at least ½ inch into the box.

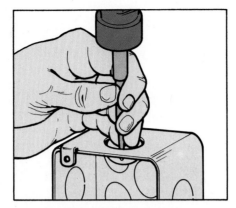

Punching knockouts. Center punch or nailset and hammer are best tools to loosen knockouts in electrical boxes. Twist off with pliers.

Pryouts. To insert a cable in a clamp inside a box, remove pryout. Insert screwdriver in slot, pry up, and twist out.

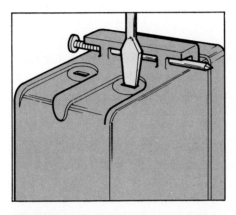

Plastic boxes. Plastic boxes for nonmetallic cable only have pryouts also, which are removed with a screwdriver.

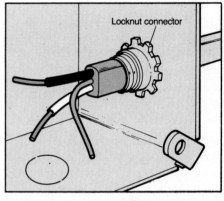

Cable connectors. Threaded collar clamped on cable extends through round knockout hole. Locknut secures collar inside box.

JUDGING JUNCTION BOX CAPACITY

Box Size (inches)	Maximum Number of Connections: AWG No. 14 Wire	Maximum Number of Connections: AWG No. 12 Wire
WALL BOXES		
3 × 2 × 2½	6	5
3 × 2 × 2¾	7	6
3 × 2 × 3½	9	8
CEILING BOXES		
4 × 1¼	6	5
4 × 1½	7	6
MAJOR BOXES		
4 × 1¼	9	8
4 × 1½	10	9
4 × 2⅛	10	9

How to use chart is explained on page 58.

Working with Switch and Outlet Boxes

Switches and receptacles must be housed in a box. There are four styles you'll work with most often:

Standard boxes with adjustable ears. This box is a simple rectangular structure with screw openings at the top and bottom front edges. The sides are straight up and down; there are no brackets or clamps. This type of box is appropriate for plastered walls, since the walls are sturdy enough to hold the box in place. The box is also used for drywall (gypsum board), along with two side brackets that you buy separately. The brackets give the box the support that the drywall alone cannot.

Boxes with side clamps. These boxes have screw-activated clamps on the front side edges. When the screws are tightened, the clamps come forward and spread out to hold the box in place. This type of box is used in paneling or hardboard that is fastened to studs. Both of these wall coverings are sturdy enough to hold the box securely.

Boxes with side flanges. A box with an external flange running along one side is used in locations in which you have easy access to a wall stud, such as an unfinished basement or attic. The box is simply nailed to the side of the stud.

This style box may have a mounting flange with metal teeth that are pounded into the stud. Set the box at a depth that will make its front edges flush with the face of the drywall or paneling that will cover the wall.

Paneling boxes. These shallow boxes hold just one switch or outlet and a single set of wires. They are mounted between ¾-inch-thick furring strips and the back side of paneling materials. Paneling boxes cannot be ganged together.

JUDGING BOX CAPACITY

Before you start the project, determine if the existing junction boxes can ac-commodate additional wiring. Any box can hold only a certain number of connections. The total number is limited both by physical space and by the provisions of the National Electrical Code.

For safety, don't crowd more wires into a box than the box can handle.

In judging what is and what is not a connection, use these guidelines:

1. Count each conductor (wire) in the box as one connection.

2. Do not count a ground wire that enters the box and is connected directly to the outlet, switch, or fixture.

3. Do not count a jumper wire as a connection.

4. Count a ground wire that is connected to the box as one connection.

5. Count cable clamps or lighting fixture mounting fittings that are inside the box, such as a nipple or hickey, as one connection for each fitting.

6. Count a receptacle or switch as one connection.

Add the total number of connections and check the chart on page 57 to determine if you can add connections to a box.

For example, a 4 × 1½-inch ceiling box in which there are two AWG No. 12 wires, one ground wire connected to the box, and a hickey for suspending a hanging fixture has a total of four connections. As the chart on page 57 shows, the maximum allowed for this box is six. So you could add two more if necessary. If more than six connections are needed, buy a new box and keep the old one for future use.

GANGING BOXES

Switch and outlet boxes are sold as singles, that is, only one switch or outlet may be mounted in the box. However, metal boxes may be ganged together to hold several switches and outlets. This technique is shown on page 59.

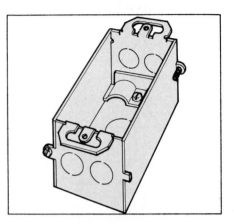

Standard boxes. Box has screw openings at top and bottom front edges. Box may be used for plaster walls and gypsum wallboard.

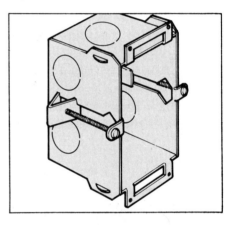

Boxes with side clamps. Box with side clamps that hold box in position in the wall. When activated, the clamps grip the edges of paneling.

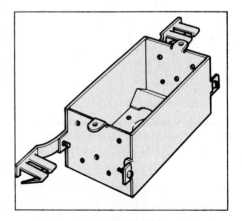

Boxes with flanges. Side flanges with metal teeth are for open construction. The teeth are hammered into the framing members.

HOW TO GANG BOXES TOGETHER

If the box you want to use is too small to hold additional switches, outlets, and wires, you can gang two or more boxes together to provide enough space.

STEP 1
REMOVING THE BOX SIDES

With a screwdriver, remove the screw along the right side of one box and from the left side of another, similar box. Lift off the sides.

STEP 2
REASSEMBLING THE BOXES

Put the open sides of the two boxes together. The notch on one box will fit into the flange of the second box. Lock these together. Then drive in the screws to hold the boxes together.

You can gang together as many boxes as you want.

INSTALLING WIRES AND CABLE INSIDE BOXES

Trim cable to expose at least 6 inches of wire. Remove a round box knockout to use a cable or conduit connector.

STEP 1
ADDING A CONNECTOR

Slip the connector collar onto the cable or conduit; let ½ inch of cable insulation extend beyond collar. Tighten the collar clamp or setscrew to hold it.

STEP 2
SECURING CONNECTOR

Insert the connector threads through the hole into the box. Screw on the locknut, then tap on its lugs with a screwdriver and hammer to fasten the connector tightly.

USING BOX CLAMPS

To use an interior box clamp, remove the pryout from the U-shaped hole where the cable is to enter. Loosen the clamp screw and insert the cable until about ½ inch of the sheath extends past the clamp. Tighten the screw to hold the cable securely. If the clamp at the other end is not used, remove it.

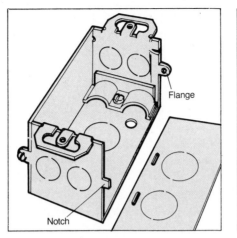

Removing the box sides. Remove left side of one box and right side of another box by backing out screws that hold sides to the boxes.

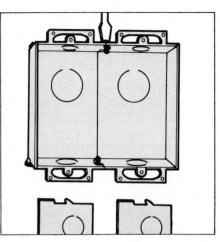

Reassembling the boxes. Put the open sides of both boxes together and lock the notch on one box into flange of other; replace screws.

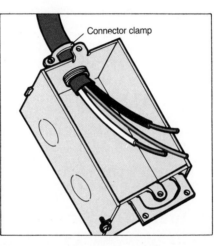

Adding a connector. Fasten the connector clamp over the cable. Let about ½ inch of cable insulation extend past the threaded end.

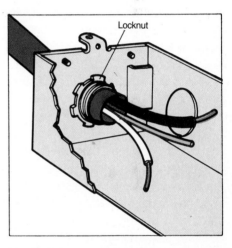

Securing the connector. Put connector into hole. Screw on locknut by hand, then tighten with screwdriver and hammer.

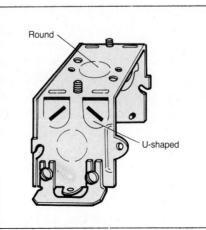

Knockouts for clamps. Remove U-shaped knockouts for saddle clamps. For conduit, punch out round knockouts in metal boxes.

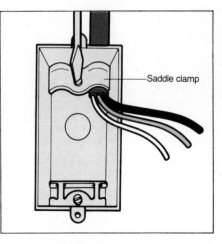

Clamps inside the box. Saddle clamps inside boxes hold wires tightly. Put wires under the clamp. Then tighten the screw to tighten clamp.

Installing Boxes in Walls and Ceilings

Replacing a switch or outlet involves simply turning off the circuit at the main panel, removing the old device, and connecting the wiring to a new one. Replacing a switch or outlet box is almost the same. Turn off the power, remove the faceplate and mounting screws, and pull the device out of the box. Make a diagram of all the connections, then unhook the wires.

Release the fasteners holding the box and work it out of the wall. Undo the cable, insert it into the new box, and secure it. Then fasten the new box into the wall. That may take some work, for space will be very tight. You may have to enlarge the hole a bit.

With the new box in place, reconnect the switch or outlet, following your diagram, and mount it in the box.

To install a switch or outlet in an existing wall, a hole must be cut in the wall for the box. After the hole has been cut, the power cable has to be fished to the opening and connected to the box and the switch and/or outlet. Fishing the wire is explained in Chapter 7.

BOXES IN GYPSUM BOARD (DRYWALL) WALLS

Plan the location of the box for the new receptacle or switch so it will fall between wall studs. If the outlet is to be placed near the bottom of a wall, position the box 12 to 18 inches above the floor surface. If you want the receptacle at a midbody height, position the box 10 to 12 inches above the surface of a nearby table or counter.

A switch is normally mounted approximately 50 inches above the floor surface.

LOCATING STUDS

The easiest way to find studs in a wall is to use an inexpensive stud finder. Some finders react magnetically to screws or nails used to hold the wall covering; others sense the density difference between studs and spaces.

Or, measure 16 inches out from a corner and drive a 3- or 4-inch finishing nail partway in. If it hits something solid, it probably is a stud. If not, try a bit to each side until it does. Mark that spot on the wall. You can fill the nail holes with spackle or drywall compound, and you will be sure of the stud location.

All other stud locations can be measured from the first stud you find with the nail. The studs will be spaced every 16 inches on center across the wall—or should be.

Another quick method is to pry off the baseboard along the wall in which you want to locate the studs. The baseboard covers the vertical untaped joints of the gypsum board. These joints are supposed to be spaced 48 inches apart. Then measure from a seam. There should be a stud 16 inches on either side of the seam.

PLASTER AND WOOD LATH

This type of construction was used in older homes; it seldom, if ever, is used in new construction.

To make a hole for an electrical box in this material, you'll have to find a stud as described above. Then, if there are no obstructions in the wall, you can use a cold chisel and hammer to remove a layer of plaster from above and below a drilled hole at the box location. This will expose the width of a single wood lath strip and portions of lath above and below it. You probably will have to chip away 1½ to 2 inches of plaster above and below the drilled hole and extend the opening ¾ inch to 1 inch out from the sides of the hole.

PLASTER AND METAL LATH

Find a stud location first, as described above.

Since you will have to cut through metal, it's best to use the box as a template, drawing an outline of it on the wall where you want the box to be located. Then remove the plaster with a cold chisel and cut the metal lath with a hacksaw blade mounted in a saber saw.

PANELING

Locate the stud positions. Use a stud finder, or look to see where the panels are nailed to the studs. This is not difficult to discover: look closely for the pattern of filled nail holes.

Turn off the power to the room at the main entrance panel, and then drill a small hole in the panel. Check through the hole for any obstructions behind the wall where you plan to locate the junction box. If you find wiring or plumbing, plug the small drilled hole with a piece of doweling and stain the doweling to match the panel so the hole won't show. Chances are good, however, that you won't run into wiring or plumbing. The next step is to use the box as a template and make the necessary cuts in the panel.

IN CEILINGS

Find the joist locations. They almost always are 16 inches on center and will run either crosswise or lengthwise over the room. Use a stud finder, or start in a corner with the nail test described above and work both ways.

If the house has an attic and the attic floor is not finished, locating the joist positions is very easy. In fact, you can work in the attic, cutting the necessary box holes from above after you determine the location from the room below.

Make sure that you have plenty of support to hold your weight on the joists. Use a sheet of ¾-inch-thick plywood as decking.

If the ceiling is tiled, you can remove tiles after finding the joists.

HOW TO INSTALL BOXES IN GYPSUM WALLBOARD WITHOUT STUD SUPPORT

If you can't locate a stud or joist, as explained on the preceding page, use the box as a template and draw an outline of it on the wall or ceiling where you want to install the box. Once the opening is made, you will have to bring the cable to this opening first. This is explained in Chapter 7.

If you do locate a stud or joist, the box is simply fastened to either framing member.

STEP 1
CUT THE PAPER COVERING

With a sharp utility knife, cut along the template lines that you drew on the wall. Be careful. Make several shallow cuts with the knife, rather than trying to make one single cut through the paper covering and into the gypsum core of the panel. If possible, cut completely through the panel with a series of cuts.

STEP 2
KNOCK OUT THE SCRAP

If the piece does not drop out of the hole, the cut may not be complete at every point. Try punching out the scrap with a short piece of 2 × 4 and a few taps with a hammer—not one blow.

STEP 3
POSITION THE BOX

Fit the box into the opening. You may have to trim the hole a bit with the knife, but the box should fit snugly.

Then slide a side bracket into the hole at one side of the box. Insert its top end and push up until the other end clears the bottom hole edge, then slide it down into position. Do the same on the other side of the box. Don't drop the brackets behind the wall!

STEP 4
SECURE THE BOX

Press the box ears firmly against the face of the wall. Pull one bracket tightly against the back of the wall and bend its tabs into the box with pliers. Repeat with the other bracket.

Cut the paper covering. Mark box location on gypsum board, and then cut along guidelines with utility knife. Use series of shallow knife cuts.

Knock out the scrap. With a short piece of scrap wood and hammer, tap out the scrap gypsum board. Let it fall between the studs.

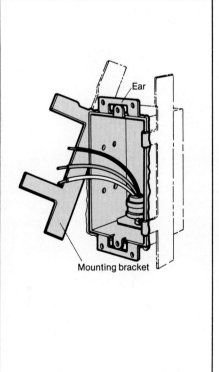

Position the box. Use side brackets to hold box in wall. Put one bracket on each side of box by tipping top of the bracket into hole.

Secure the box. When the bracket is in position between the wall and box, bend the side extensions flush inside the box sides.

HOW TO INSTALL ELECTRICAL BOXES IN PLASTER AND LATH

Many older homes have plaster and lath walls and ceilings. In this construction, lath is nailed across the framing members and then covered over with several different coats of plaster. Cut the hole after you find an unobstructed position for the box. Then, with the hole cut, bring the power cable to the opening and install the box.

STEP 1
CHISEL SMALL OPENING

At the box location, chip out a small section of plaster, exposing the width of one lath. Use a cold chisel and hammer for this job.

STEP 2
MAKE AND TRACE TEMPLATE

Make a cardboard template of a standard box. Find the center of the template and mark it. Position the template on the wall and drive an awl or ice pick through the template center point to mark the lath. Then mark the outline of the template on the wall, using the center point as a guide. Drill a hole at the point on the lath.

STEP 3
MAKE THE CUTS

Stick masking tape around the guidelines on the wall. This will help prevent the saw from crumbling the plaster. Then score the guidelines a couple of times with a utility knife. Bore ½-inch holes at the four corners of the outlines and where the ears of the box will fit. With a saber saw or keyhole saw, cut out the plaster and lath.

STEP 4
INSTALL THE BOX

Remove the masking tape and push the box into the opening, threading the wires into the box at the same time. Use the utility knife to enlarge the notches for the ears. When the box fits, screw the box through the ears to the lath. The box should be flush with the plaster.

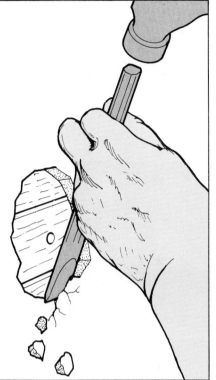

Chisel small opening. Chip a small hole in the plaster at the box location. Remove just enough plaster to expose one or two lath strips.

Make and trace template. Find the center of a box template and mark center on a lath. Mark outline of template on wall; stick on masking tape.

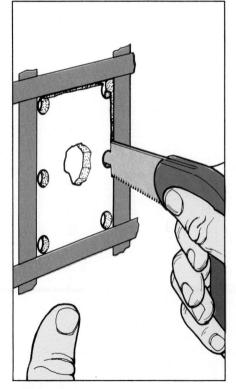

Make the cuts. Bore a series of holes in the plaster inside the guidelines. Then, with a keyhole or saber saw, cut out opening.

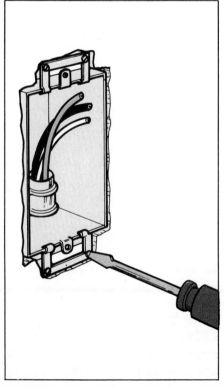

Install the box. Install the box and wires. You may have to trim plaster so ears of box fit. Screw box to lath flush with wall.

INSTALLING BOXES IN PLASTER AND METAL LATH AND PANELING MATERIALS

To install a box in plaster laid on metal lath, first determine the box position by drilling test holes to find obstructions. Then make a template, and trace the template outline on the wall. Surround the outline with masking tape.

STEP 1
REMOVE THE PLASTER

With a ⅜-inch metal drill bit, punch holes in the four corners of the guideline and at the ear openings. Then, with a cold chisel and hammer, remove the plaster.

STEP 2
CUT THE METAL LATH

Use a saber saw with a hacksaw metal-cutting blade to cut the metal lath. Or use a keyhole hacksaw.

Fit the box in the opening, making trimming cuts with the utility knife.

Insert wires into the box, push the box into the opening, and use side brackets to hold the box (see page 61).

BOXES IN WOOD PANELING

Find the location, mark it, and bring the power wires to the area.

STEP 1
MAKE A TEMPLATE

Use a cardboard template to mark the wall, tracing on the box ears.

STEP 2
BORE HOLES IN WALL

Trace the template on the wall. Then bore ½-inch holes at the corners and for the ear brackets. Cut the hole with a keyhole saw or saber saw.

STEP 3
INSERT THE BOX

Install the wires in the box. Slip the box into the hole, loosening the ear screws if needed.

STEP 4
TIGHTEN THE CLAMPS

With a screwdriver, tighten the ear screws that hold the box in place.

Remove the plaster. Punch holes with drill within template guidelines. Then remove excess plaster to metal lath with chisel.

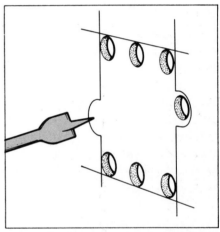

Make a template. Make a template of the box. Cut out the template and trace its outline on the wood wall at the box location you want.

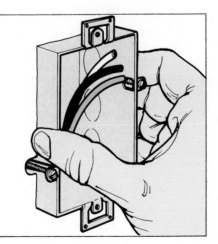

Insert the box. Fit the box in the opening and loosen the bracket screws if needed for adjustment. Box fits flush with wall.

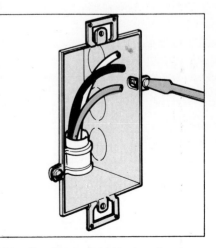

Cut the metal lath. Use a metal-cutting saw to remove the metal lath from the opening. Fit box in opening and make any trimming cuts.

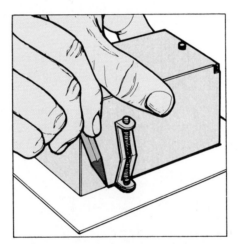

Bore holes in wall. Bore holes in the wood wall at the four corners and where ear brackets fit. Then use a saw to cut out the opening.

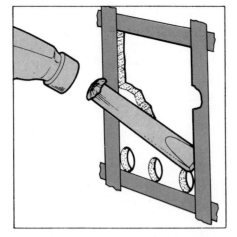

Tighten the clamps. Push box in wall and connect the wires to the box. Then tighten the ear screws to hold box in the wall.

INSTALLING BOXES ON AND IN CONCRETE AND CONCRETE BLOCK

Surface-mounting a box on placed concrete or on concrete (or cinder) block walls is easy to do. If you want to recess the box into a concrete block wall, the technique is simple, but the job is exacting.

In either type of installation, first locate the position of the box(es) and run the wires, probably in conduit, to the location.

SURFACE-MOUNTED BOXES

In an extremely damp location, use a waterproof outdoor electrical box. You can mount it directly on the concrete surface with concrete subfloor adhesive.

For a standard box, position the box on the surface and, with a nail or felt pen, make a mark through the screw holes in the back of the box on the surface, locating the positions of the mounting screws.

With a carbide-tipped masonry bit, drill ¼-inch holes into the concrete at the marks. The holes should be deep enough to accept lead, plastic, or fiber masonry expansion plugs or anchors. Tap an anchor into each hole.

Place the box with the mounting holes over the anchors and drive in the mounting screws. The anchors expand against the sides of their holes so that the screws hold the box tightly against the concrete surface.

Run the wires into the box and make the necessary connections.

FLUSH-MOUNTED BOXES

Use a power drill with a masonry bit, and a cold chisel and hammer to open the block wall to recess both the wiring and the box.

You can use a star drill and hammer instead of the power outfit, but it is time-consuming to do so.

Make a cardboard template of the box and trace the outline of the template on the block wall surface, using a felt pen. Then outline the guidelines with masking tape.

With the pen, trace a channel on the surface where the wires will be recessed, assuming that you can't fish the wires (cable) through the center holes in the blocks. The channel should be about 1 inch wide. Outline the marks with masking tape.

With the power drill and masonry bit, drill a series of holes within the guidelines. Make as many holes as you can. Then connect the holes with the cold chisel and hammer, cleaning out all concrete debris.

Fit the box and the cable into the recesses. You probably will have to do some trimming with the chisel for a good fit. Run the mounting screws into the box. Then insert the cable in the channel, mount the cable in the box, and put the box in the recess.

With a thick mixture of cement, fill the channel and recess. A small trowel or a putty knife works well. Use ready-to-mix mortar mix that's available at building material stores. Add water and stir.

When the mortar has set—at least three days or so—remove the mounting screws from the box. The purpose of the screws was to prevent mortar from entering the screw holes.

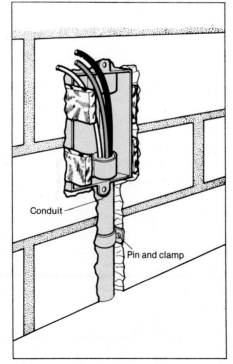

Surface-mounted boxes. Box is mounted with masonry expansion anchors. Drill holes, tap in anchors, drive screws into them.

Recessed box in block. Use drill and cold chisel to cut box and cable recesses. Front edges of recessed box are flush with block wall.

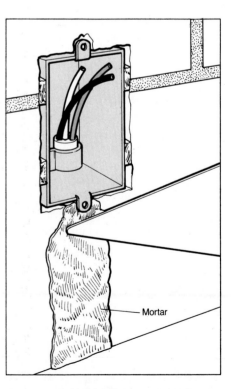

Filling in recesses. When box and cable are in place, fill all the openings around wire and box with mortar mix tinted to blend with wall.

WORKING WITH CEILING BOXES

To install a ceiling box when there is no access from an attic, you must work entirely from below. Wear goggles for safety.

There are two kinds of installations. An offset hanger bar fastened between joists lets you slide a box to any point across the width of the space, but you must open the ceiling enough to get at both joists. A stud secures the box to the bar. A box with a side flange can be screwed to the side of one joist, if the location is appropriate. This requires a smaller opening in the ceiling.

BOX IN GYPSUM CEILING

Locate the joists in the ceiling and mark the location for the box. You will have to have a 10 × 16-inch opening in the gypsum board in order to screw the bar hanger to two joists. Cut along the location marks with a utility knife and break out the gypsum board.

Fish the power cable through the ceiling to the box site. Then mount the box on the bar hanger between the joists, wire the box, and patch the ceiling with a piece of matching gypsum board with a cutout for the box.

ACCESS THROUGH ATTIC

If the attic is not finished, you can work from the attic to install a ceiling box. If the attic is rough floored, you can remove a section of the flooring and install the box. Either way, the box has to be mounted on a hanger or fastened to the face of a joist.

Drill a locating hole in the room ceiling. With an 18-inch drill extension and ⅛-inch bit, go through the hole and through the attic flooring. Stick a wire up through the hole.

In the attic, locate the wire and then cut through the rough flooring and remove enough so that you can insert and fasten the hanger or the box to the joists.

Use the pilot hole in the ceiling to locate the box. Cut a hole in the ceiling for it. In the attic, connect the cable to the box and replace the flooring.

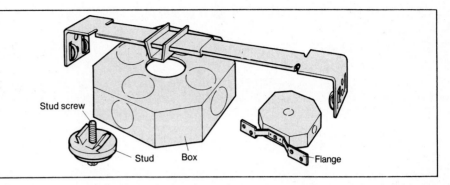

Ceiling boxes. For a gypsum-board ceiling, a bar hanger allows box to be positioned anywhere between two joists. Stud screws into the hanger through the box. Flange-type box can be screwed to the side of a joist when that is an appropriate position.

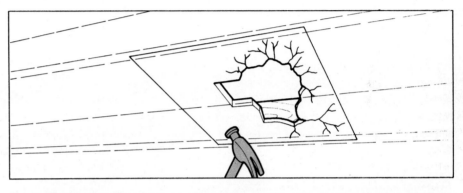

Box in gypsum ceiling. Break hole in ceiling to find joists. Draw 10 × 16-inch rectangle around hole, edges overlapping two joists. Cut rectangle with knife or saw. Fish wires; install hanger and box.

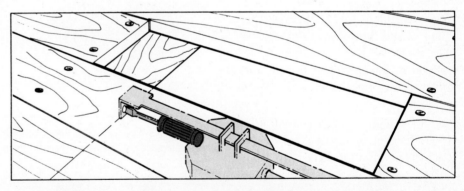

Access through attic. Bar hanger fits between joists. If attic flooring is rough, remove a section of flooring and work from above, saving lots of gypsum-board patching on ceiling below.

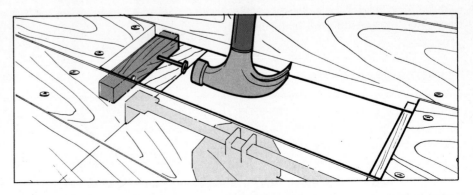

Replacing flooring. To replace flooring, fasten nailing strips to joists for flooring support. Then nail the replacement flooring to the strips.

 # Plugs, Cords, and Sockets

Replacing plugs, cords, and sockets ranks among the easiest electrical projects to do. Replacement products are readily available and inexpensive. Only basic hand tools are required.

PLUGS AND THE CODE

Many lamps and plug-in electrical devices in use today still have a standard-wired or clamp-type plug, neither of which is recognized by the current National Electrical Code. You may find them for sale, however, in electrical departments.

If you are replacing a plug, make sure that the plug meets code requirements. Do not attempt to repair a broken or damaged plug. A replacement is not costly, and you're assured that the new plug will perform properly.

Many plugs are permanently attached to electrical cords. That is, you can't disassemble the plug to disconnect the cord. In this situation, cut the cord in back of the plug, strip the insulation, and replace the bad plug with a new plug.

ELECTRICAL CORDS

A variety of line cords is available for lamps and appliances. When replacing a plug, be sure to check the cord for wear and tear. If you see damage, replace the cord along with the plug. Match the cord to the plug and appliance. For example, don't replace heater cord with zip cord.

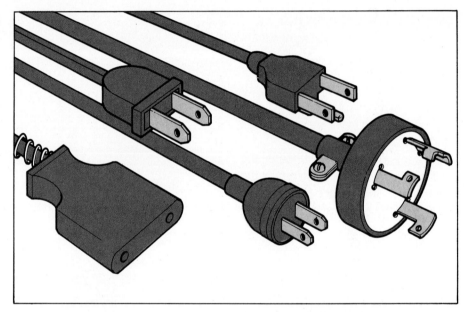

Standard-wired plugs include round-cord types, core-wired and heater plugs. The grounded three-prong is permanently attached to the wire. Heater plugs may also be so attached.

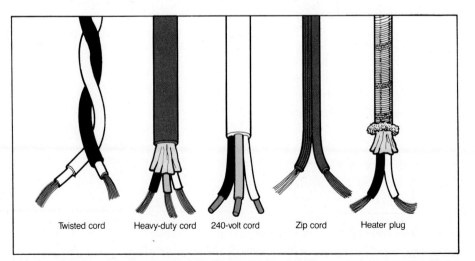

Twisted cord   Heavy-duty cord   240-volt cord   Zip cord   Heater plug

Cords may be precut and packaged in different lengths, or you may buy them by the lineal foot. The third wire in heavy-duty and 240-volt cords is the grounding wire.

Replacing a Standard Plug

Most replacement plugs are wired as shown at right, whatever wire is used; zip cord is shown here.

STEP 1
REMOVE OLD PLUG
With a knife, cut the cord in back of the plug you're replacing. Replace a worn or damaged cord.

STEP 2
STRIP INSULATION
With wire strippers, remove about ¾ inch of insulation from the wire ends.

STEP 3
INSERT WIRE INTO PLUG
Thread the cord into the plug. The cord should fit the plug opening tightly.

STEP 4
TIE UNDERWRITERS' KNOT
Split the cord and/or insulated wires inside the cord so you can tie an Underwriters' knot to prevent the cord from pulling loose from terminal screws.

STEP 5
PULL THE KNOT TIGHT
Pull hard on the ends of the wires to tighten the knot. Then pull the cord down into the base of the plug.

STEP 6
WIRE AROUND PRONGS
The wire connections go clockwise around the plug prongs and to the terminal screws in the base.

STEP 7
WIRE AROUND TERMINALS
If the wire is stranded, twist it tight and then wrap it around the terminals in the direction the terminal screws turn. Then tighten the terminals.

STEP 8
INSTALL INSULATOR
Install the cardboard insulator over the prongs and push it down flush.

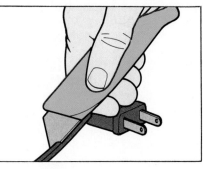

Remove old plug. Cut the plug from the cord if you can't remove it by loosening terminal screws.

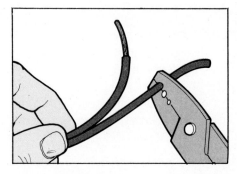

Strip insulation. Remove insulation with wire strippers. Rotate strippers around wire.

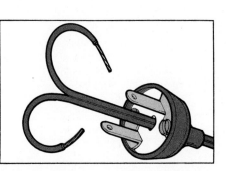

Insert wire into plug. Pull the cord through the plug. Cord should fit tightly in the plug opening.

Tie Underwriters' knot. Tie an Underwriters' knot in the wires, using this drawing as a guideline.

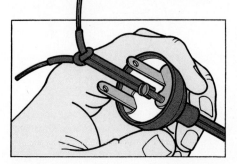

Pull the knot tight. Pull the knot tight and then pull the cord down into the base of the plug.

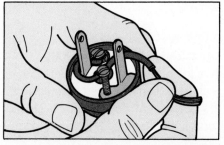

Wire around prongs. Pull the insulated wires around the prongs in the base of the new plug.

Wire around terminals. Wrap the wires around terminals in direction terminals turn. Tighten.

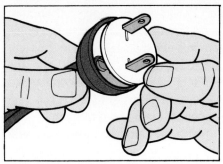

Install insulator. Slip the cardboard insulator in place over the prongs. This protects wires.

Replacing a Light Socket and Switch

This project applies to a brass lamp socket that has a rotating, push-button, or chain switch attached to the socket. Do not attempt to repair the switch or socket; replace it with a new one.

Be sure to disconnect the light from the power source before you start working on the socket.

STEP 1
REMOVE THE HARP

The lampshade is attached to the lamp with a frame, called a harp, that fits into a bracket below the socket. Slide up two finger nuts on the harp as you squeeze the harp.

STEP 2
REMOVE SOCKET HOUSING

To remove the metal housing from the socket, squeeze in on the sides of the upper sleeve just above the base cap and work it upward, out of the cap. Slip both the brass and cardboard sleeves off to expose the socket and terminal screws.

STEP 3
DISCONNECT THE WIRES

Turn the terminal screws counterclockwise to loosen the wires connected to the screws. At this point, check the cord. If it is damaged, it should be replaced. See page 69 for details.

STEP 4
WIRE THE NEW SOCKET

Twist the stranded wire as tightly as you can between your fingers. Then connect the hot copper wire to the brass terminal and the silver wire to the silver terminal. The wires should fit under the terminal screws. If not, disconnect the wires, twist them tight once again, and reconnect them to the terminals.

Place the cardboard insulation over the socket and install the brass-plated upper section. Tighten the screw holding the cord in the socket, if the socket has one. Replace the harp.

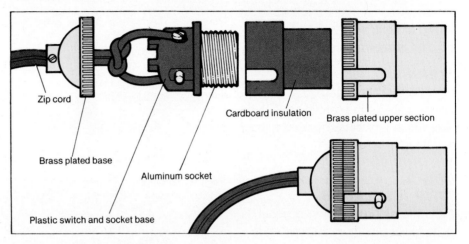

Zip cord

Cardboard insulation

Brass plated upper section

Brass plated base

Aluminum socket

Plastic switch and socket base

Anatomy of a brass lamp socket. This exploded diagram shows the individual parts of a brass socket in a lamp, in which the switch—button or chain—is included in the socket. Don't try to repair a defective socket switch or the socket. Replace it with a new socket.

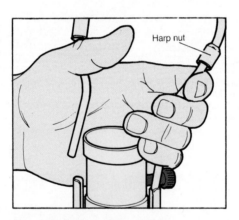

Harp nut

Remove the harp. To remove the harp, pull up on the small finger nuts while you squeeze the harp lightly. Lift the harp from bracket.

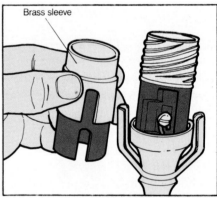

Brass sleeve

Remove socket housing. Squeeze the brass sleeve just above the base cap and slip it off along with the insulator inside.

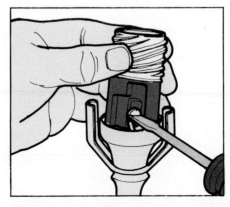

Disconnect the wires. Loosen the terminal screws and pull off the wires. If inspection shows that the cord is damaged, replace the cord.

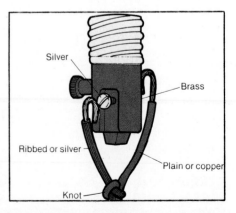

Silver

Brass

Ribbed or silver

Plain or copper

Knot

Wire the new socket. Attach the copper wire to the brass terminal and the silver wire to the silver terminal. Reassemble socket.

Replacing Lamp Cord

If you notice that the cord on a lamp is damaged (with or without a damaged switch or socket), replace it.

The simple procedure is described and illustrated here.

1. Unplug the lamp from the power source.

2. Remove the harp from the base of the socket (see page 68.)

3. Remove the brass shell and insulation jacket from the socket.

4. Unscrew the terminals holding the wires. Then loosen any screws holding the wire in the cap of the socket. Untie the knot at the cap, if there is one.

STEP 1
REWIRING THE LAMP

With electrician's tape, join the new wire with the old wire at the socket connection. Make a tight joint.

Then carefully pull the old cord out of the lamp and the new cord into the lamp at the same time. When the new cord appears, unwrap the tape.

STEP 2
REPLACE THE PLUG

It's a good idea to install a new plug on the new wire. Strip about ¾ inch insulation from the wire, slip on the new plug, and tie an Underwriters' knot in the wire.

STEP 3
SEAT WIRE IN THE PLUG

Pull the wire into the base of the plug and connect the bare wires to the terminals. Then rewire the brass socket. Also see pages 67 and 68.

STEP 4
CORD WITH POLARIZED PLUG

If your home is equipped with polarized outlets, replace the lamp cord with a polarized plug and cord set. Buy at least one foot more cord than the total you need. The UL-listed polarized cord should be the same size as the cord already in use: No. 18 gauge wire.

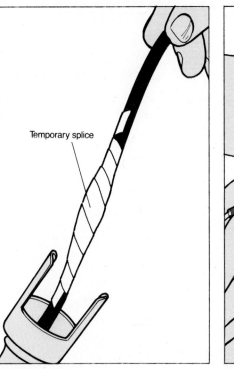

Temporary splice

Rewiring the lamp. Splice the new wire to the old wire and pull both through the lamp at the same time after wire is unscrewed.

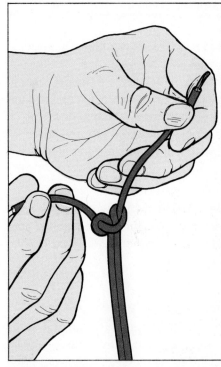

Replace the plug. Install a new plug on the wire. Strip off ¾ inch insulation for terminal connections. Then tie a UL knot in wire.

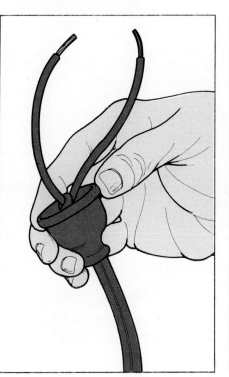

Seat wire in plug. Pull the knot into the base of the plug. Wrap insulated wire around prongs; screw bare ends to terminals.

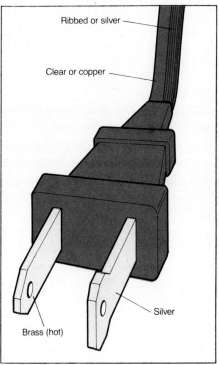

Ribbed or silver

Clear or copper

Silver

Brass (hot)

Cord with polarized plug. Large prong of polarized plug goes to the silver wire; small prong goes to hot copper wire. Plug and wire are a unit.

HEAVY-DUTY, APPLIANCE, AND FLAT PLUGS

Under code provisions, new plugs for home lamps and appliances must be molded in plastic around the cord; they cannot be removed or replaced. Plugs must also be polarized: the prongs are two different shapes that fit a polarized outlet only one way.

If the line cord is damaged only at plug, disconnect cord, cut off the damaged part, and attach a new plug. If both plug and cord are damaged, replace both with polarized products.

STEP 1
HEAVY-DUTY 125V PLUGS

Removable twist-lock plugs are used on some appliances. Loosen the cord clamp, unhook the wires, and pull the cord out.

STEP 2
CONNECT NEW PLUG

Insert the cord and lead the wires around the blades. Hook the black wire to the brass terminal, white wire to the silver terminal, and green wire to the green terminal. Tighten the cord clamp.

STEP 1
APPLIANCE PLUGS

You may not be able to find this type of plug on the market. If you can, unscrew the clamshelllike cover and remove wire from terminals.

STEP 2
CORD SPRING AND HOOKUP

Slip the cord spring onto the cord and into the grooves in the plug base. Then connect the wires to screw terminals. Assemble plug.

STEP 1
CORE-WIRED PLUGS

Remove the insulator from a flat plug; pull the core out of the housing and remove the wires. Pull wire through the new plug and separate it.

STEP 2
WIRES GO TO TERMINALS

Fasten wires to the screw terminals on the core. Seat the core in the housing and replace the insulator.

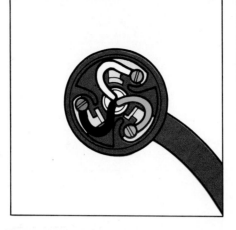

Heavy-duty 125V plug. With screwdriver, loosen terminal screws and unhook the wires. Pull the cord out through the neck of the plug.

Connect new plug. Insert cord through neck. Connect black wire to brass terminal; white wire to silver terminal; green to green.

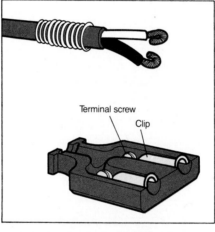

Appliance plug. Don't throw old appliance away. Buy new cord assembly or plug. Unscrew cover; release wires from terminals.

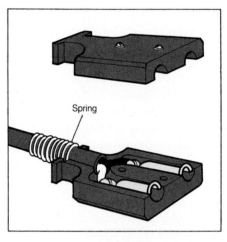

Cord spring and hookup. Slip cord spring on cord and into grooves in plug base. Fasten wires to terminals. Screw together plug halves.

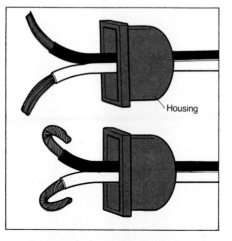

Core-wired plugs. Remove insulator or core from flat plugs, pull the core out of the housing, and remove the wires from terminals.

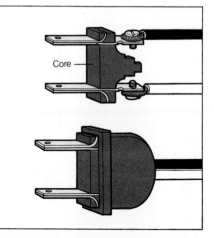

Wires go to terminals. Draw the cord through the housing and separate. Fasten stranded wires to terminals; replace core in housing.

Replacing Multisocket Lamp Switches

Two-socket lamps usually have one on-off switch that controls both sockets. Three-socket lamps may have individual switches or a single on-off switch.

SOLDERED TWO-SOCKET

The sockets are molded together. Wire connections run internally between the sockets. The switch turns both sockets on or off at the same time. If one socket won't light, undo the wire nuts holding the switch and the power wires together. Detach the switch wires from the power wires. Connect new switch.

SEPARATE SOCKETS

In this two-socket lamp, the sockets are wired separately and can be replaced individually. The switch turns both bulbs on or off at the same time. The wiring arrangement is more complex, because jumper wires connect sockets. With the exception of the jumpers, the replacement is the same as above.

SOCKETS WITH SWITCHES

Three-socket lamps with individual switches are repaired this way. Remove the wires from the socket's terminal screws, withdraw the old socket, and reattach the wires to the terminal screws of the new socket. Since three sockets receive current through one power cord, there are jumper wires from the line cord to the terminal screws of each socket.

ONE-SWITCH SOCKETS

A three-socket lamp having one four-way switch is shown bottom right. The first position turns on socket No. 1 only; the second position turns on sockets No. 2 and 3. The third position turns on all sockets. A black wire connects the switch to the line cord, a black wire connects the switch to socket No. 3, and a black wire connects the switch to socket No. 1. Remove the switch by disconnecting wire nuts. Then reconnect them to new switch wires.

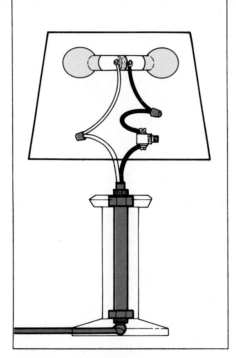

Soldered two-socket. To replace a soldered double socket, remove wire nuts and release splices. Rewire as shown, following color code.

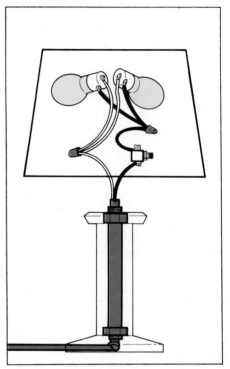

Separate sockets. If lights work independently, replace either socket separately. Release wire nuts; install the new socket or switch.

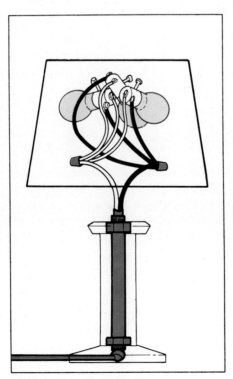

Sockets with switches. If each socket has its own switch, each is replaced separately. Just release wire from nuts and rewire with nuts.

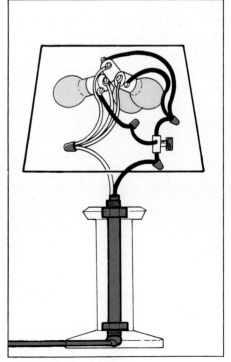

One-switch sockets. To replace single-switch on a multisocket fixture, attach a white wire to each socket; then attach hot wire to each.

INSTALLING GFCIs

A Ground Fault Circuit Interrupter (GFCI) is a safety device that continually compares the amount of current flowing on the black and white wires of a fixture or appliance circuit. Any imbalance indicates leakage in the system. If the GFCI detects as little as .005 amp difference in the current flows, it breaks the circuit in a fortieth of a second.

GFCIs are now required by many local codes in kitchens, bathrooms, utility rooms, other wet or damp locations, and exterior installations. There are three basic types: plug-in and wired into a conventional box—which you can install—and a main panel, whole-circuit model. Leave that to a professional.

PLUG-INS

Simply plug the GFCI device into a standard wall receptacle. It has plug blades on the back.

WIRED-IN-BOX TYPE

1. Turn off the power to the circuit and remove the old receptacle from the box.

2. Make sure the bare wire ends are safely away from the walls of the box, then turn on the circuit power. Use a voltage tester to identify the incoming (feed) power line. Touch one probe to a bare black wire, the other probe to the box. When the tester lights, that wire is the feed. *Turn off the power*. Label the feed black and white wires.

3. Measure the box in the wall. If it is less than 2¼ inches deep, mount the spacer supplied with the GFCI unit on the front of the box.

4. Connect the GFCI black and white leads labeled LINE to the feed (power cable) wires of the same color. Connect the GFCI leads labeled LOAD to the outgoing wires in the box. If there are no outgoing wires, tape a wire nut on each GFCI LOAD lead.

5. Connect the green GFCI grounding wire with a pigtail to the box grounding terminal.

6. Mount the GFCI on the spacer or box and screw on the faceplate.

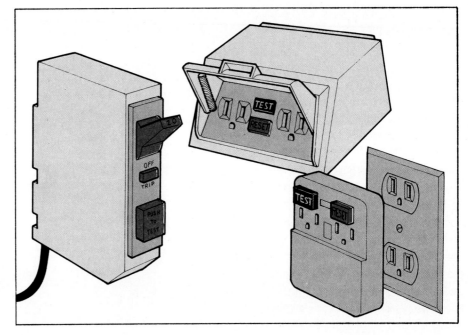

Types of GFCIs. Plug-in GFCI (right) has blades that fit into slots of conventional outlet. Circuit breaker GFCI is installed in main panel to protect all outlets on a given circuit. Weatherproof model is for outdoor installation. Wired-in-box model is shown below.

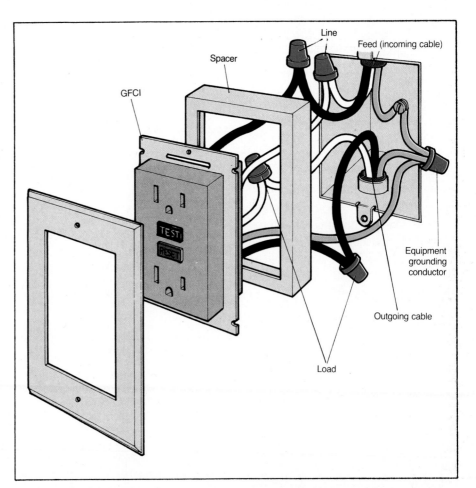

Wiring a GFCI in a switch or outlet box. Wiring diagram for middle-of-the run GFCI. Two key wires are LOAD and LINE. GFCIs are sold in a complete package, ready for installation. Many codes now require them, especially in circuits subject to dampness and moisture conditions.

 # Wiring in New Construction

If you are building anew or remodeling old construction where the framing members are exposed (not covered with gypsum wallboard, plaster, paneling, or tile), wiring in new circuits and fixtures is extremely easy and well within basic do-it-yourself skills.

Tools are easier to operate and electrical materials are easier to install between the open framing of new construction. However, you may spend more money for materials because it may be easier to take the long way to new circuit hookups than shortcuts.

You should run the wiring yourself and then let a professional electrician make the hookups at the power source. The pro's charges are not prohibitive, and the pro will check your work so you will be assured that it is safe and sound. In this chapter, you'll find the basic techniques for installing circuits.

DRAW A PLAN

We recommend that you make a wiring plan of the project first, in order to save money and complete the work faster.

Draw a plan of the room or area on a piece of graph paper, putting in accurate dimensions. Then mark where you want lights, outlets, switches, and other fixtures in the overall plan, and where and how the room wiring is connected to the power cable coming from the main service panel. This way, you will have a rough estimate of the materials that you will need when you go to the store to buy them.

ELECTRICAL PERMITS

A wiring permit may be required by code in your community. If so, you can get one at the city or county building commission office.

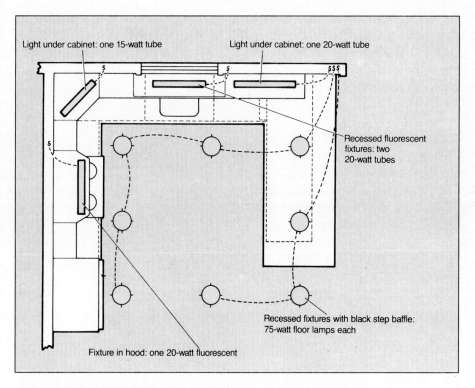

Light under cabinet: one 15-watt tube

Light under cabinet: one 20-watt tube

Recessed fluorescent fixtures: two 20-watt tubes

Recessed fixtures with black step baffle: 75-watt floor lamps each

Fixture in hood: one 20-watt fluorescent

This plan shows where the lighting goes in a new kitchen. Your plan doesn't require electrical symbols (unless you want to use them), but you should identify fixtures, switches, and outlets, so you can determine material needs.

Running Cable Through Wall Framing

There are several techniques that you can use. All are easy, especially if you own a portable electric drill with variable speed and reversing capabilities.

DRILL HOLES FOR CABLE

You'll need a power drill or hand brace and a ⅝- or ¾-inch bit to make holes through studs. The hole should be not less than 1¼ inches from the facing edge of the stud.

ADD PLATES, IF NEEDED

If you can't leave 1¼ inches of space between the hole and the edge of the framing member, put a steel plate on the framing member for the necessary support. The plates are available at stores selling electrical supplies.

CUT NOTCHES FOR CABLE

The framing members can be notched at the edge with a chisel to accept the cable. Make two parallel saw cuts ¾ inch deep and 1 inch apart in the framing. Cut out the excess wood between cuts with a chisel.

Once the cable is in position, cover the notch with a steel plate to protect the cable and strengthen the framing member.

CURVE THE CABLE

To avoid kinking the cable, gradually change the position of holes in the framing across a wall. Kinking won't choke the flow of electricity, but it can crack the cable insulation.

HOLES AT BOTTOM PLATE

The cable is best supported in holes drilled in framing members along the bottom plate of the wall. The same hole location requirements apply here.

HOLES IN TOP PLATE

For circuits supplying power to switches and outlets fastened to studs, the wiring may be run through the top plate of the wall and down the studs.

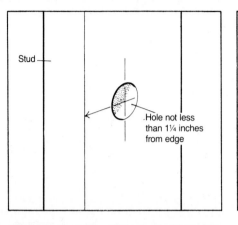

Drill holes for cable. Holes for electrical cable drilled in studs should be placed at least 1¼ inches away from any stud face.

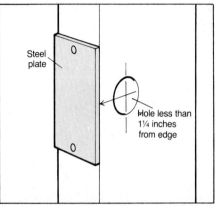

Add plates, if needed. If less than 1¼-inch space is available, you should support hole and framing member with a steel plate made for this.

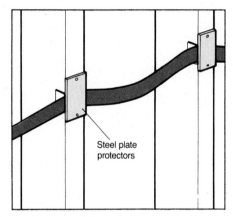

Cut notches for cable. Notches instead of holes for cable may be cut with a saw and chisel. Cover the notch with a steel plate for safety.

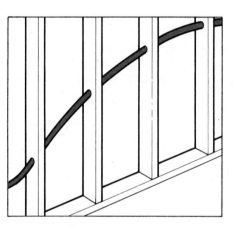

Curve the cable. Avoid kinking the cable by raising and lowering holes gradually in wall framing materials. Let the cable curve.

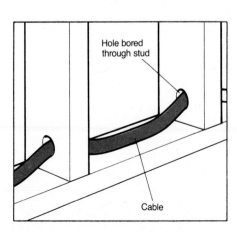

Holes at bottom plate. Cable also may be installed through holes in framing near the bottom plate of the wall. Drilling space may be tight.

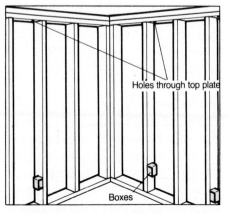

Holes in top plate. For switches and outlets on individual circuits, run the wire through top plate of the wall and down the studs.

Running Cable Through Open Ceiling

The technique for stringing wire and cable through joists and rafters is very similar to running it through wall framing. Some helpful techniques are explained below.

CABLE RUNNING AT RIGHT ANGLES TO JOISTS

In this installation, the cable must be routed through holes or notched in the joists to protect the cable. Use ¾-inch holes; minimum spacing for the holes is 1¼ inches from the joist edge. If you drill closer than this, reinforce the framing members with steel plates.

RUNNING CABLE IN UNFINISHED ATTICS

You can run cable at right angles over the tops of ceiling joists, but you must nail 1 × 4 furring as guard strips spaced just far enough apart to form a channel for the cable.

You can also run cable along the length of ceiling and floor joists or wall studding, centered on the broad side and stapled at appropriate intervals.

RUNNING CABLE IN UNFINISHED BASEMENTS

If you are running cable in an unfinished basement, most codes let you fasten the cable to the edges of the joists facing the basement—*provided* the cable is No. 8 gauge or larger.

If you use smaller cable, drill holes in the joists, or run a furring strip continuously across the underside of the joists and staple the cable to it. Fastening cable to the undersides of the joists may prevent finishing the ceiling gypsum board or furred-out tile, but will work for a suspended ceiling.

CABLE ANCHORING AT BOX

As you install cable either in wall or ceiling framing, keep in mind that the cable must be anchored with staples or straps within 12 inches of a box. Leave enough cable slack.

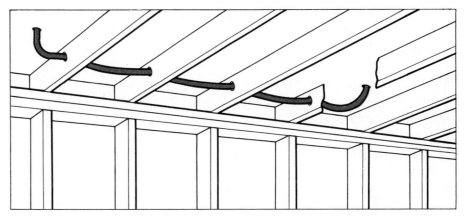

Cable running at right angles to joists. If the cable runs at right angles to the joists in a finished space, you must bore holes through the joists to support and protect cable. Recess holes at least 1¼ inches from edges.

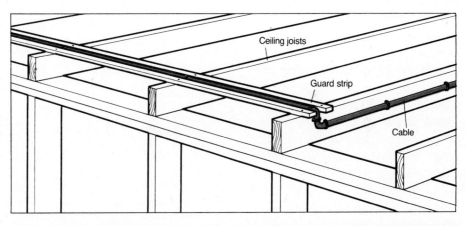

Running cable in unfinished attics. You can run across the joists, but you must make channels with two 1 × 4-inch furring strips—or strips as thick as the cable—to protect the cable from damage.

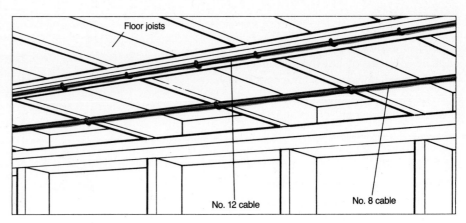

Running cable in unfinished basements. You can fasten cross-joist runs of No. 8 or larger cable directly to the joists. For smaller cable, drill holes, or run a board as shown and fasten cable to it.

Working with Outlet Boxes

Outlet boxes are similar to switch and junction boxes in the design of their knockouts, brackets and mounting devices, and cable clamps. They are either square or octagonal, and that's how you can generally tell them from switch boxes (see page 78).

OCTAGONAL BOXES

These are used mainly for ceiling lighting fixtures and other applications where more space is required within the box. With a bar hanger and stud fitting, an octagonal-shaped box may be mounted anywhere between joists.

There are two basic types of hangers for these boxes: drywall and offset for shallow spaces.

You also can buy flanged boxes. This type is attached by screws or nails through the flange to the ceiling joists.

SQUARE OUTLET BOXES

These are known as outlet and device boxes. You can buy covers for square boxes that close the box, raise the device in the box, or extend the box.

Extension rings are used when boxes are mounted behind plastered or tiled ceilings or walls. A ring extends the edge of a box so it is flush with the finished surface.

BOX SIZING

By code, you may install only a certain number of wires in a box. The table on page 57 will help you buy the right size. Keep in mind, however, that the space is reduced by the studs, clamps, and grounding wires installed in the box. Here's how you figure it:

● One stud: subtract one wire from the figure in the chart.

● One clamp: subtract one wire. If there already is a clamp in the box do not reduce the number.

● One strap: subtract one wire.

● One ground: subtract one.

● One hickey: subtract one.

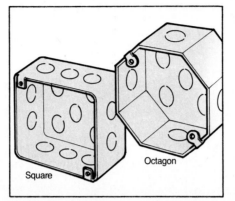

Box shapes. Outlet boxes are octagonal or square in shape. They're manufactured from metal or plastic in many different sizes.

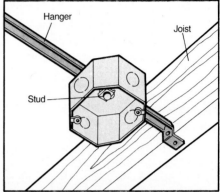

Ceiling hangers. For ceiling fixtures, the best choice is octagonal boxes that can be mounted on hangers with studs to span joists.

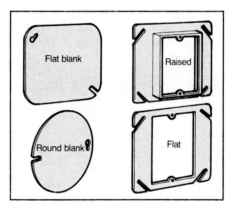

Covers for boxes. Typical covers for outlet boxes include these. The covers are attached to the fronts of boxes with mounting screws.

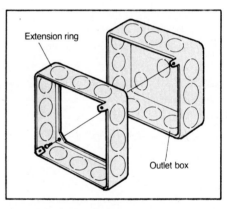

Box extension. If the finished ceiling or wall surface lies beyond the box front or you need more space, add an extension ring.

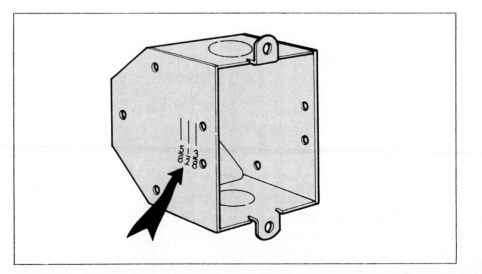

Depth gauge on boxes. Line markings on box side serve as a depth gauge for setting box to extend past the face of a framing member. Depths are for standard gypsum board thicknesses: 3/8, 1/2, 5/8 inch.

INSTALLING OUTLET BOXES

Cable running to outlet boxes must be anchored to the framing within 12 inches of the outlet. Also, on a 120-volt circuit, you should have at least one junction or major box to accommodate the circuit wiring since there will be a different number of wires going to and from the outlet boxes. A $4 \times 4 \times 2\frac{1}{8}$ inch box usually provides enough space for these additional wires.

FACE-NAILED BOXES

If the box will be nailed to the face of a framing member, buy one that has a bracket running parallel to the side.

EDGE-NAILED BOXES

If a box is to be nailed to the edge of a framing member, it should have a front bracket extending out from the box.

BOXES BETWEEN FRAMING

Ceiling boxes often must be mounted between framing members instead of being nailed directly to them. You will need bar hangers.

STEP 1
REMOVE THE KNOCKOUTS

With a punch and hammer, remove the center knockout in the box for the hanger stud. Then remove the knockouts necessary for the cable.

STEP 2
FASTEN BOX TO BAR

With a screwdriver, remove a clamping screw and stud from the adjustable bar hanger.

STEP 3
INSTALL THE BOX

Set the box over the bar fitting and tighten the clamping screw just enough to hold the box to the bar.

STEP 4
MEASURE AND TIGHTEN

Measure between the framing where you want the box to be located. Then tighten the box mounting screw. Or install the hanger between the framing, position the box, and tighten the screw.

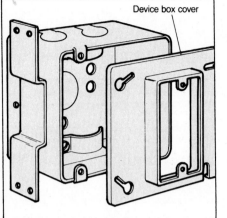

Face-nailed boxes. Face-nailed box fastens to the face of a framing member. Cover for box fits flush with material covering the framing.

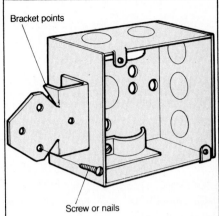

Edge-nailed boxes. Edge-nailed box fastens to the edge of framing member. Bracket is attached to box to prespace it for wall covering.

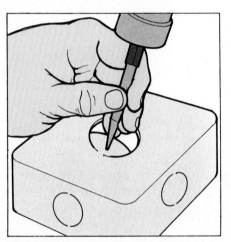

Remove the knockouts. Remove center knock-out for hanger stud. Also remove knockouts you'll need to install the wires in box.

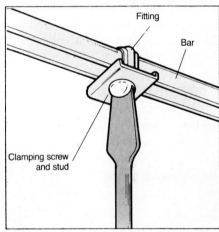

Fasten box to bar. Remove clamping screw and stud from bar hanger with screwdriver. Fitting runs in a track, so it may be adjusted.

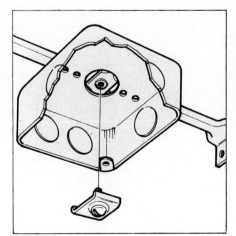

Install the box. Loosely mount box on hanger with stud and screw, so it can slide on hanger to the position you want it.

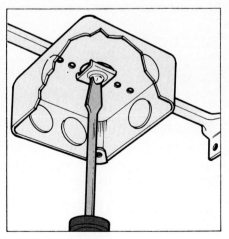

Measure and tighten. Tighten clamp screw when box is in correct position. Best way is to install the hanger, then adjust the box.

Working with Switch Boxes

Switch boxes are rectangular in shape and, like outlet and junction boxes (sometimes called major boxes), have little wire-holding devices, special clamps, mounting brackets, and knockouts. You can buy metal or plastic boxes, and a model called a handy box (see page 79). Plastic and handy boxes cannot be ganged together.

DEPTH GAUGE ON BOXES

Many switch boxes have depth gauge markings on the side of the box. The markings let you position the boxes on framing members without measuring.

Boxes must not be recessed more than 1/4 inch from the surface of gypsum wallboard, plaster, or concrete.

COMBUSTIBLE MOUNTING

Boxes must be mounted flush with the surface of combustible materials, such as wood paneling.

PLASTIC BOXES

Plastic boxes are mounted on framing members with nails driven through brackets on the boxes.

Cable clamps are not necessary inside the boxes, if the cable is stapled or anchored a maximum of 8 inches away from the point that it enters the box. Also, the full outer insulation of the cable must enter the box at least 1/4 inch.

CABLE CLAMPS

These metal devices are especially designed to hold cable and wires inside boxes. Several styles are available.

GROUNDING CLIPS

These devices clip onto the edges of boxes and are used to connect cable grounding wires to the box.

QUICK CLIPS

With quick clips you don't need to tighten a screw to hold the cable or wire in position. Just wedge the conductors into the clips.

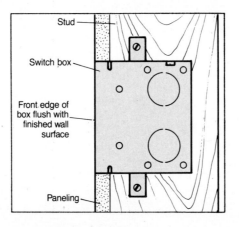

Combustible mounting. Boxes must be mounted flush with combustible materials, according to National Code.

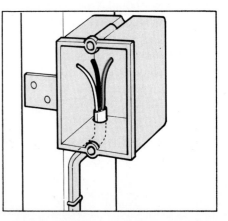

Plastic boxes. Plastic boxes don't have cable clamps. You must anchor cable within 8 inches of box entrance, according to code.

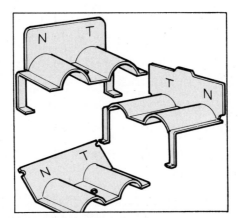

Cable clamps. Clamps inside boxes are of various designs. A single screw holds a clamp and tightens it against the cable.

Grounding clips. If a metal box doesn't have a grounding wire terminal, you can use a clip to attach the wire to the edge of the box.

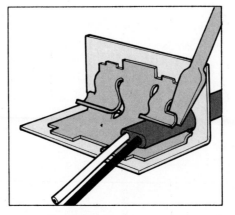

Quick clips. These clips use leaf-spring pressure to hold a cable. Lift with a screwdriver to insert cable, then release.

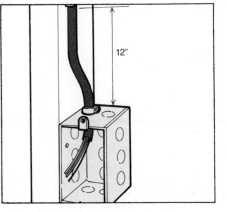

Cable in metal boxes. Support cable in metal box with connector; staple to framing within 12 inches, then every 4 1/2 feet.

INSTALLING SWITCH BOXES

In most construction, the codes dictate where and how switch boxes are installed. In new construction, cables must be anchored (stapled) every 4½ feet along sills, joists, rafters, and studs. If they run at right angles through notches or holes in the framing, cables are considered to be anchored.

CABLE IN METAL BOXES

Staple cable to a framing member no more than 12 inches from a metal box.

CABLE IN PLASTIC BOXES

If you are using nonmetallic boxes, a cable must be stapled within 8 inches of entering a box, and the sheathing (outer insulation) must extend into the box ½ inch. Check your electrical code to see if a snap-in cable connector is required.

BOXES BETWEEN STUDS

Where possible, switch boxes should be fastened directly to framing members. If this is not possible, you can suspend the boxes between studs on 1 × 2-inch wooden furring strips cleated and nailed between the studs. The 1 × 2s are spaced the height of the switch box, and the box is fastened to these strips.

STEEL SUPPORT BARS

An alternate to furring strips for suspending boxes between studs is steel support bars (similar to ceiling box hangers) that span the studs and are nailed to them.

HANDY BOXES

These single-switch boxes have to be fastened directly to a framing member. The best way is to use screws driven by a portable electric drill with a screw-driving bit.

MASONRY SURFACES

The best way to mount boxes on any kind of masonry surface is with masonry anchors and screws. Measure, mark, and drill holes in the masonry, insert anchors, and mount the box.

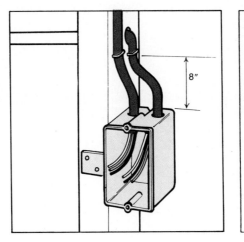

Cable in plastic boxes. At nonmetallic boxes, cable must be anchored within 8 inches of box. ½ inch of sheathing must enter box.

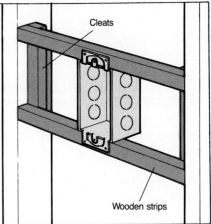

Boxes between studs. Secure boxes between framing members with furring strips spaced the height of the box. Screw box to strips.

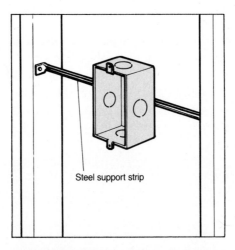

Steel support bars. You can buy steel support bars to suspend boxes between framing members. Boxes screw to the bars.

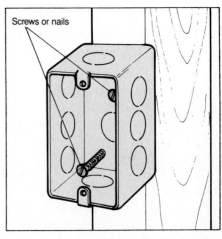

Handy boxes. Fasten handy boxes directly to framing members. It may be easier to fasten the boxes with screws driven by a drill.

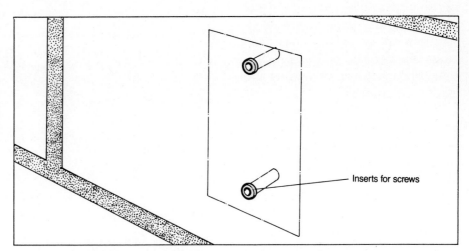

Masonry surfaces. On any solid masonry surface (concrete, brick, stone) fasten box to masonry anchors inserted in drilled holes. (For recessed boxes in concrete or cinder block, see page 64.)

Wiring in Existing Construction

Stringing wire and cable through existing walls and ceilings is akin to fishing in a muddy creek: you can't see where the line is going, and you have to have lots and lots of patience. However, fishing wire and cable through walls and ceilings is within your home maintenance and improvement skills, and in this chapter, we'll show you some tricks of the trade to make the job easier.

ANATOMY OF A WALL

No matter what a wall or floor is made of, the inside framework is the same.

The *studs* are the vertical wood beams, generally 2 × 4s mounted 16 inches apart, center to center. All wall materials are fastened to studs. In some localities, where high humidity has an adverse effect on wood, metal studs are used. The best electrical installations are those in which junction boxes are mounted on the side of a stud, although this is not required and may not be possible.

The *joists* are the horizontal wood beams mounted 16 inches apart, center to center, in attics and basements. Ceiling materials and flooring are nailed to joists. Cable often runs either parallel or at right angles to the joists.

FROM TOP OR BOTTOM

If you have access to walls from a basement or attic, you can get power into walls by fishing the cable down or up instead of across.

In many installations, going the long way around to make the connections may be easiest, although you may have to spend more money for cable. The cost of the cable may be less expensive than ripping into walls and ceilings, however.

If you have to run cable across the framing, you almost always will have to chisel into or remove the wall covering in order to position the cable or wires.

Take time at the beginning to examine and study the different routes that might be open for the cable. Then make a rough sketch or map of the route the cable will take. A little work early on can save you plenty of time and money later.

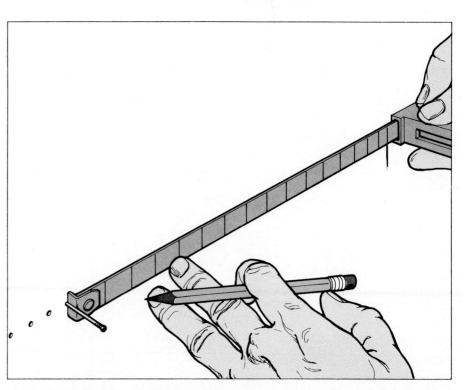

A *sure* way to find framing members is to start at a corner and measure out 16 inches. Then drive a small finishing nail through the wall covering until you find the framing member. Mark this spot and measure out 16 inches for other framing locations.

Opening Walls and Ceilings

Usually the first step in running cable is to open a wall or ceiling where the switch, outlet, or junction box will be located. Then you route or fish the wire or cable to this point.

IN GYPSUM WALLBOARD
Openings in gypsum wallboard (trade name Sheetrock) and drywall are cut with a keyhole saw or portable electric saber saw with a wallboard blade.

Outline the opening on the wall and mask the outline with tape. Then drill holes in the material so you can insert the saw. Make the cut on all four sides and either remove the scrap or knock it back between the framing members.

IN PLASTERED WOOD LATH
Make the outline drawing and remove the plaster within the outline with a cold chisel. Then cut the lath with a keyhole or saber saw after drilling a hole to start the blade.

THROUGH METAL LATH
Outline the opening and chisel out the plaster. Use a keyhole hacksaw or a hacksaw blade in a saber saw.

THROUGH WOOD PANELING
Outline the opening, drill a series of holes along the outline, and then connect the holes with a keyhole saw or saber saw.

IN HOLLOW BLOCK
Outline the opening and drill holes inside the outline using a masonry bit in a portable electric drill or a star drill and baby sledge hammer. Clean out waste with a cold chisel and sledge. Wear gloves and safety glasses.

ON SOLID MASONRY
You can't open this material. The wiring and boxes must be surface-mounted on the material. Drill holes for masonry anchors and insert the anchors.

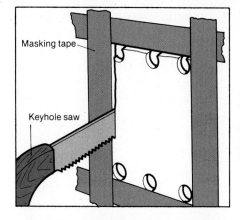

In gypsum wallboard. Outline the opening, using the box as a template. Mask these lines. Drill holes to start the saw, and connect the holes.

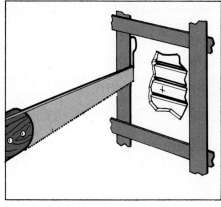

In plastered wood lath. Chip away the plaster with a cold chisel and hammer. Then X the center lath as benchmark. Make the keyhole saw cut.

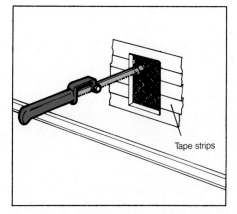

Through metal lath. Cover area with strips of tape; mark hole. Open it with chisel and hammer, cut metal lath with hacksaw.

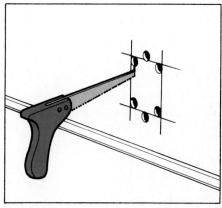

Through wood paneling. Drill holes at the corners of the outline marks and for the box ears. Then connect the holes with a saw cut.

In hollow block. Drill holes in hollow block walls with a masonry bit. Then chisel out the waste material within the outline marks.

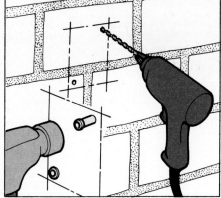

On solid masonry. Outline the box on the surface and mark screw holes inside the box. Drill holes for masonry anchors; drive in anchors.

Closing Walls and Ceilings

Once the boxes are installed in gypsum board or plaster walls, the ragged edges of the holes usually are covered by faceplates over the boxes. However, you may have to do some small patch work along cable routes and around boxes and fixtures. And you may discover that you cut the hole in the wrong place and have to repair it.

General patching procedures for gypsum wallboard and plaster are illustrated below.

PATCHING AROUND BOXES

1. Use a utility knife to make a clean edge; don't try to enlarge the hole.

2. Use ready-mixed drywall taping compound, or mix a batch of spackling compound to a thick mud consistency.

3. Stuff the area between the wall and the box with mineral wool insulation. The insulation fibers will catch on the wall and hang in place.

4. Fill the open area with the taping compound or spackle, but do not dislodge the insulation. Let this filling dry for a day. It will shrink a bit.

5. Once again, fill the opening with taping compound or spackle. Smooth the filling with a putty or drywall taping knife so that the patch is slightly higher than the wall surface. This will allow for normal shrinkage.

6. When the spackling is dry, sand the area lightly so it is level with the surrounding surface. You don't need to paint this concealed patch.

PATCHING LARGE AREAS

If you have to run cable through the wall studs and must patch them over, follow this procedure:

1. Whether the wall is plaster or drywall (gypsum board), cut patches from a piece of drywall. Fasten them to the studs with drywall nails or screws.

2. With a 6-inch taping knife, spread a thin layer of drywall compound around the cracks and embed joint tape in it, covering the cracks. Cover with a thin coating of compound. Let dry overnight. Cover with a second coat of compound; feather out the edges smoothly onto the patch and the surrounding wall.

3. Let the finish coat dry 24 hours, then smooth with medium-grit abrasive paper. Use a sanding block, and do not rough up any exposed paper surface of the patch. Finish with paint or recover with wallcovering.

NAIL-HOLE REPAIRS

Fill any small holes you made to find framing members, as follows:

1. Mix a small amount of spackle to the consistency of thick mud, or use ready-mixed drywall taping compound.

2. Press compound into each hole with a putty knife and level it.

3. Let dry for an hour or so; sand; spot finish with a dab of paint.

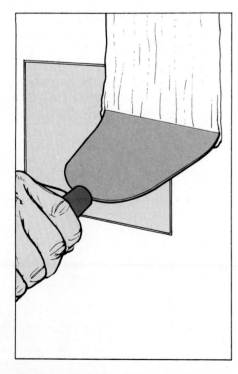

Fill area with patch. Fasten drywall patch in opening. Embed and cover joint tape in thin layers of taping compound.

Sand patch smooth. When second layer of compound is dry, sand smooth. Do not rough up surface of drywall patch.

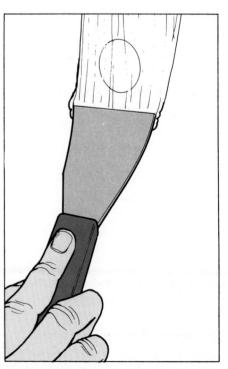

Small hole repairs. Fill holes with taping compound. When dry, sand and spot-paint with small brush or cotton swab.

Fishing Cable at Floor Level

In this situation, you are stringing cable or wire through a basement or crawl space up through the floor into the room above, for example, from an existing receptacle to a new one.

The tools that you need include a hand brace, long electrician's bit and/or wood bit assortment, fishwire, keyhole saw, electrician's tape, tape measure, and equipment to cut through the walls for boxes (see page 60).

START WITH A HOLE

After you have made the opening for the new receptacle or switch in the wall, follow this procedure:

1. Remove the baseboard below the existing receptacle.

2. In line with the receptacle, drill a ¹⁄₁₆-inch hole at an angle through the floor at the base of the wall. Insert a thin wire down through the hole.

3. In the basement or crawl space, find the wire.

4. Next to the wire, locate the bottom plate, which is the support for the wall studs. The plate will be about ½ inch in from the wire directly under the wall.

5. In line with the wire, use a spade or wood bit to drill a hole up through the bottom plate large enough for a cable connector to pass—at least ¾-inch diameter, but check with your connector to be sure. The hole will extend into the empty space between wall studs.

6. Repeat the locating and drilling procedure below the opening for the new box or boxes.

TIME TO GO FISHING

You now have a route for the cable to follow up through the floor.

1. Thread an electric fish tape, which is hooked on the end, through the knockout opening of the old box and into the wall space. Have a helper in the basement push another fish tape up into the wall space through the hole that was drilled in the bottom plate.

Maneuver the tapes until they hook together. Then draw the end of the upstairs tape down through the hole in the bottom plate and into the basement. Unhook the tapes.

2. Strip off 3 inches of plastic sheathing insulation from the cable and remove the wire insulation.

If you are using BX cable, remove 12 inches of the armored sheathing. Install a plastic protector around the wires.

If you are using two-piece cable connectors, install the piece that will be outside the box onto the cable. Then strip away about 3 inches of insulation from the cable wires.

3. In the basement or crawl space, thread the bare wires through the fish-tape hook. Bend back the ends of the bare wires over the hook and wrap masking or electrician's tape around the cable wires and the fish tape to join them.

4. Pull the fish tape and cable up through the wall, into the box. Secure the cable connector box.

5. At this point, connect the new cable to the wiring in the old box. Box and fixture hookups are explained on pages 56–65.

BACK IN BASEMENT

In the basement or crawl space, run the cable along the joists to the area below the new opening. Repeat the procedure detailed above to bring the cable up through the new receptacle location.

When the cable is fished up into the new box, you can connect it to the receptacles or switches that you have planned.

If you have to run cable at right angles to the joists, drill a ¾-inch hole through each joist and thread the cable through the holes. If you have to run cable parallel to a joist, fasten the cable to the faces of the joists. Use staples or clamps spaced about 48 inches apart.

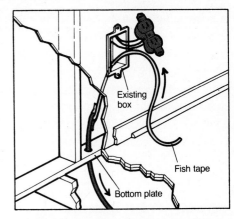

Connecting fish tapes. Push one tape through the knockout and into the wall; push the other up through the plate hole. Join both tapes.

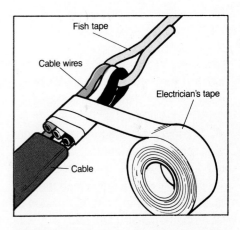

Joining cable to tape. To fasten cable to fish tape, remove 3 inches of sheathing and insulation. Loop wires through hook and tape.

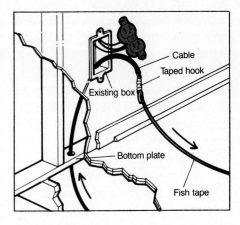

Pulling cable. Pull fish tape and cable up into room. Remove tape. Strip 8 inches of outer insulation from cable for hookup.

Fishing Cable Along a Wall

In this situation, the room is on the upper floors of the house or there is no attic, basement, or crawl space. You will have to cut access openings along the walls. The process requires extensive repairs, but, in most cases, you don't have a choice. *See the procedure for lath and plaster walls below before you start*.

OUTLET, THEN ACCESS

Locate and cut a hole for each new box. Then:

1. Remove the baseboard so you can find the stud position.

2. Locate each stud lying between the boxes you want to join. Once you have located the first one, the process should be fairly simple. In standard construction, studs are 16 inches on center. They sometimes are spaced 12 to 18 inches apart.

3. At each stud, mark off a rectangle centered on the stud and 2 inches high and 4 inches wide. The width is critical so you can insert a drill. Once the rectangle has been cut out, both sides of the stud should be exposed.

4. Use a utility knife to cut out the rectangular access holes, if drywall. If not drywall, see cutting details on pages 60–65.

5. With the studs exposed, use a bit to drill a ¾-inch hole from side to side in each stud. You may need an angled drill chuck for this.

6. Fish the cable from the first box to the access hole in the wall. Then thread the cable through the hole in each stud until you reach the opening for the next box.

7. Make electrical connections to the outlets or switches.

8. Now make patches to cover the access holes in the wall. This involves cutting out appropriately sized rectangles from a panel or drywall. The procedure is explained on page 82.

LATH AND PLASTER WALLS

If you are working on a lath and plaster wall, you can extend the cable behind the baseboard. This keeps the work hidden from view.

1. Remove the baseboard from under the existing box to the opening(s) for the new box(es).

2. Just above the floor and aligned with the existing outlet, chip out a hole that is 1 inch high and deep enough to break through the plaster and lath.

3. Continue chipping out until you form a channel that extends from the existing box to the position(s) of the new one(s). This channel should be 1 inch high and ½ to ¾ inch deep.

4. Drop one fish tape into the wall through the knockout hole in the box and push another fish tape up into the wall through the channel opening just below it. Hook the two together.

5. Fish the cable down through the knockout hole to the channel. Run the cable along the channel to the area of the new box(es); push the cable into the wall. At the opening for the new box(es), use fish-tape to pull the cable up the wall into the opening.

6. When the new box(es) have been installed and the wiring completed, cover the channel with a ¹⁄₁₆-inch-thick metal plate fastened in place with small screws. Attach the baseboard with subfloor adhesive, or nail into studs well above the cable notches.

GOING AROUND DOORWAYS

If a doorway is in the path of the cable, you will have to run the cable up and around the door frame.

1. Remove the trim or molding from around the door. Carefully pry it up and off and pull the nails from the trim through the back side using pliers.

2. Notch out door frame spacers with a chisel. Then string the cable in the spaces and fasten it with staples.

3. Replace the trim.

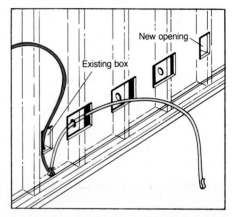

Cable across walls. To route cable across a wall, cut out rectangles to expose studs. Drill holes in studs for cable; fish it through holes.

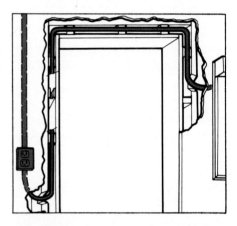

Cable around doorways. Remove the trim and make a patch to route cable around a doorframe. Notch out channels for the cable in framing.

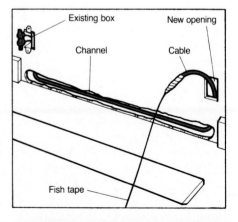

Cable behind baseboard. You may be able to go across with cable by removing baseboard and cutting notches in the framing for it.

Fishing Cable in Ceilings

If the ceiling is open framing in an attic or crawl space, you can fish the cable up through the wall and work unobstructed from above. If the ceiling is not open, you will have to cut openings to fish the cable up the wall and along between the joists.

CUTTING PLATE HOLES

To get access for working:

1. Follow the joists from the ceiling fixture opening to the place where the cable will turn to come down the wall.

2. At that spot, mark and cut adjoining 2 × 4-inch openings in the ceiling and wall to expose the wall top plate.

3. Use a keyhole or saber saw and a chisel to cut a notch ¾ inch wide and 1 inch deep in the top plate.

FISHING THE CABLE

With two short fish tapes, feed one into the wall at the ceiling and one from below. When their ends hook, draw the upper tape down, hook on the cable at floor level, and pull it up to the top of the wall. Unhook and secure the cable temporarily. Repeat with the two tapes through the ceiling openings, ending with the cable pulled to the fixture opening.

With a long fish tape, the following is easier. Feed the tape in through the ceiling fixture opening and along between joists until you can grab it at the top of the wall. Tie a weight on a stout cord (or use a plumb bob) and drop it down through the wall to the lower opening. (If it is stopped by a crossbrace between wall studs, mark the cord, pull it out, and measure down to that point on the outside. Cut a small opening in the wall and notch the brace for the cable.) When it does hit bottom, tie it to the fish tape above and pull the tape down and out the lower opening. Fasten the cable to the tape and pull it up the wall, across the ceiling, and out through the fixture opening.

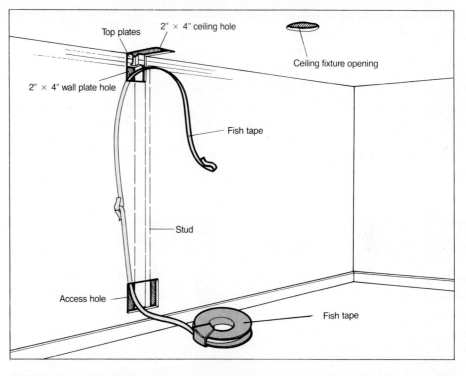

Fishing with two tapes. Feed one tape in from top of wall, one from the bottom. When they hook, draw top tape down, hook on cable, pull it up to top opening, and secure temporarily. Repeat across ceiling to get cable to fixture opening. Staple cable to framing at openings.

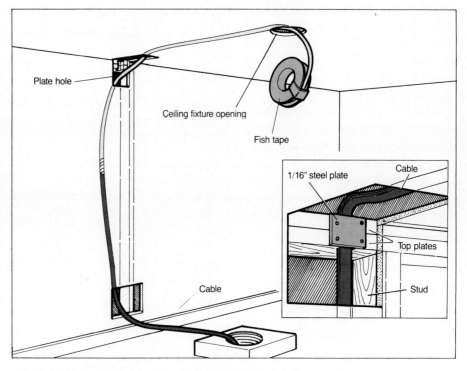

Fishing with one long tape. Feed tape through ceiling fixture opening to wall plates. Drop weighted cord to lower opening and use it to pull fish tape down. Hook on cable and pull up through wall and across ceiling. Inset: Protect cable with metal cover plate over notch.

Installing Surface Wiring

Surface wiring, or more specifically, installing wires in a raceway, eliminates behind-the-wall cable fishing and all the work that goes with it. Raceways are like protected extension cords: the wiring is enclosed in a protective plastic or metal casing. The casing is permanently attached to walls, baseboards, ceilings, or floors. Raceway wiring can include outlets, switches, or ceiling fixtures.

Special connectors turn corners or provide intersections for extending branches from the basic pathway. A raceway is grounded with an equipment grounding conductor, a metal casing, or both.

RACEWAYS AND THE CODE

The National Electrical Code limits raceway use to dry locations not subject to physical damage. The sections must form a secure mechanical and electrical coupling to protect wires inside the raceway. Screws that hold the raceways against surfaces must be flush with the channel surface to avoid cable abrasion. Plastic raceway must be flame-retardant, resistant to moisture, impact, and crushing, and be installed in a dry location.

Before you purchase any materials, be sure to check local codes for special restrictions concerning their use.

SHOP FIRST, THEN PLAN

It's a good idea to first take a look at a raceway system in a store, paying attention to all available parts.

Then at home, sketch out on graph paper a plan of the route that the raceway will take, carefully measuring and marking distances, box locations, junctions, and so on. Then go back to the store and purchase the materials needed.

THE COMPONENTS

Measure the total distance that the channel will travel, and purchase channel lengths to equal that plus an extra 5 to 10 feet to allow for possible breakage and miscuts.

At the same time, buy the housings for the receptacles, switches, and fixtures. All these pieces must be compatible with the raceway.

You also may need a raceway elbow connector and T-connector junction box. The elbow is used to connect two pieces of raceway that join at right angles. The T-connector box is used for new middle-of-the-run receptacles. You will need reducing connections to connect larger junction and fixture boxes to smaller raceway openings.

The wire used is two-wire with ground: black-, white-, and green-insulated. Install Type TW with the same amperage rating as the wire to which you will connect it. Connections are usually made to an existing switch or outlet, although the raceway system may be on a circuit of its own. Add about one third more wire to your total for hookups and general waste. You will need wire nuts and plastic electrician's tape.

TOOLS REQUIRED

You'll need a screwdriver and masonry or wallboard anchors. Wear gloves.

To cut the raceway to size, use a hacksaw with a fine-tooth blade that

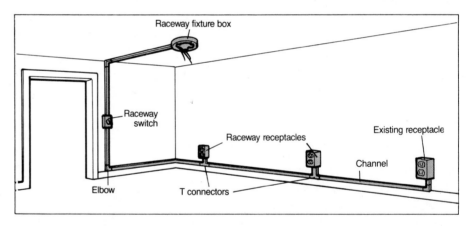

Raceway wiring is all on the surface. Surface wiring adds receptacles, switches, and fixtures without breaking into walls or ceilings. Metal or plastic channel holds two or more individual insulated wires, not cable; special housings and fittings couple with channel.

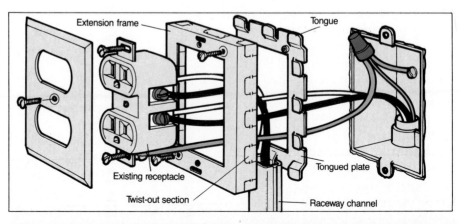

Raceway receptacles are conventionally wired. Existing outlet box is extended with a plate and extension frame to accommodate the raceway channel. Once the raceway channel is in position, you can connect the wires. If using existing switch box, the same extension parts are used for hookup.

has forty teeth per inch. You will need a wire cutter and stripper to finish the wire connections. To pull the wires through the raceway, use a fish tape.

THE POWER CONNECTION

Raceway can connect with an existing fixture, switch, or outlet. Wiring connections are the same as in other installations. A backing plate and extension fit over the box; the switch or outlet mounts on them, as shown on page 86.

New installations (right) use plates that mount directly on the surface. Raceway channel ends slip over tongues on the plates; unneeded tongues are removed. Outlets and switches mount on protruding arms. Deep covers enclose all components.

CHANNEL CONNECTIONS

The ends of channel sections slip onto surface-mounted extension (straight-line), elbow, and T plates. The joints are covered with snap-on covers.

LARGE T CONNECTORS

These connectors receive wires from opposite directions and provide room to house connections between them. The middle leg takes a reducing connector.

RECEPTACLE INSTALLATION

A middle-of-the-run installation needs a large T plate. At the end of a run only one elbow or one extension connector is needed. Screw the receptacle back plate to the wall. Mount the connector plates. Slip the raceway channels onto the connectors and the appropriate tongue of the wall plate, and fish the wires through. Wire and mount the receptacle. Twist out the required opening in the cover and mount it. Snap on the connector joint covers.

FIXTURE INSTALLATION

A fixture plate mounts on an existing fixture box or directly on the surface. The fixture mounts onto an extension cover of the plate. A reducing connector cover joins a twist-out opening in the extension to the raceway channel.

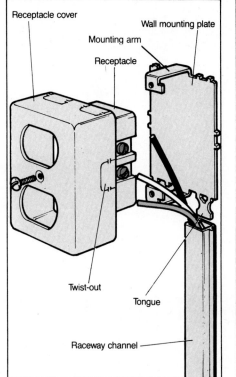

The receptacles. Mounting plate screws to wall with outlet fastened to it and connected to wires in channel. Cover fastens to outlet.

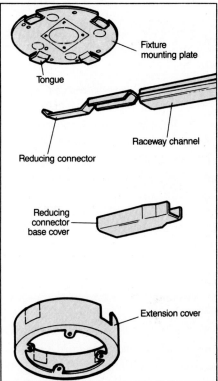

Fixtures. Mounting plate goes on surface. Extension cover provides depth for wire connections. Fixture mounts on cover.

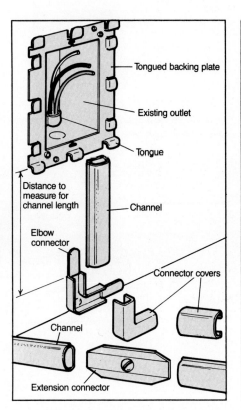

Channel connections. Various fittings join channel sections. Wires are fished through before connector covers are added.

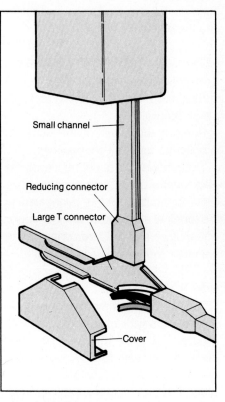

Large T connector. T connector is large enough for wires to turn or be joined. Set all devices, then wire.

240-Volt Electrical Connections

Clothes dryers and some air conditioners require lots of power in the form of 120/240-volt, 30-amp connections. The appliance plugs in when the receptacle is in place. The plug-in cords are sold in sets similar to extension cords.

120/240-VOLT, 30-AMP OUTLET

Red and black wires to this outlet provide 240-volt power; either one and the white wire form a 110-volt circuit. The outlet has no ground terminal; the cable grounding wire (green) connects to the box.

To make cable wire connections, strip ¾ inch of insulation from the wire, insert it in the terminal slot, and tighten the terminal screw. Connect the white wire to the terminal marked WHITE, then connect the red and black wires to the other terminals. It doesn't matter which goes to which unless the terminals are labeled.

A prefabricated plug and cord set connects to the appliance and plugs into the outlet.

SURFACE-MOUNTED OUTLET

If an outlet box is not available, you can surface-mount a 120/240-volt receptacle on the wall.

Remove the cover of the outlet to expose the terminal connections.

The ground wire is connected to the back of the outlet with a screw. The white or neutral wire is connected to the terminal so marked, and the power wires, black and red, are connected to the other two terminals in the outlet.

240-VOLT OUTLET

A 240-volt outlet (without a 120-volt circuit) is wired with a two-wire cable with ground. The white wire must be taped black. It connects to one brass terminal; the black wire connects to the other. The bare or green cable grounding wire is pigtailed to both the outlet and box ground terminals.

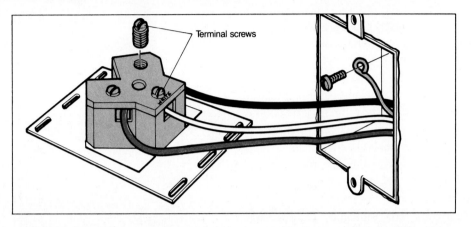

120/240-volt, 30-amp outlet. Black and red wires are connected to brass terminals; white goes to terminal so marked. Ground goes to box.

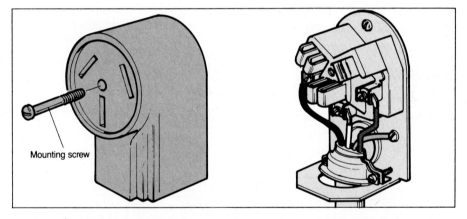

Surface-mounted outlet. Cable ground is connected to back of outlet. White goes to neutral; power goes to brass terminals.

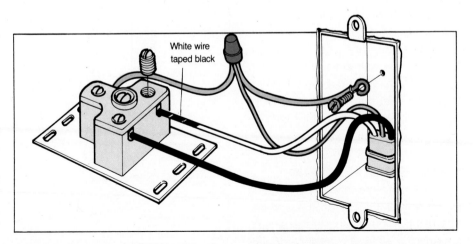

240-volt outlet. This outlet uses a two-wire with ground cable, with the white wire taped black. Grounding wire is pigtailed to outlet and to box. Before wiring this hookup, check your local code.

Hooking Cable to Existing Circuits

Any new wiring can be connected to an existing circuit, *provided* that the circuit will handle the additional power load. You can figure this according to the formula on page 9; you should do so before adding the new wiring. If you find that the existing circuit will not handle the extra load, you can have a pro connect it directly to the main electrical panel, creating a new circuit.

Any wiring can be connected as a new circuit to the main electrical panel of your home. Have a professional electrician make this connection.

JOINING NEW CABLE TO EXISTING CIRCUITS

Once the new cable is fished through, hook up the wires to existing circuit. Turn power off first. Most situations will require at least one wire splice. Splices can be made only in a box using wire nuts and electrician's tape.

AT AN END-OF-RUN OUTLET

This is the easiest hookup to complete. Attach the black wire of the new cable to the unused brass screw. The white wire goes to the unused silver-colored screw. With a wire nut, splice the green ground wires together.

AT A MIDDLE-OF-RUN OUTLET

This hookup requires three wire nuts and two jumper wires—one black and one white—each 4 inches long.

Identify the black and white wires of the power source cable (see next page) and unhook them from the outlet. Splice the black power wire together with the new black cable wire and the black jumper. Attach the jumper to the brass outlet terminal. Splice the two white cable wires with the white jumper and connect the jumper to the silver outlet terminal. Finally, splice the two cable grounding wires together with pigtails/jumpers to the outlet and to the box terminal.

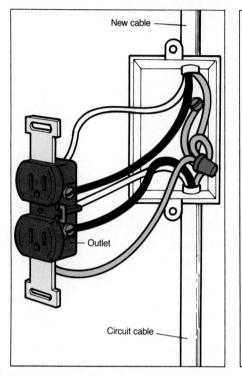

End-of-run outlet. To hook up new cable to an end-of-run outlet, attach the black and white wires of the new cable to the unused brass and silver terminals.

Middle-of-run outlet. To hook up new cable to a middle-of-run outlet, add jumpers from black, white, and green wire. Cap the splices with wire nuts and tape.

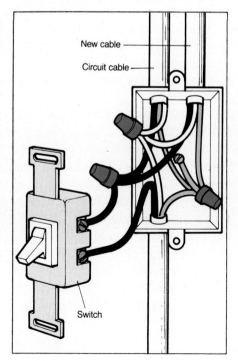

Middle of-the-run switch. Identify the incoming circuit cable. Connect it to the new cable as shown and as explained on page 90.

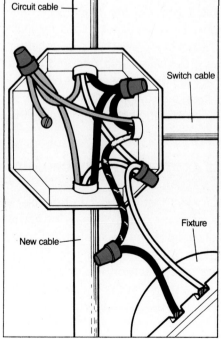

Ceiling fixture. Identify the switch and power (circuit) cables. Connect the new cable to the power cable; see text page 90.

AT A MIDDLE-OF-RUN SWITCH

There will be two sets of existing wires in a switch. One set comes from the service panel. The other set runs to the fixture or outlet that the switch controls.

Before you can hook up the new cable, you must find out which set comes from the main service panel. Otherwise, your new outlet will have power only when the switch is on.

To determine which cable comes from the service panel, use a voltage tester. Disconnect the wires to the switch. Then, and only then, have a helper turn on the circuit at the service panel. Put one probe of the voltage tester against the metal box. With the other probe, touch one of the exposed black wires. If it is the feed wire (the one coming from the service panel), the bulb of the voltage tester will light. If the bulb does not light, test the other black wire. The one that lights the bulb is the one you want. Then turn off the circuit again before you continue work.

Make two 4-inch-long jumper wires—one black and one green. Splice together the black wire that lit the bulb, the new cable's black wire, and the black jumper. Fasten the black jumper to the brass terminal on the switch. Fasten the black wire that doesn't light the tester bulb to the other terminal of the switch. Splice together the green wires with one end of the green jumper, and secure the other end of the green jumper under the screw at the back of the box. Finally, splice the three white wires.

AT A MIDDLE-OF-RUN CEILING FIXTURE

You must first find which of the black wires in the existing cables is live and is not controlled by the light switch.

This black wire comes from the service panel. Turn off the circuit at the service panel. In the fixture will be at least two splices that connect black

wires. The black wire coming from the service panel will not be in the splice holding the black wire coming from the light fixture. Look for the other black wire splice.

Disconnect this splice and separate the wires. Make sure the bare ends do not touch anything. Turn on the circuit at the service panel and use the voltage tester. The black wire that turns on the test light is the one to connect to the black wire of the new cable. Turn off the circuit.

Splice together the black wire from the new cable and all black wires contained in the original splice. With the circuit still off, take apart the white wire splice and add the white wire from the new cable.

Finally, splice all green wires and one end of a 1½- to 2-inch green jumper. Fasten the other end of the green jumper under the box screw.

TAPPING JUNCTION BOXES

Several circuits may pass through a junction or major box. Have a helper turn off the circuits one by one, as you use a voltage tester to determine which cable controls the circuit you want to tap.

Once you have found the source, turn off the power and then splice the wires together: black to black, white to white, ground to ground.

TAPPING POWER FOR CEILING FIXTURES

You have three choices: a middle-of-the-run ceiling box, a wall switch, and an end-of-the-run outlet.

If a ceiling fixture has a built-in switch, the easiest way to get power to it is to connect to an existing middle-of-the-run ceiling box. If the new fixture requires a switch, connect from the power wire in the existing box to the switch, then up to the new fixture. Connect fixture white to existing white.

A MIDDLE-OF-RUN WALL SWITCH FOR A FIXTURE

If the new ceiling fixture requires a wall switch, it's best to get power from an existing middle-of-the-run switch in the same room. Run two-wire cables from the old switch and the new fixture to the new switch box. Connect the switch to the two black wires, and connect the whites together. At the old switch, connect the new white and black to the power cable white and black.

A SWITCH LOOP FOR A NEW FIXTURE

Tapping into power is no problem in this situation, but if you want a separate switch control for a new fixture you have a choice of wiring.

If you are tapping a ceiling fixture, add the new cable into the splice containing the feed hot wire. If you are tapping a switch, cut a 4-inch black jumper wire. Splice together the jumper, the feed hot wire, and the new cable wire.

Attach the loose end of the jumper to the brass terminal on the switch. Then wire the switch as for an end-of-the-run switch.

HIGH-VOLTAGE WIRING

Every 120/240-volt or 240-volt outlet must be on its own circuit, running directly to the main panel. You may not tap into that circuit, or add another outlet. You can of course replace an old outlet; wire it as shown on page 88. If you are running cable for a new circuit, connect the outlet, but have a professional make the main panel hookup.

Codes usually permit the white wire in cable to be used for grounding the device. In Canada, codes require a fourth wire for grounding. In the 120/240-volt hookup, the 240 volts run the appliance while the 120-volt connection runs accessories, such as timers and pilot lights.

8 Lighting Repair and Installation

An incandescent light produces light by passing electricity through a thin wire called a filament. As the wire heats, it produces a white glow called incandescence.

Inside a fluorescent tube the electricity jumps from an electrode at one end of the tube to another electrode at the other end of the tube. The tube contains mercury and argon gases. The current causes the gases to emit an ultraviolet light. To make the light visible, the tube is coated with a phosphor powder that glows or fluoresces when hit by the ultraviolet light.

INCANDESCENT LIGHT TROUBLES

When an incandescent light isn't working, here are some ways to identify the problem:

If the bulb doesn't light:

1. The plug has been pulled from the wall outlet. Push the plug back into the outlet.

2. The bulb is loose and isn't making contact with the socket. Tighten the bulb.

3. The bulb is burned out. Replace the bulb.

4. The line cord is damaged. Replace the line cord.

5. The switch is defective. Replace the switch.

If the bulb flickers:

1. The bulb is loose and barely makes contact with the socket. Tighten the bulb.

2. There is a loose wire at the socket terminal. Turn off the power to the circuit or unplug the lamp. Then secure the wire.

3. The switch is defective. Replace the switch.

If the lamp blows a fuse or trips the circuit breaker:

First, make sure there is not an overload or short circuit at the main service panel.

1. There is a short in the line cord. Replace the line cord.

2. The plug is defective. Replace the plug.

3. The socket is defective. Replace the socket.

(Fluorescent light problems are discussed on pages 107–111.)

SPOTTING SYMPTOMS

How can you tell if any of the above problems apply in your case?

Usually, there are signs to let you know if a plug, switch, or line cord is faulty. A defective plug normally has visible damage, such as cracks in the plug housing or loose, broken, or bent prongs.

A bad switch usually feels loose as you turn it on and off, or the bulb may flicker as the switch is jiggled. A damaged line cord often looks frayed.

HOW TO CHECK FOR BROKEN WIRES

Sometimes there is a broken wire within the line causing problems. You can test it, as explained below. *Do not test* it if the cord is frayed or a bare wire is exposed.

1. Plug the lamp into a wall outlet and turn on the lamp switch.

2. Flex the line cord back and forth over its entire length. If the bulb flickers, a wire in the cord is broken.

Flexing the cord opens and closes the two ends of the broken wire. When a faulty plug, switch, or line cord has been located, replace the bad part.

HOW TO SOLVE LIGHTING PROBLEMS

This chapter tells you how to solve a wide range of lighting problems—from replacing a broken cord to repairing a switch to installing new lighting devices, such as dimmer switches, track lights, and fluorescent fixtures.

As in any electrical project, turn off the circuit to the project before you start work. In the case of a table lamp, be sure to unplug the lamp first.

To complete these projects, you will have to handle wire, switches, outlets, and other electrical devices. The techniques you need are explained earlier in this book. Refer to them as you go through the steps of repair and replacement.

Rewiring Freestanding Lamps

Table lamps, pole lamps, pedestal lamps, and others that are freestanding and individually wired, are all assembled in almost the same way: a cord running up through a base is connected to a socket.

Heat from the bulb in the socket eventually causes the socket to malfunction, requiring replacement. Wear and tear on the plug end of the cord requires replacement of the plug and cord. Switches also wear out and must be replaced. The procedures for replacing individual sockets, switches, and plugs are explained in Chapter 5, page 66: Plugs, Cords, and Sockets.

The procedures for rewiring a lamp from start to finish are shown here and on the following pages.

First, unplug the lamp and set up the rewiring project on a workbench or table surface with tools and materials handy. Materials that you will need include cord, sockets, switches, glue, and plastic electrician's tape. Tools include a screwdriver, pliers, wire strippers, and a sharp utility knife, pocketknife, or paring knife.

REMOVE HARP ASSEMBLY

Remove the lamp shade, which is held by a decorative nut either at the top of the shade or where the shade joins the body of the lamp. If the shade is supported by a harp, slide up the small finger nuts at the base of the harp bracket with one hand and lift off the harp with the other.

REMOVE BASE COVERING

Most table lamps have a felt pad covering the bottom of the lamp. The covering usually is glued to the bottom of the lamp. Remove this covering by first breaking the glue seal with the blade of a utility or pocket knife, and then peel back the covering so you have access to the cord and/or switch in the base of the lamp.

Most pole and pedestal lamps don't have this covering; the cord runs directly into the lamp housing.

If the lamp has a nut that holds the lamp cord secure in the bottom of the lamp, remove it. This is a flat nut and washer assembly, and the nut turns counterclockwise to loosen.

Some pole lamps have a cord locking nut, which is removed the same way. However, in other pole lamps, the cord may be simply threaded into the housing. Most pole lamps have a cord locking nut just under the shade. Remove this nut to remove the shade and loosen the cord when you want to replace the socket/switch.

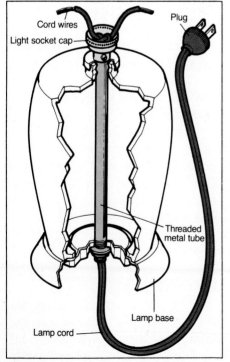

Anatomy of table lamp. Cord runs through base of lamp, sometimes completely through a metal tube, and attaches to socket terminals.

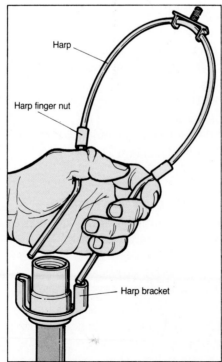

Remove harp assembly. Slip finger nuts holding harp to bracket upward. Then squeeze harp in your fingers and lift it out of the harp bracket.

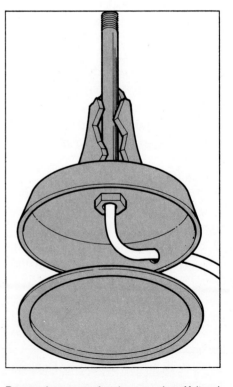

Remove base covering. Loosen edge of felt pad with a knife and then peel back the pad. This will reveal the locking nut securing the tube.

REMOVING WIRES FROM SINGLE SOCKETS

Lamp sockets have a thin brass housing. To remove the outer shell, squeeze in on the sides, just above the base cap. (Pry with a thin blade if necessary.) Pull up to expose a cardboard insulating sleeve. Remove that, loosen thé terminal screws, and unhook the wires. The copper lamp cord wire always goes to the brass socket terminal, or to a switch lead (see below). The silver wire goes to the silver terminal.

LAMPS WITH MULTIPLE SOCKETS

The wires are connected to the sockets the very same way as on single sockets. However, to replace the cord, you will also have to disconnect the wiring connections in a storage housing near the sockets. The connections are spliced with wire nuts; remove these nuts after you note which wires are connected to each other. You can identify them by the color of the insulation.

SOCKETS WITH SINGLE SWITCHES

The lights may not be controlled by switches on the sockets. Instead, a single switch controls the lights.

In order to remove the sockets and the cord, you will have to disassemble the connections, which are made with wire nuts. Make a careful diagram of how the wires are joined.

LAMPS WITH BASE SWITCHES

If the lamp has a base switch that controls the light sockets, the wiring connections will be located in the base. Make a wiring diagram.

On pole lamps, the lights may be controlled at the socket. Or a single switch may turn on all lights at the same time. In this case, you will have to disconnect the switch assembly in order to remove the cord. Note the connection, which usually is black wires connected to the switch with the white wires bypassing it.

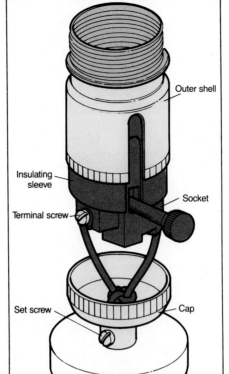

Single-socket wiring. Remove brass socket housing from cap to expose socket terminals. Then remove wires by loosening terminals.

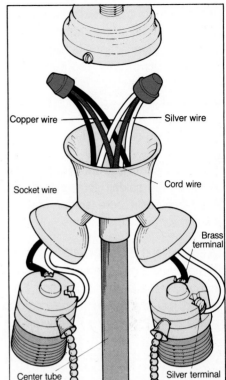

Multiple sockets. For lamps with two or more sockets, remove brass housing and wires from terminals. Then remove switch wires.

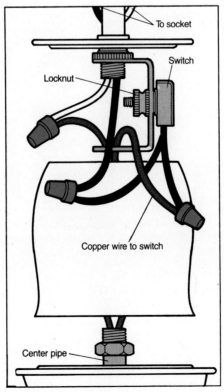

Single switches. A single switch may control two or more lights. It will be below the sockets. Diagram the hookup as you disconnect wires.

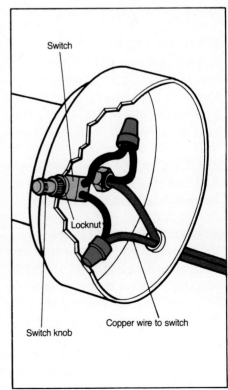

Base switches. If lamp has a base switch, disconnect the wires here and at the socket(s). Note wiring plan for hookup later on.

SOLDERED CONNECTIONS

When you take a lamp apart you may find solder connections between wires and brackets or tabs. The best way to disconnect these is to heat the solder, not the wire, with a soldering gun until you can pull the wire free.

When you reassemble the connection, you may be able to reheat the solder the same way and reuse it. If not, heat the old solder, scrape it off, and then use rosin core solder (noncorrosive) for new connections.

REMOVING THE CORD

Temporarily attach the new cord to the old cord at the socket connection. Strip a bit of insulation from the new cord to make a tight joint, and then wrap the joint with a couple of layers of electrician's tape so the connection won't pull apart.

Untie any knots or loosen any set-screws in or around the cord on its route through the lamp.

Then pull the old cord out of the lamp base and thread the new cord into place. Disconnect the old cord and discard it.

UNDERWRITERS' KNOT

At the socket end, split the insulation (if it's zip cord) and tie an Underwriters' knot in the cord, leaving approximately 3 inches of loose wire at the end of the knot. Make a loop in each wire and thread the end of each wire through the opposite loop. Pull the knot tight. The knot prevents the wire from pulling loose from terminals in the socket.

SOCKET CONNECTIONS

Strip about ¾ inch of insulation from each wire. With your fingers, twist the stranded wire as tightly as possible. Then wrap the bare wire around the socket terminals in the direction the terminal screws turn down—clockwise.

When you replace wire nuts, twist the wires together as tightly as you can, insert the wires into the base of the wire nut, and twist the wire nut. Then wrap the nut and wires with a couple of layers of electrician's tape.

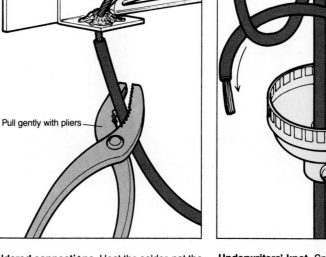

Heat with soldering gun

Pull gently with pliers

Soldered connections. Heat the solder, not the wire, until it melts and pull wire out. To reassemble, use noncorrosive solder.

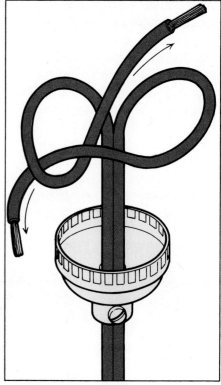

Underwriters' knot. Split the wire or divide the wires and make two fairly large loops. Thread end of one wire through opposite loop.

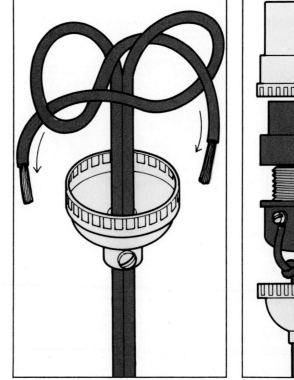

Pull UL knot tight. Thread other wire through the opposite loop, forming loose knot. Pull wire ends apart, making a tight knot.

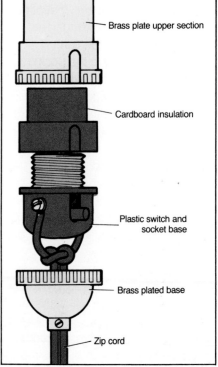

Brass plate upper section

Cardboard insulation

Plastic switch and socket base

Brass plated base

Zip cord

Socket connections. Hook bare wire ends around terminals clockwise and tighten screws firmly. Reassemble socket.

Installing Dimmer Switches

A dimmer switch allows you to select different intensities of light to create a mood or to conserve electricity. You must not use them to control receptacles into which you may plug appliances or power tools. This could result in damage to the dimmer switch.

A *hi-lo dimmer switch* has a toggle that lets you select one of three positions: OFF, LOW, and HIGH.

A *rotary dimmer* switch has a rotary, rather than a toggle, control. You can set the control for light output that is fully on, fully off, or any intensity in between.

A *line dimmer* switch has a rotary dial that sets the light output. This switch comes in a cord set for use with table or freestanding lamps. You will have to rewire the lamp (see pages 92–94) so the lamp can be dimmed properly.

Fluorescent lamps may be controlled by a special *fluorescent dimmer switch and ballast* combination.

INSTALLING INCANDESCENT DIMMERS

Decide whether you need a single-pole or a three-way switch. A single-pole is connected the same way as a conventional single-pole switch. Turn off the power first.

In a three-way circuit, you replace only one of the two conventional switches. To function correctly, a three-way dimmer must be paired with a conventional three-way toggle switch. Turn off the power. Tag the black wire on the common terminal. Then disconnect the old switch. Connect the hot wire of the dimmer switch to the tagged hot wire in the box. Connect the two traveler or switch wires of the dimmer to the two traveler wires in the switch box.

STEP 1
SINGLE-POLE DIMMER

Turn off the power and remove the faceplate and switch from the box. Disconnect the wires. Then connect the same colored wires of the dimmer switch to the wires in the box. Wire nut and wrap them with electrician's tape.

STEP 2
ATTACH THE SWITCH

Push the wires and the back of the switch into the box. Fasten the dimmer housing to the holes in the switch box. Then install the faceplate and the control knob.

END-OF-RUN 3-WAY DIMMER

If the dimmer goes into an end-of-the-run box, the connections are made as shown below. If the switch doesn't have a built-in ground, hook the switch's ground wire to the box.

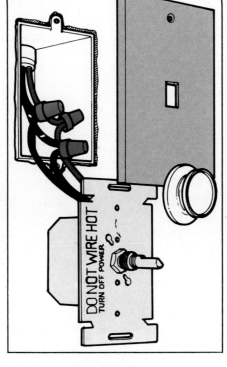

Single-pole dimmer. Remove the old switch and replace it with dimmer switch. Splice wires with wire nuts and tape.

Attach the switch. Fasten housing to box and install faceplate and control dial. Turn switch so light is brightest; reseat dial on shaft.

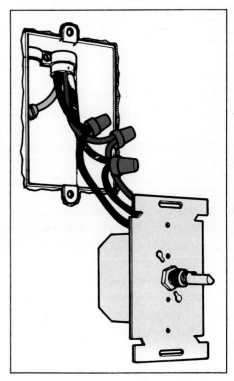

End-of-run switch. End-of-run dimmer connections. If the dimmer has just two wires, ground box with an equipment grounding conductor.

FLUORESCENT DIMMER SWITCHES AND BALLASTS

Fluorescent fixtures with external or instant-start starters require extensive work to adapt them for dimmer switches. Here you'll find directions for installing a dimmer to control a 40-watt rapid-start fluorescent light.

STEP 1
REMOVE THE BALLAST

Turn off the power to the circuit and remove the fluorescent lamp and metal lid that covers the ballast and wiring. Remove the terminal screws.

Remove the wire nuts and untwist the wires. Don't disconnect the equipment grounding conductor.

Unscrew the ballast locking nuts. Lift out the ballast and terminals.

STEP 2
UNHOOK LAMP TERMINALS

Notice the wiring setup. Two sets of wires extend from the ballast, one from each end. The wires at one end have the same color insulation. At the other end they are white, black, and a third, different color.

Disconnect all of these wires from the lamp terminals. Align the new dimmer ballast wires with those in the old ballast, so the new hookup will be identical with the old. If there is a short white wire protruding from one of the lamp terminals, connect it to the white wire from the dimmer ballast. This terminal is prewired.

STEP 3
HOOK UP DIMMER BALLAST

Wire the new dimmer ballast to the lamp terminals by pressing the clamps, pushing the wires into the respective slots, and releasing the clamps.

Attach the dimmer switch ballast to the fixture with the locking nuts. Reinsert the two lamp terminals and fasten them in. Then connect the ballast wiring to the house wiring by splicing the hot wires together, and the neutral wires together. Reinstall the fixture cover and fluorescent lamp.

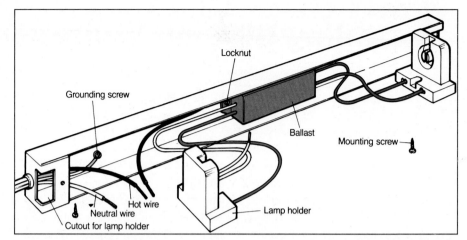

Remove the ballast. Turn off the power on the circuit. Remove the fluorescent tube and cover plate. Unscrew the ballast locknuts and remove the ballast. Then slip the lamp holders out of their retaining brackets. Dimmers are easy to install on rapid-start units.

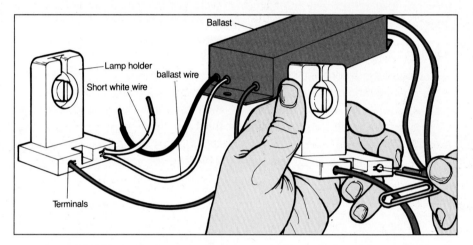

Unhook lamp terminals. Disconnect the lamp holders by inserting a stiff wire, such as the end of a paper clip, into the opening beside the ballast wire to release the circuit wire. Note color-coded wires so you can reassemble the unit with the new dimmer-type ballast.

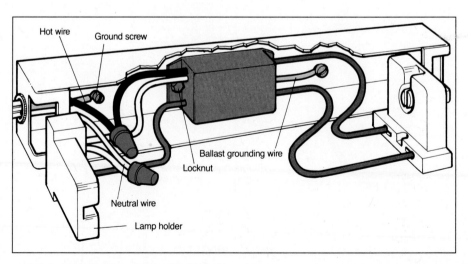

Connect dimmer ballast. Attach the ballast wires to the lamp holders; slip the holders into position, and then fasten down the ballast. Splice the house and ballast wires using wire nuts and electrician's tape. You must now install a dimmer switch.

INSTALLING THE DIMMER SWITCH

A dimmer switch for a fluorescent light can control as many as eight fluorescent bulbs simultaneously. However, the ballast of every fluorescent fixture you want to control must be replaced with the special dimmer ballast. A dimmer switch also is somewhat larger than most conventional or special switches. It will fit into a standard box. You may need to replace an old-style box with a larger one to accommodate new switch and wires.

Dimmer switch markings are similar to those on conventional switches. A dimmer switch also has data that tells you the total maximum bulb wattage that may be used with the switch. Buy a switch that can handle your fixtures.

Mechanically, a fluorescent dimmer switch is installed the same way as an incandescent one. Turn off the power to the circuit. Remove the faceplate and then the switch. Remove the wires from the terminals.

STEP 1
CONNECT NEW SWITCH

Splice the leads on the switch to the incoming hot wire in the box and to the outgoing wire to the fixture. One of these will be black, the other will be white taped black. Use wire nuts and tape them in place. Then mount the switch in the box.

STEP 2
SET THE DIMMER

Turn on the power. Push the dimmer control knob onto the dimmer switch shaft. Then turn the control knob so the light is turned down to its low lighting capacity. Now turn the knurled adjustment nut, located at the base of the shaft on which the control knob fits, counterclockwise with pliers until the lamp flickers. Then turn the nut clockwise until the lamp stops flickering. The adjustment is made.

STEP 3
INSTALL COVER PLATE

When the control knob is set to your satisfaction—high to low light—remove the control knob and mount the faceplate on the switch housing. It screws on just like a conventional faceplate. Then reinstall the control knob. Test the light from high to low. When the knob is on the high setting, the light should be fully on. When it's on low, the light should be at its lowest level. If not, you will have to remove the faceplate and adjust the nut.

INTERFERENCE TROUBLE

The addition of a dimmer switch may cause interference with television, radio, and phonograph systems. Although dimmer switches usually have a filter to block out signals created by the switch, some signals can penetrate the filter.

One way to lessen interference is to plug television, radio, and stereo equipment into a circuit other than the one serving the dimmer switch. If this does not work, purchase a power-line filter from a TV supply store and attach it, as directed, between the equipment and the receptacle into which you plug the equipment. A power-line filter traps interfering signals created by dimmer switches.

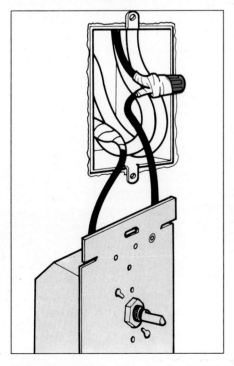

Connect new switch. Join the switch leads to the incoming power and fixture hot wires. Power and fixture white wires join directly.

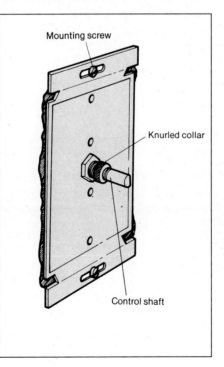

Set the dimmer. Adjust dimmer so lights work as you want. Do this by manipulating the knurled nut on the control shaft of switch.

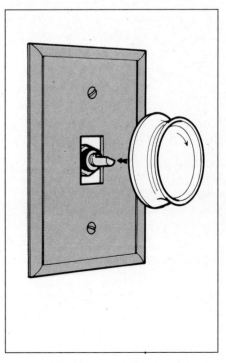

Install cover plate. The cover plate goes over the switch housing. Push the control knob on the projecting shaft and test the full range of the light.

Eliminating Pull-Chain Lights

Owners of older homes often want to replace a pull-chain ceiling light with a light operated by a wall switch.

You will need to run new two-wire with ground cable from the ceiling light to a wall switch, which requires fishing the wire through the ceiling and down the wall. Besides the cable, you will need a new switch, switch box, wire nuts, electrician's tape, fish tape, wire stripper, needlenose pliers, and, perhaps, a voltage tester. To install the box, you will need a keyhole saw and drill bit for holes to start the saw. You can install a new fixture or leave the old.

AT THE CEILING

Turn off the power to the light and remove the fixture.

If you find only two wires, the job is simple. If there are more than two wires, you will have to determine which wire is hot and which is neutral. If the wires from the power source are connected to fixture wires, unscrew the wire nuts to bare the wires. If the wires are connected to fixture terminal screws, do not loosen them.

Hold one probe of a voltage tester against the box. Touch the other probe to the bare ends of one of the wire connections or to one of the fixture terminal screws. Have a helper turn on the current. If the bulb in the tester lights, you have located the hot wire. If not, touch the probe to the bare ends of the other wire connection, or to the other fixture terminal screw, to verify that it is hot. Tag this hot wire.

FISHING THE NEW CABLE

Run the new two-wire with ground cable between the ceiling fixture and switch. The procedure is to cut a hole for the switch box, then fish the wire from the ceiling box to the switch box and connect the switch, as shown.

The easiest way to fish the wire may be from the ceiling to the switch. Run

the fish tape through the channel formed by parallel joists (see page 85). Where the joists meet the wall, cut a small hole in the ceiling and wall so you can turn the tape downward. You may have to notch the framing members to accept the cable. Hook the cable to the tape at the switch and pull it up the wall, around the wall–ceiling corner, and into the ceiling box.

THE CONNECTION

At the fixture, connect the black wire from the power source to the white-taped-black going to the switch. Connect the power cable white wire to the silver fixture terminal. Connect the black wire from the switch to the brass fixture terminal. Pigtail the grounding wires to the fixture box.

At the switch, connect the black and white-taped-black wires to the switch terminals. Connect the grounding wire to the box.

Complete the project by patching the holes cut in the wall and ceiling. Then install the ceiling fixture and the switch faceplate.

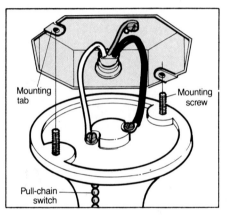

At the ceiling. Incoming power wire is black-insulated. You may have to use voltage tester to find hot wire if box has more than two wires running in it.

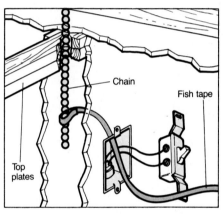

Fishing new cable. To fish through a box knockout, drop a chain from above and snag it with a fish tape. Draw it into the box, hook on the cable, and pull up to the ceiling.

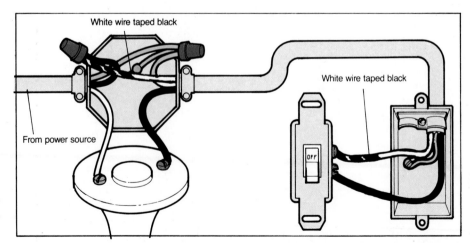

The connection. Here's the wiring connection between the ceiling light and the switch. The incoming power wire bypasses the fixture (tag white wire black) and goes to switch. The black wire from switch terminates at the fixture. Ground wire is connected to both boxes.

Hanging a New Chandelier

Replacing a ceiling light, such as one over a dining table, with a chandelier, is a very simple job—one some pros call a "change-out."

The procedure involves removing the old fixture, modifying the ceiling box to handle the weight of the chandelier, and making the necessary electrical connections.

STEP 1
REMOVE OLD FIXTURE

Turn off the power to the circuit. Remove the fasteners holding the old fixture to the ceiling box. If the old fixture is heavy, have a helper steady the fixture for you while you disconnect the wires at the terminal screws on the old fixture.

STEP 2
MAKING THE CONNECTION

If the new chandelier weighs more than 10 pounds and the fixture you are removing weighs less than 10 pounds, you will need to fasten the new one with a stud, a nipple fitting, and a hickey. A stud is a short piece of threaded tubing that screws into the center of the box. A hickey screws onto the stud, the nipple screws into the hickey, and the collar of the chandelier screws onto the nipple. You may need to replace the ceiling box for this arrangement (see Chapter 3, page 36: Switches and Outlets).

STEP 3
THE WIRING CONNECTIONS

Chandeliers are prewired. Splice the black-insulated wire to the black-insulated wire in the ceiling box. Do the same with the white neutral wires. Cover all the splices with wire nuts and wrap the nuts with plastic electrician's tape.

The chandelier canopy or ceiling escutcheon fits over the ceiling box and is held with a collar nut that screws onto the threads of the nipple in the box.

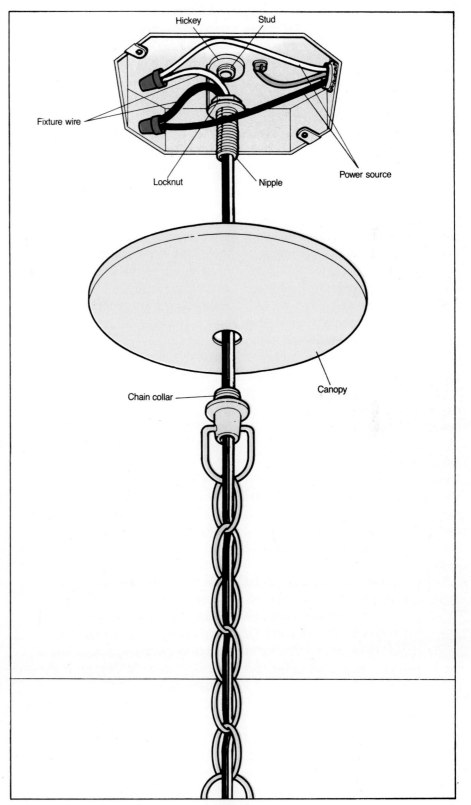

Chandelier-hanging hardware includes a stud, hickey, and nipple that supports the extra weight of the fixture. A box knockout accommodates the stud. Wires are spliced black-to-black and white-to-white with wire nuts. Make sure box is secure to framing.

Adding New Ceiling Fixtures

The artificial lighting in your home falls into two categories: general lighting—which illuminates a room as a whole—and local lighting—which focuses on areas where you perform specific jobs. Local lighting is needed over a kitchen sink, a chopping block, a range or cooktop, or above a desk or dining area.

Ceiling fixtures commonly supply the general lighting in a home. To increase general lighting, you can add a central ceiling fixture. This can be recessed, flush with the ceiling, suspended from a canopy base on the ceiling, or a hanging fixture designed in styles ranging from a simple lamp to an elaborate chandelier.

Regardless of the type of lighting that you elect to use, you will need to run power into the ceiling (it probably is already there or close by) and to a ceiling fixture box or multiple boxes. The next three pages show how these boxes are installed.

RECESSED FIXTURES
If you want diffused lighting throughout the room, consider distributing several recessed multiple ceiling fixtures evenly throughout the room. To do this, you will have to work around the joists in the ceiling.

Multiple power sources tend to be expensive to install and to operate. They require extra fixtures and supplies, and they consume more energy than a single fixture. Because the lights are recessed, they provide only direct light.

CEILING GRIDS
One innovative way to handle recessed ceiling lights is to create a grid of crisscrossed strips of wood, metal, or plastic. The bulbs are hidden in grid openings. The openings can be small enough to house only a single bulb or large enough to make squares with the beams of a beamed ceiling.

Another way to increase general light is to transform part or all of the ceiling into a luminous light panel by suspending a ceiling of hanging translucent acrylic panels below a grid of fluorescent lights. This installation is fairly simple. You can buy luminous ceiling kits, or you can construct your own. If you decide on such a plan, provide 40 watts for each 12 square feet of floor area.

THE SWITCHES
When installing a ceiling fixture where there was none previously, you also must decide on the kind of switch that will control the fixture.

Selecting a fixture that has a built-in switch simplifies the job, because that eliminates routing cable to a switch location, installing the switch, and routing cable from the switch to the power source. With a built-in switch, you simply mount the ceiling box, run the cable between it and the power source, and connect the fixture to the box.

THE POWER SOURCE
The power source for a new ceiling fixture is usually a ceiling junction or major box to which you have access in the attic. If there is no attic, power is normally drawn from an existing receptacle or outlet in the room in which the fixture is to hang.

Tapping into this existing power involves fishing cable from the power source to the ceiling boxes. This is explained in detail in Chapter 7, starting on page 80.

You can also create a new circuit for ceiling lights, and this could be easier than fishing for power. If you opt for a new circuit, we suggest that you run the cable from the main electrical service panel, make the necessary connections along the line, and then have a professional electrician inspect your work and make the power hookup at the main service panel.

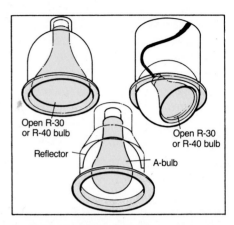

Incandescent bulbs can be recessed in single-bulb fixtures built into ceiling. Single ceiling boxes are utilized for this.

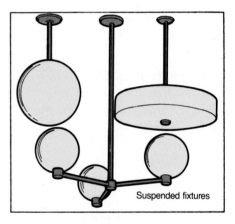

For diffused room lighting, the fixtures can hold one or more bulbs of different wattage. Bulbs are suspended in ceiling fixtures.

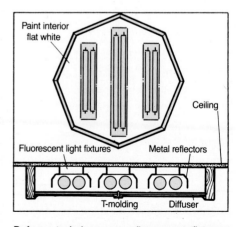

Defuser technique uses fluorescent fixtures, 1 × 6-inch boards to house lights, and diffuser panels. Lights hook to ceiling boxes.

TYPES OF CEILING BOXES AND THEIR INSTALLATION

In stores you will find a huge selection of ceiling boxes from which to choose. Your job will be matching the box to the location. The more popular box styles are described on this page.

TWO-PIECE BOXES

If you are working with open framing, the two-piece box is ideal. A bar spans the joists and is connected to the joists either with prepunched nail tabs in the bar hangers or with regular nails. The bar is adjustable to joist widths, and the box mounted on the bar can be moved with a screw clamping device into any position you want.

OFFSET BAR HANGERS

This product is also a two-piece bar combination, except that the bar hanger is offset to fit up into the joist openings and the bar is nailed to the edges of the joists. The bar has a box clamp fitting that can be moved to any position across the bar.

PANCAKE BOXES

This is a flat box, shallow in depth, that is nailed or screwed directly to the edge of a joist. It is designed for open-beam construction, but you can adapt it to covered ceilings.

FLANGED BOXES

Another ceiling box design is the flanged box. The flange is fastened directly to the edge of the box and it may or may not have prepunched nail tabs to attach the box to a joist. All boxes, however, will have nail and/or screw holes for mounting purposes.

CUT-IN BOXES

These are lightweight boxes that are pushed through a hole you cut in gypsum board or wood paneling. The boxes have a spring device that holds the box in position against the back side of the ceiling material. The boxes also have metal extensions that are installed inside the box to hold fixtures. Observe these boxes' weight limits.

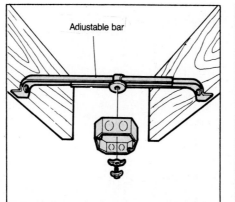

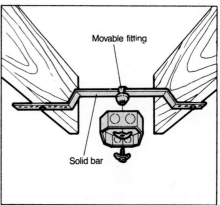

Two-piece boxes. A two-piece box has an adjustable bar hanger. Box can be positioned anyplace along bar with a screw clamp.

Offset bar hangers. An offset bar hanger recesses the box between joists, although the bar is nailed directly to the edges of the joists.

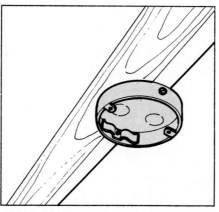

Pancake boxes. If the joist or beam is exposed, or there is little working room between joists, you can use a pancake box nailed to joist edges.

Flanged boxes. Nail or screw box directly to joist face. Set rim of box flush with ceiling covering.

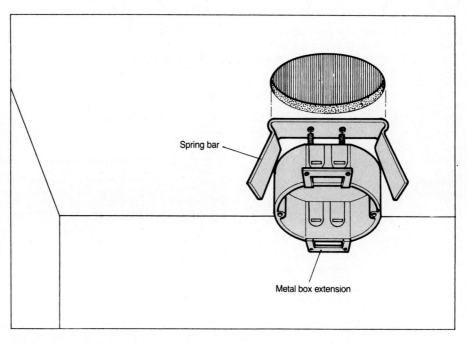

Cut-in boxes. In gypsum board and in wood ceiling paneling, you can use a cut-in box. Spring device holds it in position against ceiling material. Attachments are installed in the box to handle wires and fixtures. Box can't support extra heavy fixtures.

Make initial cut. Locate joists where you want box. Then cut a hole about 8 × 8 inches next to a joist or between two joists as a pilot hole.

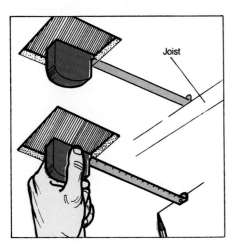

Make joist measurement. Slip a tape measure inside the pilot hole and measure the distance to the joists. Transfer measurements to the ceiling face.

Cut square opening. Cut a hole 17½ inches square. The cut will be in the center of two joists. Trim the cut edges as square as possible.

INSTALLING BOXES IN GYPSUM BOARD CEILINGS

You'll need a keyhole saw, a drill bit to start the hole into the ceiling material, a tape measure, safety glasses, and the wiring materials. First, find the joists (see page 60).

STEP 1
MAKE INITIAL CUT

After you locate the joists, cut an 8 × 8-inch-square opening in the gypsum board ceiling material.

STEP 2
MEASURE JOIST

Inside the hole you made, determine the exact distances to the joists. Note the measurements; transfer them to the face of the gypsum board ceiling. Add ¾ inch to this mark; this shows you where the joist centers are located.

STEP 3
CUT SQUARE OPENING

With a square, mark a 17½-inch-square opening on the ceiling that splits the centers of the joists. Then, using a straightedge and a sharp utility knife, cut out the square.

STEP 4
MAKE A PATCH

From a piece of gypsum board the same thickness as the ceiling material, cut a 17½-inch-square patch to fill the opening. In this patch, locate the opening for the box and cut out the opening.

STEP 5
INSTALL BOX AND PATCH

Fasten the ceiling box on its hanger to the joists. Then position the box so it fits the hole in the patch. Test it. Then pull the new cable into the box; fit and nail patch in opening.

STEP 6
PATCH THE PATCH

With joint tape, a taping knife, and drywall taping compound, seal the patch into the ceiling. Use at least three coats of compound, letting each dry. Sand smooth at the end.

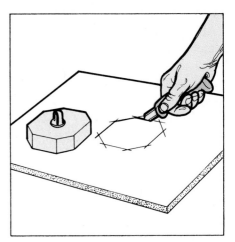

Make a patch. Make a patch to fit the hole in the ceiling. Then locate box position in the patch. Cut a hole for it. Check sizes as you go.

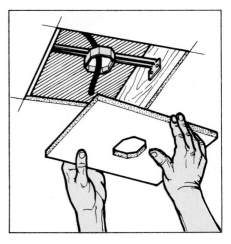

Install box and patch. After you position box between joists on a hanger and nail the hanger to the joists, pull the cable into the box and fasten it. Test the patch for fit.

Patch the patch. Cover edges of patch with joint tape and taping compound. Use three coats of compound. Sand smooth. Paint to finish.

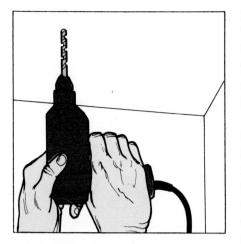

Locate the box. Determine the box location. Use an extra-long bit or an extender shank to drill a small hole through ceiling and floor above. Stick a wire through the holes.

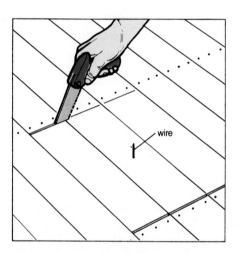

Cut hole in flooring. Using wire in hole as a guide, mark a square on the floor and cut out flooring between joists. If floor is tile or sheet material, cut out a square; patch later.

Drill box guide holes. Center the ceiling box on the underside of the ceiling material, and trace its outline. Drill small holes at the box points.

INSTALLING CEILING BOXES THROUGH FLOORS

When working from a second-story floor through the ceiling below, first locate the joists on either side of the new box location (see page 60).

STEP 1
LOCATE THE BOX

On the ceiling, drill a ¼-inch hole between the joists through the ceiling material, joist space, floor sheathing, and floor covering above, exactly where you want the ceiling box to be.

STEP 2
CUT HOLE IN FLOORING

Run a stiff piece of wire up through the ceiling hole. Locate this wire on the floor upstairs. If the floor is covered with tile or resilient flooring, remove a tile or a square of flooring. With a square and the wire in the hole as a guide, measure, mark, and cut out a small square.

STEP 3
DRILL BOX GUIDE HOLES

Carefully position the center of the ceiling box over the hole in the ceiling. Then mark the points of the box on the underside of the ceiling. Drill ¼-inch holes at these points.

STEP 4
MAKE CUT IN CEILING

Downstairs on the face of the ceiling, draw an outline of the electrical box, using the holes to position the box correctly. Then saw out an opening.

STEP 5
INSTALL THE BOX

Back upstairs, position the box in the hole in the ceiling; nail the bar hanger to the joists. Trim the ends of the bar if necessary. Run in the electrical cable.

STEP 6
PATCH THE FLOORING

With small pieces of 2 × 2 or 2 × 4, cleat the faces of the joists so a flooring patch may be nailed to the cleats. Then cut new flooring to fit the opening. Or use plywood sheathing.

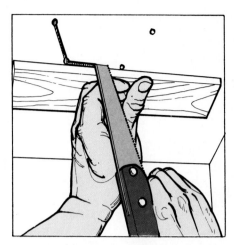

Make cut in ceiling. Downstairs, match the box to the drilled holes, draw an outline of the box on the ceiling, and make cut for box in ceiling.

Install the box. Upstairs, install the box in the ceiling hole using a bar hanger. Adjust the box with the screw clamp to fit perfectly in the hole.

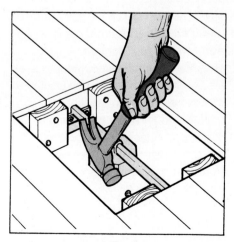

Patch the flooring. Nail cleats to the joist faces. Then install flooring or sheathing patch. Nail it to the cleats; re-cover patch with tile or sheathing.

CHANGING A CEILING FIXTURE

Replacing an old ceiling fixture with a new one is easy—just a matter of determining which mounting devices are needed for the project depending on fixture weight. The different devices are illustrated at the right.

Turn off the power, then:

STEP 1
REMOVE OLD FIXTURE

Depending on the style of the fixture, remove the globe, light diffuser, and bulbs from the fixture. The canopy, escutcheon, or fixture base is held to the ceiling electrical box with a locknut or fixture bolts. Remove these fasteners; turn them counterclockwise. This will expose the contents of the ceiling box.

STEP 2
DISCONNECT WIRING

Have a helper hold the fixture while you disconnect the black and white wires from the fixture. If a helper isn't handy, you can make a hook support from a bent coat hanger to hold up the fixture.

If there are more than two wires in the box, note the configuration and connections. The other wires could be switch and grounding wires.

If the fixture is held by a hickey and nipple or a nut and stud, unscrew these connectors, releasing the fixture.

STEP 3
INSTALL NEW FIXTURE

Have a helper hold up the new fixture or support it with a coat hanger arrangement while you connect the fixture wires to the circuit wires. Most fixtures are prewired; remove ¾-inch insulation from the wires for connection.

Mate and twist the black wire of the fixture to the black wire of the circuit; do the same with the white wires and ground wires, if any. Use wire nuts and tape them.

STEP 4
MOUNT THE FIXTURE

The fixture is supported by mounting devices in or on the box, as shown.

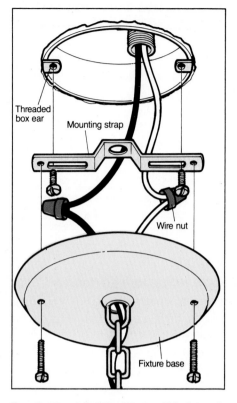

Four types of fixture mounts. This fixture is held with a mounting strap spanning the ceiling box. Screws hold strap to box and base to strap. Stud is not needed.

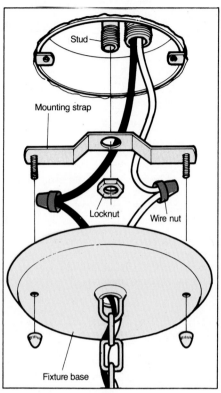

Less than 10 pounds. Mounting strap is held to stud with locknut, and fixture base is screwed to strap. Use this arrangement for fixtures weighing less than 10 pounds.

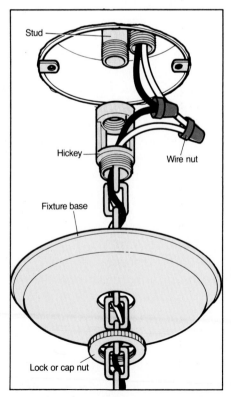

From 10 to 20 pounds. Heavy fixture is mounted on hickey that is screwed to stud in box. Cap nut only secures fixture base to hickey; it doesn't hold fixture up.

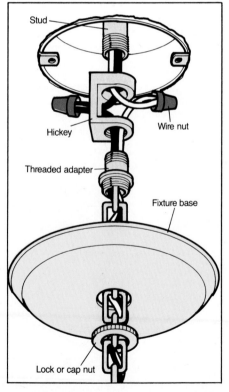

Over 20 pounds. Here, stud, hickey, and threaded adaptor are used to mount very heavy fixture. The necessary parts usually are packaged with the fixture.

Installing Track Lighting

Track lighting creates a theatrical mood. It can be formal and informal at the same time, and it can be installed in open ceilings and on finished ones.

If you install track lighting in an open ceiling, you can spray the joists and sheathing above flat black and the track lights will seem to float on the ceiling surface.

You can add local lighting with track lights, which, in many ways, are similar to raceway lighting. The basic part is a length of surface wiring that can be tapped anywhere for a fixture. Because of its flexibility, you can place it in almost any room. The track comes with various adaptors that enable you to add outlets or, in some cases, even a fairly heavy chandelier.

THE POWER SOURCES

Track lighting is connected to the house wiring, like any other ceiling fixture. You probably will have to add a ceiling junction box to install this style of raceway, since the existing boxes will not be close enough to the track.

LIGHTING SUGGESTIONS AS YOU GO SHOPPING

Track lighting installation procedures vary according to the manufacturer and model. Be sure that you read all the instructions carefully *before* you buy the system. You can start with the basic system and add to it as your budget or decorating scheme dictates. Make sure that the brand of track lights you buy will accommodate your plans for the future.

If the track-lighting channel is attached to a ceiling, use toggle or Molly® fasteners to ensure the stability. If the track is mounted on open framing, you can attach the track to edges of joists or along a joist edge. In some situations you can recess the track and the lights between the joists in a straight line.

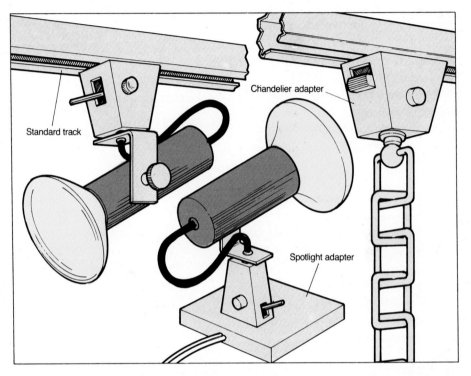

Track lighting is available with myriad fittings—from standard lights to spotlights to chandeliers. The lights also come in different designs to match most decors.

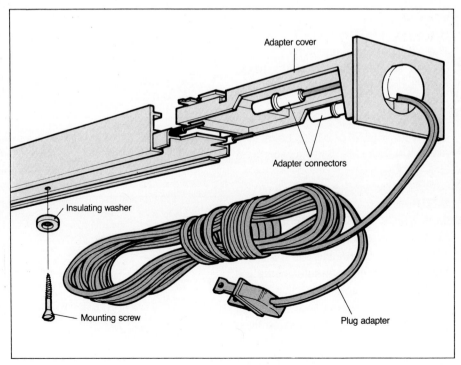

You can buy a plug-in track-lighting kit that eliminates the need to make wiring connections. Or you can buy track that must be connected to a wired ceiling or junction box.

CONNECTING TRACK LIGHTS TO HOUSE POWER

Turn off the circuit on which you will be working. Roughly plot the position of the track on the ceiling. Install a ceiling junction box, if none exists, at one end of the track's location and fish cable to the box. The technique involved is explained starting on page 85.

If you are using a plug-in track lighting system, install the track as described below and simply plug it into an existing wired outlet.

STEP 1
CONNECTOR PLATE

The track adaptor plate covers the junction box and holds the track connector and the electrical housing. Assemble these pieces. Splicing like-colored wires together, hook up the track wires to the cable wires. Then fasten the adaptor assembly to the junction box ears with the screws provided.

STEP 2
PLOT THE TRACK

Working from the center slot of the track connector, draw a line along the ceiling to pinpoint the track's location.

STEP 3
INSTALL TRACK CLIPS

The track is held in position by special clips spaced evenly along the track. Hold the clips in place on your line, and mark pilot holes in the ceiling.

Drill the pilot holes and attach the clips with toggle or Molly bolts to a drywall surface or with screws to a wooden surface.

STEP 4
CONNECT THE CHANNEL

Connect the track channel solidly to the electrical connector; slip the channel into the track connector. Snap the track channels into the clips. Then tighten the setscrews along the sides of the clips to hold the channels firmly in position.

To complete the project, install the raceway cover and attach the track lights anywhere you wish.

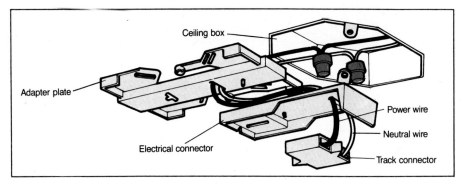

Connector plate. Connect the track wiring to the house wiring, using the metal adaptor plate. Wire nut the splices and wrap them with plastic electrician's tape. Fasten assembly to ceiling box.

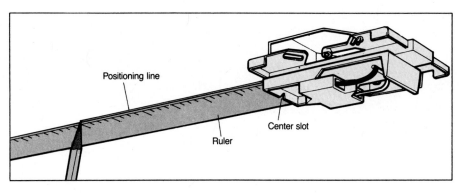

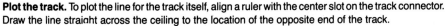

Plot the track. To plot the line for the track itself, align a ruler with the center slot on the track connector. Draw the line straight across the ceiling to the location of the opposite end of the track.

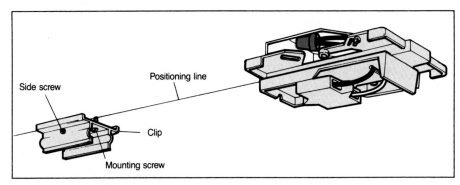

Install track clips. The track will be held along the line by plastic clips. Center the clip on the line; draw a mark for the screw hole. Then install the clip using toggle or Molly bolts or wood screws.

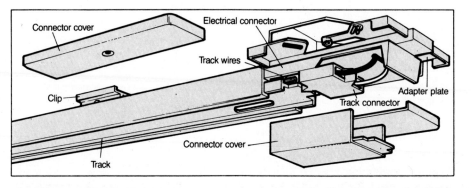

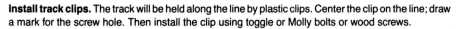

Connect the channel. Hook up the track to the track connector. The track itself supplies power for the track lights. Make sure that the track connection joints are butted tightly together. Then attach lights.

All About Fluorescent Fixtures

The three main parts of a fluorescent fixture are the fluorescent tube, which may be straight or circular, the starter, and the ballast. Defects in these components cause most fluorescent fixture problems.

THE TUBE

A fluorescent tube produces light in this way: Inside a tube, the electric current jumps or arcs from a cathode at one end of the tube to an anode at the other end. The tube is filled with mercury and argon gases. As the arc passes through the gases, it causes them to emit invisible ultraviolet light. To make the light visible, the inside of the tube is coated with phosphor powder that glows when hit by ultraviolet light.

THE STARTER

The starter is a switch that closes when activated by electric current. After a momentary delay, the starter allows current to energize gases in the tube. There are two types of starters: *replaceable* ones, which are about ¾ inch in diameter with two contacts protruding from one end. The other is a *rapid-start* fixture. The starter is built into the ballast and can't be replaced independently of the ballast.

THE BALLAST

The ballast is a boxlike component usually about 6 to 7 inches long. It is a kind of governor that holds electric current to the level required to provide proper light operation. There are two types of ballasts. *Choke* ballasts limit the amount of current flowing through the tube. Fixtures that hold long fluorescent tubes have *thermal-protected* ballasts that incorporate transformers and choke coils. When the light is turned on, a transformer steps up the voltage to deliver a momentarily high surge of electricity to get the tube to glow.

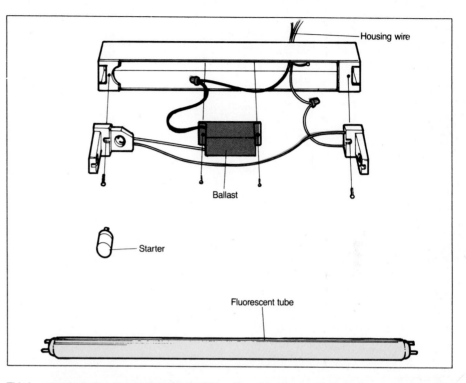

This is a standard straight-tube fluorescent fixture. The wiring for a separate ballast and replaceable starter is illustrated. The starter fits into a contact seat in the fixture housing.

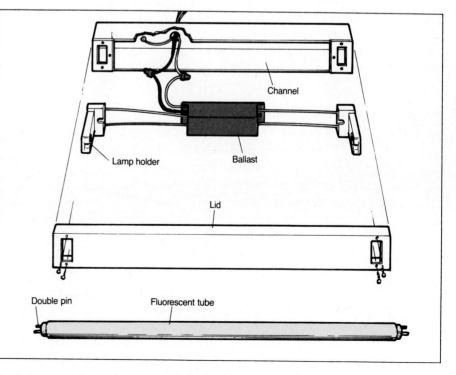

This fluorescent fixture has a rapid-start ballast and starter in one unit.

REPLACING A FLUORESCENT BALLAST

Turn off the circuit breaker or remove the fuse that supplies power to the circuit. Then remove the tube(s), and take off the cover. Jot down the number codes on the old ballast and take them to the store with you, just to make sure you buy the right ballast replacement.

STEP 1
DISCONNECT THE WIRES

Remove the wire nuts or loosen the terminal screws to disconnect the ballast wires. The wire connections of the ballast you are replacing are the same or similar to one of those shown on this page. Notice that ballast wires are color-coded. A ballast wire of a given color is always connected to the fixture wire of the same color.

A thermally protected ballast must be connected in the same way. If the complexities of the wires confuse you, make a simple color-coded diagram before you disconnect any wires.

STEP 2
REMOVE THE BALLAST

The ballast you are removing is heavier than you might think. Be careful. Have a helper hold the ballast while you remove the fasteners that attach it to the fixture.

Note carefully the alignment of the ballast in the fixture and then take it down.

STEP 3
CONNECT NEW BALLAST

Again with a helper holding the new ballast, line up the ballast so that it is in the same position as the old ballast was. Screw the new ballast to the fixture.

Match the color codes of the wires and twist these wires together with your fingers or pliers. Then thread the connected wires into wire nuts. Wrap the wire nuts with a couple of layers of plastic electrician's tape.

As a final step, before you replace the cover, turn on the power and test the light.

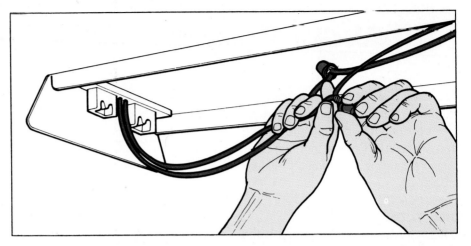

Disconnect the wires. When replacing a ballast unit, first make a color-coded diagram of the wiring. Then remove the wire nuts from all connections and disconnect the splices. Note color-coding of wires and numbers on ballast for purchasing purposes.

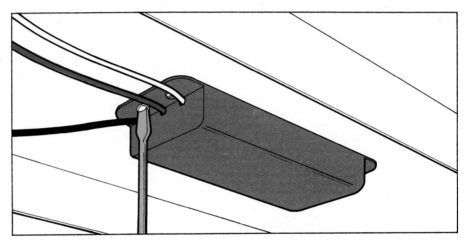

Remove the ballast. Loosen the screws that hold the ballast in the fixture. Have a helper hold the heavy ballast while you do this. Then remove the ballast from the fixture, noting its exact position.

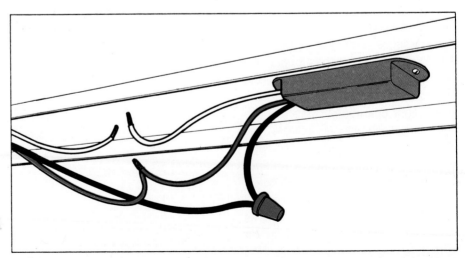

Connect new ballast. Don't worry about the maze of wires. Connections are made by matching colors, splicing wires, and securing splices with wire nuts wrapped with plastic electrician's tape.

FLUORESCENT FIXTURE INSTALLATION DATA

To replace a fluorescent fixture, first turn off the power to the circuit and remove the old fixture from the ceiling. To add a new fixture, install a ceiling box; run in the cable. The techniques are explained on pages 101–103.

STEP 1
CIRCULAR FIXTURES

In the center of the ceiling box, add a threaded stud, if one is not present. The fixture hangs on this stud. Add a reducing nipple to the stud. Have a helper hold the fixture while you connect the power wires: black to black, white to white. Wire nut the splices and wrap them with electrician's tape.

Push the wires into the box, thread the nipple through the hole in the center of the fixture, and secure the fixture with a cap nut.

STEP 2
ONE-TUBE FIXTURES

You will need a hickey and nipple if the box has a stud. If not, you can attach the fixture to a nipple and strap screwed to the ears in the box.

First splice the fixture wires to the house wires, wire nut the splices, and wrap the splices with plastic electrician's tape. Then attach the fixture to the ceiling box with the nipple, a washer, and a locknut.

Have a helper hold the fixture while you assemble and fasten it to the ceiling box. When the fixture is stable, drive a couple of sheet-metal screws through the fixture housing into the ceiling at each end.

STEP 3
LARGE FIXTURES

Fixtures with more than two tubes usually have a center cutout that is used when hanging the fixture from an *octagonal box*. The fixture uses a stud, hickey, nipple, and a mounting strap inside the housing. The assembly is held with a locknut. Connect the wiring with wire nuts. Then push the wires into the box and secure the fixture.

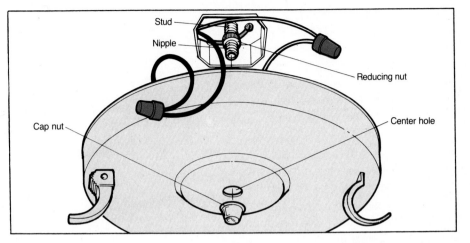

Circular fixtures. Circular fixture (Circline) is connected to a stud and nipple inside the ceiling box. Complete the wiring first with wire nuts, then hang fixture with cap nut on nipple. Install the tube.

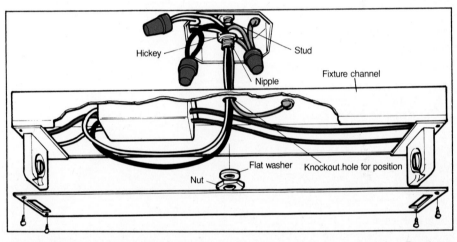

One-tube fixtures. Knockouts in housing let you position fixture almost anywhere over box. Punch out knockout. Connect wiring. Fasten to ceiling. Add screws through housing at ends to support fixture.

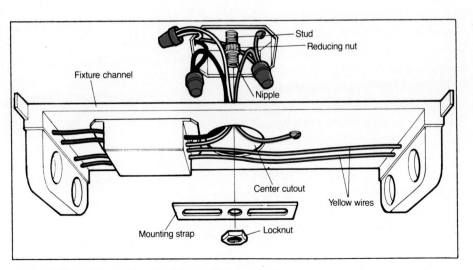

Large fixtures. Strap inside fixture helps support weight. The assembly order is: stud, reducing nut, nipple, fixture, strap, and locknut tightener. Cover plate slips into channels along sides of fixture.

REPLACING DEFECTIVE FLUORESCENT SWITCHES

Most fluorescent lights are wired integrally with the housing wiring and are controlled by wall switches. Some fixtures have built-in switches that can fail. Here's how to replace them.

PULL-CHAIN REPLACEMENT

With pliers, loosen and remove the knurled nut and locknut that hold the switch in the fixture housing. Disconnect the switch wires. If they can't be disconnected, cut them, leaving a couple of inches for reconnection.

Lift out the entire switch. Make wiring connections with wire nuts. Tape the nuts, then set the new switch in place. Secure it with locknuts.

TOGGLE SWITCHES

The technique is the same as for chain switches, except that power wire terminal screws are attached to the switch. Remove the wires, install a new switch, and rewire it.

SWITCHING A PUSH SWITCH
STEP 1
REMOVING THE SWITCH

With a wrench or pliers, remove the nut holding the switch in the housing. Then slip the switch out of its socket.

STEP 2
DISCONNECT THE SWITCH

When the push switch has been loosened and removed, disconnect the wire nuts and break the splice.

STEP 3
RECONNECT THE SWITCH

Install the new switch, connecting the electrical wires with wire nuts. Wrap the wire nuts with a couple of turns of plastic electrician's tape. Then set the switch in the housing and locknut it tight to the housing.

FLICKERING PROBLEMS

If a tube has the flickers, remove it. Straighten bent pins with pliers. Then burnish the pins lightly with fine-grit abrasive or steel wool.

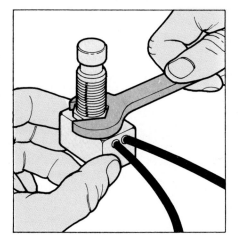

Pull-chain replacement. To replace a pull-chain switch, remove the knurled nut and locknut. Break the splices. Put in new switch and reconnect the splices.

Toggle switches. To replace a toggle switch, release the locknuts on the old switch. Attach wires to the terminal screws of the replacement switch.

Switching a push switch. At the fixture housing, remove the locknut holding the defective switch in place. Then slip the switch out of its socket.

Disconnect the switch. Break the splice by removing the wire nuts. Note the wiring pattern: it usually involves two wires, but it could have three.

Reconnect the switch. Install the new switch with the same wiring pattern as the old one. Twist the wire nuts tightly over the splices and wrap with tape.

Straightening the pins. If the tube flickers on and off, the pins, not the switch, may be the trouble. Straighten the pins and then shine them with abrasive.

TROUBLESHOOTING GUIDE TO FLUORESCENT LIGHTS

For the most part, fluorescent fixtures are easy to repair. However, when the cause of the problem is not obvious, troubleshooting can be a hit-or-miss proposition. If you are unsure of the cause, replace one component after another until you find the one that's causing the trouble.

The chart at the right lists possible fluorescent fixture failures and their causes and repairs. Causes are listed in the likely order of occurrence, and repairs are listed in the order in which they should be made.

USING YOUR SENSES

Fluorescent troubles you can't see often can be heard and smelled. Here are some examples that may be helpful in finding the problem.

VERY LOUD HUMMING

You won't mistake it, although a low hum is normal. Suspect loose wires first, then the ballast, which may be burning out. Or it may be the wrong ballast for the fixture.

AWFUL SMELL

Tubes on their way to permanent darkness can emit an acrid odor. So can ballasts. The smell may persist for several days before the component gives out completely.

NO LIGHT OR THE BULB FLICKERS

The fixture seems to work except on certain days when the room is cold. A low temperature—sometimes down to 50 degree F—can prevent gases in the tube from igniting. A low temperature sometimes can cause the light to flicker until it warms up. Flickering càn also be caused by bent and/or corroded tube pins.

NO LIGHT

Don't be too quick to blame the fixture. Check the main service panel for a blown fuse or for a circuit breaker that has tripped.

FLUORESCENT FIXTURE TROUBLE SHOOTING

Type of Failure	Causes	Repairs
Tube fails to light	1. Fuse has blown or circuit breaker has tripped	1. Replace fuse or reset circuit breaker. If problem recurs, check house wiring.
	2. Tube not seated correctly in sockets	2. If tube is straight, rotate off and reseat into sockets. If tube is circular, remove and reinstall; all pins should fully engage socket.
	3. Defective starter	3. If starter is independent of ballast, replace starter. If starter is part of ballast replace the tube before you replace the ballast.
	4. Defective tube	4. Replace tube with one of correct wattage, which is marked on old tube. If marking is unclear, check voltage marked on ballast.
	5. Defective ballast or starter in ballast	5. Replace the ballast. Check ballast connections.
Light flickers and swirls around in tube	1. New tube	1. Normal in new tubes; should clear up in a short time.
	2. Defective starter or ballast	2. Replace starter if it is independent of ballast; if problem remains, replace ballast.
Light blinks on and off	1. Low room temperature (below 50°F)	1. To eliminate, install a low-temperature starter and ballast or replace entire unit with one designed for low temperature locations.
	2. Tube not seated properly	2. If tube is straight, reseat securely in sockets. If tube is circular, remove and reinstall. All pins must fully engage socket.
	3. Tube pins bent	3. Examine the tube pins. If bent, straighten with long-nosed pliers. Sand pins lightly; wipe away foreign matter. Insert pins securely into sockets.
	4. Sockets deformed or dirty	4. Turn off circuit (see Chapter 1). Socket contacts of a long fixture should lean inward. If deformed, try repairing them by bending with long-nosed pliers. Sand contacts lightly; blow foreign matter from sockets with an ear syringe.
	5. Loose connections	5. Turn off circuit; remove fixture cover. Remove wire nuts and check all wire splices. Reinstall wire nuts securely.
	6. Defective tube	6. Replace tube.
	7. Defective ballast	7. Replace ballast.
Ends of tube light; center does not glow	1. Defective starter	1. Replace starter.
Tube seems to burn out rapidly	1. Fixture turned on and off at frequent intervals	1. Avoid turning fixture on and off so frequently.
	2. Incorrect ballast	2. If short tube life occurs after replacing ballast, ballast may be incorrect type for the fixture. Check ballast and fixture types. An electrical parts dealer can help you.
	3. Incorrect ballast wiring	3. Turn off circuit. Remove fixture cover and trace wire connections. Use earlier illustrations as guides.
	4. Mating tube failure	4. Replace a burned-out tube immediately, especially in some rapid-start fixtures holding two or more tubes. Otherwise, the other tube usually will fail prematurely.
	5. Defective starter or ballast	5. Replace starter; if condition continues, replace ballast.
Discoloration at tube ends	1. Normal condition	1. Brown or gray bands about two inches from tube ends are normal.
	2. Worn out tube	2. Gradually enlarging black bands at tube ends indicate tube is going bad. Replace tube.
	3. Defective starter or ballast	3. If black bands develop on new tube, replace starter; if condition continues, replace ballast.
Humming	1. Normal	1. Some humming is normal.
	2. Loose ballast wires	2. Loose wires can cause humming. Turn off circuit. Remove wire nuts and check connections. Secure wire nuts.
	3. Incorrect ballast	3. If humming started after installing ballast, it may not match the fixture type. Check ballast and fixture types.

Match the fluorescent fixture problem you're having with the troubleshooting chart above. Tubes and starters usually go bad before ballasts and other parts of the fixture.

9 Heating, Cooling, and Ventilating

In the last few years, manufacturers have improved the designs of heating, cooling, and ventilating products with the do-it-yourselfer in mind.

This chapter explains the installation, replacement, and repair of the more simple heating, cooling, and ventilating products.

Turn off the power at the service panel before starting to work.

ROOM CEILING FANS FOR COOLING AND HEATING

Although it is powered by electricity, a ceiling fan can be a real energy saver. In air-conditioned rooms, for example, the cool air pools on the floor. But with the paddles of a slow-turning ceiling fan stirring the air, cool air is distributed throughout the room.

The same holds true in heating situations. A room may be comfortable at floor level, but uncomfortably warm near the ceiling—in a sleeping loft or the upper berth of a bunk bed, for example. A ceiling fan corrects this by circulating the rising warm air throughout the room. Used with either air conditioning or heating, the fan can distribute costly cold or heat for just pennies. And with both heat and cooling turned off, a ceiling fan often provides plenty of comfort by itself—also for pennies.

CEILING FANS ARE QUIET AND EASILY INSTALLED

Most ceiling fans are isolation-mounted. That is, the ceiling fan is installed on a ball-and-socket device that lets the fan run quietly and with less vibration to ceiling and fan.

You can buy a ceiling fan that is installed with a bracket over an existing electrical ceiling box. The hookup is to the wires in the box. Or you can wire in a new box as the power source. No matter what you do, check that the installation conforms to local electrical codes. When purchasing a fan, verify that the product has been tested according to current electrical standards by a recognized laboratory. Call your local electrical inspector for questions.

You have plenty of fan designs to choose from: there are four- and five-blade models with and without lights, reversing blade features for summer and winter use, and many styles to match any decor.

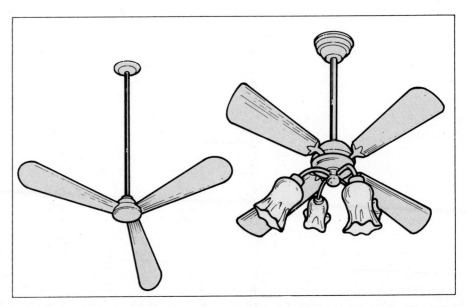

Ceiling fans come in many designs, from clean-line three-blade models, to elaborate four-blade styles with single or multiple built-in light fixtures. Wiring options are explained on following pages.

Installing a Ceiling Fan

Ceiling-fan installation involves two critical measurements. You must have at least 7 feet of clearance from the floor to the blades of the fan in the room in which the fan will be installed. The blades must also be free to rotate; there can be no obstruction in the path of the rotation. Check the vertical space in the room. Also check the length of fan blades for proper blade clearance.

HOUSEPOWER HOOKUP

Ceiling fans operate on regular housepower. No electric transformers or special switching devices are needed. You can connect them directly to the wires in a ceiling box listed for this purpose. If you are running cable to a new ceiling box for the installation, the wire size should correspond with the wire size that you are tapping into. If you are creating a new circuit, the wire size should be AWG No. 12/2 with ground. How to install new wiring is explained on pages 60–65.

SWITCHING CHOICES

Switching is another consideration. If the room in which the fan is installed has a ceiling light controlled by a wall switch, the fan hookup is simple: remove the light fixture and substitute the fan. If the light fixture has a switch on it, you can buy a fan that also is controlled by its own switch. To control the fan with a wall switch, you will have to wire this switch by (1) tapping into a source of power elsewhere in the room (usually an outlet), (2) tapping into the fan, or (3) by running a switch loop from the ceiling box to the wall.

If you have an attic crawl space in your home and you have access to the crawl space, you may be able to tap into the wiring in the crawl space, either in the existing ceiling box, at another nearby ceiling box, or by breaking a power wire (after turning off the power) and adding a junction box from which the ceiling box and fan receive electricity.

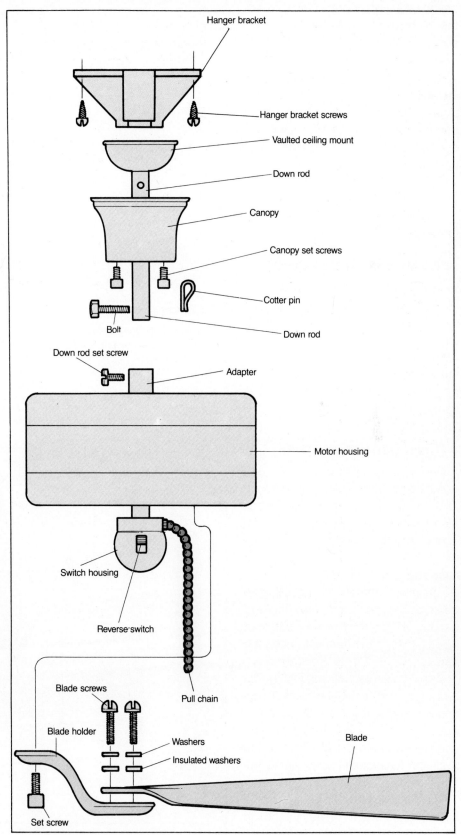

This is how a typical ceiling fan is assembled. Your model may differ slightly. The key to installation is to firmly secure the ceiling electrical box to the joists. The box must be rigid to support the fan.

CEILING-FAN MOUNTING OPTIONS

To install a ceiling fan, first make certain that you have turned off the power on the circuit serving the ceiling box or tap-in connection. If you're not sure the power is off, use a voltage tester to make certain (see page 53).

Be sure to follow the manufacturer's instructions and check to see that the product meets current electrical standards. Hanger pins with a swivel suspension must be attached to the ceiling framing.

To install any ceiling fan in an existing ceiling outlet, remove the ceiling light and disconnect the wires to the light terminals.

SECURE BOX TO FRAMING

Brackets must be attached to the framing and the electrical box must be listed for this specific use. Check the box. It must be securely attached to the joists. If the box feels loose, drive a couple of round-head wood screws through the mounting holes in the box into the framing members.

J HOOK (ISOLATION TYPE)

If the fan is mounted on J hooks and hanger pins, the pins must be fastened into the ceiling framing, not into the box alone. Make sure the ceiling box is securely fastened to joists.

SURFACE MOUNTING

If you mount the fan on an exposed beam ceiling, position the fan between beams, using a 2 × 4 or 2 × 6 length of wood between the beams to hang the fan.

You also can use a Hang Fast (trade name) bracket (or similar bracket), not shown. There must be 6 inches of space for the bracket. It also may be used where attic crawl space is not available for mounting and wiring the fan.

The blocking between beams can be spiked to the beams. Install the box to the wood beams. The fan is mounted on the box or a J hook also screwed into the box.

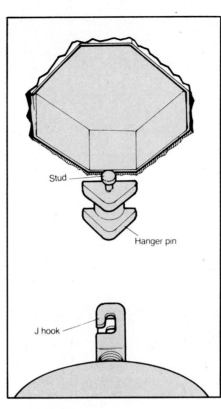

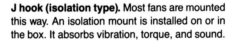

J hook (isolation type). Most fans are mounted this way. An isolation mount is installed on or in the box. It absorbs vibration, torque, and sound.

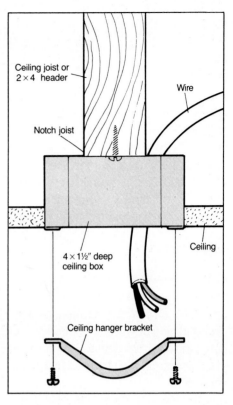

Flush mounting. Ideally the box for the fan is attached through the ceiling with screws to a framing member.

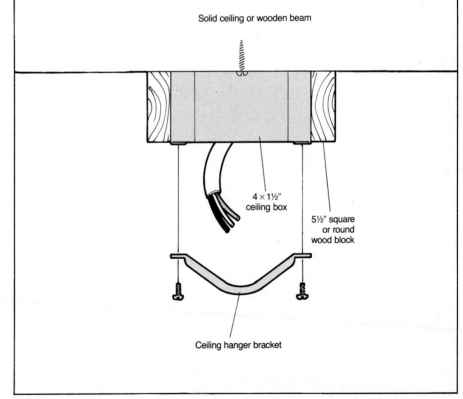

Surface mounting. If you find it necessary to mount the fan-mounting ceiling box on the surface, you can frame the box in wood or other materials to hide it. If you decide to do this, make sure that the box is screwed directly to a framing member through the ceiling covering.

FLUSH MOUNTING

To install the fan on a finished ceiling where there is no outlet or wiring, you must open the ceiling and add framing between joists to fasten the box to. Do not use an adjustable hanger bar, it may not be strong enough.

CEILING-FAN ASSEMBLY AND MOUNTING TIPS

Most ceiling fans are assembled the same way. There may be slight variations between fan manufacturers, but the differences will be noted in the instructions enclosed in the fan package. Wire colors may also vary.

AT THE CEILING BOX

Turn off the electric power to the ceiling box at the main electrical service panel. Do not flip a wall switch and assume that the power is turned off. Go to the main service panel and flip the appropriate circuit breaker or remove the fuse. If there is any doubt, use a voltage tester, as described on page 53, to make sure there's no power on in the box.

Remove the ceiling fixture and disconnect the black and white wires from the terminals or wire nuts.

If the ceiling light is controlled by a wall switch, the fan also may be controlled by the wall switch. If the light is not controlled by a wall switch and you want to control the fan with a wall switch, you will have to fish cable through the ceiling and down the wall to create a switch loop. This is explained on page 98. If you want to control the fan with the fan switch, you simply connect the fan to the power wires inside the ceiling box.

We want to stress that the ceiling box must be securely mounted to the ceiling framing. Double-check to make sure it is. The best insurance is to drive a couple of screws through holes in the box into solid material.

Assemble the mounting bracket according to manufacturer's instructions. Attach the bracket into the ceiling framing, not to the ceiling box alone. Be certain the product conforms to electrical codes.

If the box is mounted on a pitched ceiling or beam, you have to use either a swivel hanger or an angle kit that you can buy at the store. The kits are not furnished in the fan package. An angle hanger lets the fan hang level although the box sits at an angle.

The fan can be supported by a hook, but you will need a block of wood to drive the hook into. We recommend a short length of 4×4. Predrill it and bolt it to the beam or ceiling. The power wire can be stapled along the top or bottom edge of a beam and then connected into the electrical ceiling box. You can paint or stain the cable so it matches the beam.

DOWN-ROD ASSEMBLY

Position the down rod through the canopy of the fan, using the diagram on page 113 to help you.

Then run the electrical wires from the fan through the down-rod assembly. Use a stout string to pull them through if necessary. There will be power circuit wires and a switch wire. There may also be a fourth, grounding, wire, depending on the brand and type of fan you are installing. The usual insulation colors identify the power circuit wires: black for the hot line and white. The switch wire is usually blue-insulated, but may have red insulation in some fans. The grounding wire will be bare or have green insulation.

Now insert the down rod into the motor adaptor and fasten it. Insert the bolt provided and insert and spread the cotter pin. Tighten the setscrew counterclockwise to complete the job.

MOUNTING THE FAN

With a helper, lift the fan into position at the ceiling without the blades attached. Put the vaulted ceiling mount or swivel into the hanger bracket. The fan now should be supported on the ceiling with a swivel-type ball-and-socket bracket or J hook.

Make the necessary electrical connections as shown on page 116.

LIGHT-KIT ASSEMBLY

If the fan has a light kit, remove the switch housing on the fan and the center screw. Screw the light kit onto the bottom plate.

You'll need a helper to hold the kit assembly in position while you connect the fan's blue wire to the light's black wire and the fan's white wire to the light's white wire. Use wire nuts for splices and wrap the wire nuts with electrician's tape. Screw on the bottom plate and light, and attach the glass.

CONNECTIONS AND CHECKS

Put the fan blades into the holder. Then fasten the holder to the fan motor. The unit is now assembled.

Connect the fan to power. In a general hookup, the white wire goes to white, and black goes to black. The ground wire connects to the ceiling box via a screw or clip. Or the ground is spliced to an incoming ground wire.

Turn on the power and make sure that the fan operates in all speeds, forward, and reverse. If the fan has a light kit, turn on the lights.

If you notice any blade wobble, measure from the ceiling to the tip of each blade. If the blades are not even, exert light pressure on the blade that is out of alignment so it matches the other blades. You may have to loosen setscrews that hold the blades in position, if the fan has them. If not, just push the blades gently until they are even. All blades must be uniform. Otherwise, the blades will wobble and jump and exert extra wear and tear on the fan mounting assembly.

TROUBLESHOOTING

If the fan doesn't run or the lights don't work, you can make these checks:

● Is the power turned on at the main service panel? Has a fuse blown or breaker tripped while you were connecting the fan?

● Is the wall or fan switch in the proper mode?

● Is the light switch on the fan in the proper mode?

● Are the power wires properly connected in the ceiling box?

● Are the switch wires properly connected in the ceiling box?

CEILING-FAN WIRING CONNECTIONS

Wiring variations used for connecting ceiling fans include:

FAN SWITCH ON FAN

If the fan has a three-speed pull chain near the bottom of the motor, the blue and black fan wires are connected to the black-power wire in the box. The white-insulated wires are joined; the green ground wire is fastened to the ceiling box. Use wire nuts and tape.

LIGHT SWITCH ON WALL

In this connection, the light is controlled by a wall switch. You control the fan with the three-speed control on the fan. You also can have a separate wall switch to control a ceiling-fan light kit. The black wire in the fan connects to the incoming black power wire and to another black wire going to the switch. The blue switch wire connects to the blue fan wire. The white wire in the fan connects to the white wire in the box. The green wire connects to the green wire in the box or to the box itself.

FAN AND LIGHT SWITCH ON WALL

In a dual-control wall switch, the black power wire is connected to a black wire going to the switch. The black and blue fan wires also connect to the switch. Connect the white wires; connect the green wires. If the box doesn't have a green grounding wire, connect the green fan wire to the box.

TRANSFORMER AND SWITCH ON WALL

If the fan has a three-speed transformer, you can control it with a wall switch or variable control. Connect the fan's black wire to the black switch wire. The blue wire is connected to the incoming black power wire and connects to the fan's blue wire. The white wires are connected and the green wires are connected. If you want variable speed on the fan, leave the pull chain on the fan at the high-speed setting.

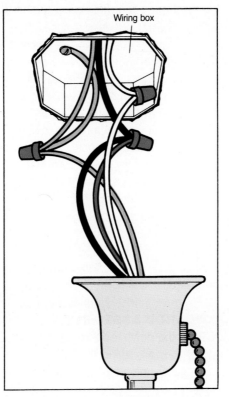

Fan switch on fan. Wiring hookup is for a three-speed pull chain. It provides for optional light kit, which is operated independently of the fan by a pull-chain switch.

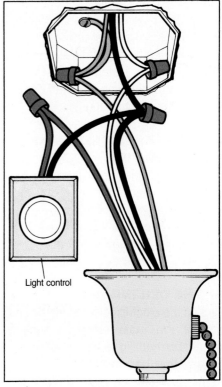

Light switch on wall. The light is controlled from a wall switch in this arrangement. You control the fan speed with its three-speed control, and the light from the separate wall switch.

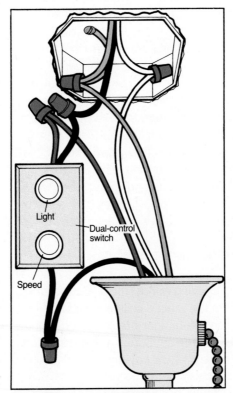

Fan and light switch on wall. To control the fan and light from a wall switch, use a dual-control switch. Put pull chain on fan on high speed, although it may be on any speed.

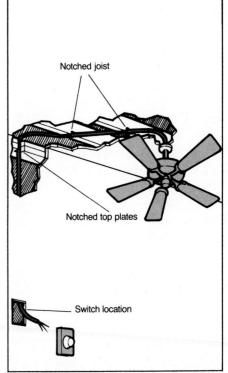

Transformer and switch on wall. For a supplemental variable control with a standard wall switch and three-speed transformer, use this hookup. Leave pull chain on high speed.

How to Install a Bathroom Fan

Most building codes require ventilators in bathrooms without windows. The window and ventilator help remove moisture and excess heat, as well as odors. Many bathrooms should also have a fan. Using an exhaust fan to remove excess moisture and heat that would otherwise build up will also lower air-conditioning costs. Opening a window may remove odors, but it wastes fuel in the winter and power in a centrally air-conditioned house.

Exhaust fans also preserve interior and exterior paint. Moisture vapor will damage paint in an unventilated bathroom; it will also penetrate the walls, popping paint off exterior siding.

An exhaust fan can operate from a wall switch that is independent of the light, or integral with the light. Some codes require that in windowless bathrooms a ventilator go on automatically when the light is switched on.

FAN SIZE
Ventilation engineers suggest a fan with the capacity to make from six to twenty complete air changes per hour. Fans are rated in cubic feet per minute (cfm).

INSTALLATION OPTIONS
Ventilating ceiling fans are installed between ceiling joists and are ducted either through the roof, the eaves, or the outside wall. Wall fans can exhaust directly to the outside when mounted on an outside wall, or through ducts to the roof, eaves, or outside wall.

The fan should discharge directly to the outside, either through a duct or a passage that is part of the fan unit. Many older installations merely exhausted into the attic. Usually a duct can be retrofitted to these fans so they exhaust to the outside. Codes in your area may permit exhausting into an unfinished attic space. If so, the job will be easier.

Mounting a fan in a wall is similar to the technique used for a ceiling installation. The fan should be mounted as near to the ceiling as practical, since that is where the heat accumulates. Cut the opening for the switch. Above it, cut the opening for the fan. Run a No. 12/2 or 14/2 with ground cable from an existing receptacle to the switch. Then run cable from the fan opening to the switch. Complete the necessary wiring hookups. This information is given on pages 60–65.

Fan Capacity *CFM	Laundry or Family Room Sq. Ft.	Kitchen Sq. Ft.	Bathroom Sq. Ft.
40	50		35
50	62		45
60	75		55
70	87		65
80	100		75
90	112		85
100	125		95
110	137		105
120	150	60	115
140	175	70	135
160	200	80	
180	225	90	
200	250	100	
250	310	125	
300	375	150	
350	435	175	
400	500	200	
450	560	225	
500	625	250	
550	685	275	

Note: Ceiling height of 8 feet is assumed.
*Cubic feet per minute

Fan capacity. Use this chart to determine fan capacity sizes needed for bathrooms, kitchens, and laundry areas.

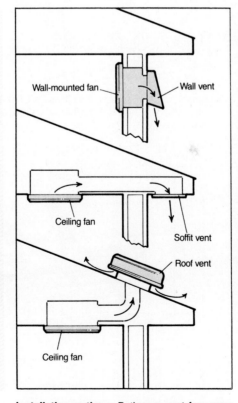

Installation options. Bathroom vent fans may be mounted in the ceiling or wall. They can exhaust through the wall, ceiling, or a vent mounted on roof.

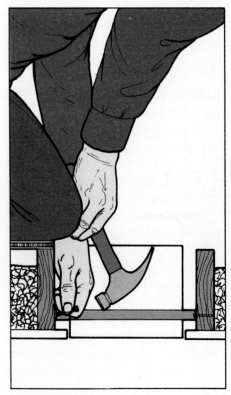

Mounting procedures. To mount fan in ceiling, cut hole for it between joists or studs. Then mount the fan on brackets. Make fan level and flush with wall, ceiling surfaces.

VENTILATING (EXHAUST) FAN HOOKUP DETAILS

Installing the fan through a ceiling or wall is a big project, although it is not difficult. You have to make the cut between joists or studs, removing the interior and exterior coverings. Trim pieces seal and hide the cuts. If you install the fan in a ceiling, you may be able to exhaust it into an attic space; otherwise the fan will have to be ducted outside. For some wall installations, you can buy through-the-wall fans that don't require ducting, if the fan is mounted in an outside (exterior) wall.

Flexible ducting like that used to vent clothes dryers often may be used for exhaust fans. Check codes and the store where you buy the fan for information on flexible ducting.

FAN WITH SWITCH ON IT

If the fan has a switch on it, you will need just two wires for connection. You can tap into an existing outlet for the power. Connect black wires together, or hook the black fan wire to a brass receptacle terminal. Connect white wires, or hook the white wire to a silver terminal. Hook the grounding wire to the fan housing and the outlet box.

FAN/HEATER CONNECTION AT THE WALL SWITCH

Wiring connections for fans with heaters, as used in a bathroom, require a new 15- or 20-amp circuit. You will need a two-wire hookup at the switch and four wires from the switch to the fan.

At the switch connect the white wires together. Pigtail the black power wire to all switch terminals on one side. Hook wires of three colors to the other side. Add a grounding wire as shown.

FAN/HEATER CONNECTION AT THE FAN/HEATER UNIT

Pigtail the white wire to the silver terminal of each outlet. Connect the grounding wire to the unit housing. Each outlet must connect to the proper switch. Check which color wire goes to each switch and connect to the appropriate brass outlet terminal.

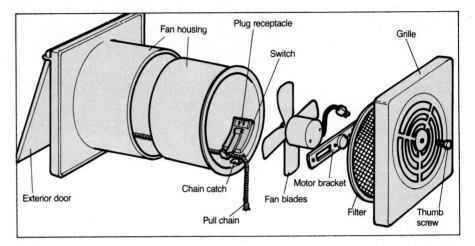

Anatomy of through-the-wall fan unit. The grille is mounted inside the house and a spring-loaded door on the outside. A pull chain opens the door. Most fans have a dust or grease filter. The units may be used in any rooms where moisture and odor need to be removed.

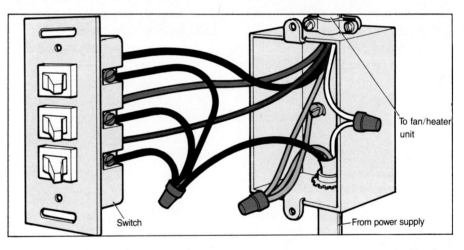

Fan/heater connection at wall switch. Switch box has black, white, and ground power cable wires coming in. You add three switch wires, a white wire, and a grounding wire for the fan/heater hookup. Use different color UF wires for the switch, to make connections at the unit easier.

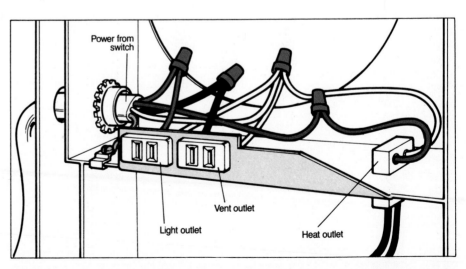

Fan/heater connections at the unit. Pigtail the incoming white wire to all outlets. Connect the grounding wire to the unit housing. Use the insulation color identification to connect the switch wires to the appropriate outlets: light switch to light outlet, vent to vent, heat to heat.

Installing a Whole-House Attic Fan

Before you select a whole-house fan, figure your ventilating requirements. The fan should be able to change the volume of air in the selected area fifteen to twenty times an hour. When you do not want to move all the air in the house, as when only one or two rooms are to be ventilated, a two-speed or variable-speed fan will save power.

GIVE IT ROOM

Leave sufficient clearance between a ceiling-mounted fan and the roof or other obstructions above it. Otherwise, the fan will create back pressure, which reduces the efficiency of the fan and increases its noise level.

The clearance requirements vary with the size of the fan and its manufacturer, but generally are from 24 to 36 inches.

There must be enough vent area in the roof to allow the air to be exhausted outdoors with no restrictions. The vents may be gable-end louvers, roof vents, or soffit vents. The net free area should be 1 square foot of opening for each 750 cubic feet per minute (cfm) of fan capacity. For example, if your fan has a capacity of 3,600 cfm, there should be 4.8 square feet of net free vent area.

If you install any other ventilating fans that exhaust into the attic, these must be ducted through to the outside. Otherwise, the whole-house fan will force air from the attic back into the living area.

CONSIDER ACCESSORIES

Three accessories that should be considered for a whole-house fan are an automatic temperature control, a timer, and a high-temperature switch. For safety, automatic shutters should always be used.

CONSTRUCTION STEPS

Hooking up a whole-house fan to electric power is very simple. Installing the fan in the ceiling is the big job, although it is well within do-it-yourself skills.

Tools for the construction part of the installation include a stepladder, carpenter's square, level, tape measure, keyhole saw, drill and drill-bit assortment, hammer, carpenter's crosscut saw, and safety glasses. You will need a length of lumber (probably 2×6) to match the width and thickness of the ceiling joists. This material will be used to make headers to support the fan.

The purpose of the construction is to create a square framework in which the fan housing sits. There is not much more to it than this. The fan can be connected to existing power in the attic, or you can run a new circuit. How this is done is explained in detail on pages 73 to 91.

We recommend UF-type cable in No. 12 gauge with ground. However, check the codes in your area; codes may require conduit of some type: EMT or BX, for example.

You probably will be able to tap into power in the attic, especially if the attic or attic crawl space has open framing.

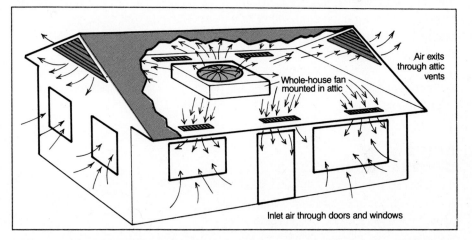

Circulation pattern for attic fan. A whole-house attic fan draws air in from the windows and doors you have open and then forces the air into the attic and out the attic vents. The fan may be operated manually or automatically by a thermostat.

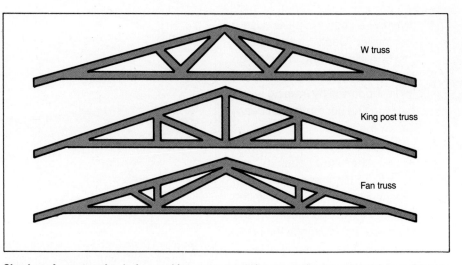

Check roof construction before making any cuts. Before you make any cuts in joists, make sure that the joists are not part of a roof truss system. If you don't know, consult a builder or architect. Cutting a joist could weaken the roof structure.

BUILDING THE FRAMEWORK FOR A WHOLE-HOUSE FAN

Make a rough sketch on graph paper to locate the fan's position in the ceiling and to route the source of power to the fan. Measure accurately so that you buy adequate materials.

STEP 1
CUT CEILING OPENING

Using the shutter grille, make a template on light cardboard and tape the template to the ceiling in the position you want the fan to be located. Make the opening a tad smaller than the actual overall size of the shutters to allow the shutter to trim the opening.

Drive four nails, one in each corner of the marked opening. Then go up into the attic and locate the nails. They should not be near electric wiring or ducts or located on the edges of joists. Either move any wiring that interferes or relocate the fan. Create the opening so there is at least 1½ inches clearance from one joist.

STEP 2
CUTTING THE JOISTS

If you are sure that cutting the joists will not weaken the roof structure, cut the joists 1½ inches shorter on each side of the opening to allow a header to be nailed to them. The header should be the same size material as the joists.

Since the attic space is unfinished, lay down a working platform of ¾-inch-thick plywood across the joists. Use a 4 × 8-foot panel. Don't try to straddle the joists; one slip and you'll go through the ceiling below. Also, make sure the platform is supported by framing members that won't be cut for the fan headers. Spread the load.

The best tool for making the joist cuts is a saber saw. Saw almost through the framing and then finish with a crosscut or keyhole saw (with the blade mounted upside down in the handle) so you don't damage the backside of the ceiling covering. Use a square to mark the cutting lines on the framing members.

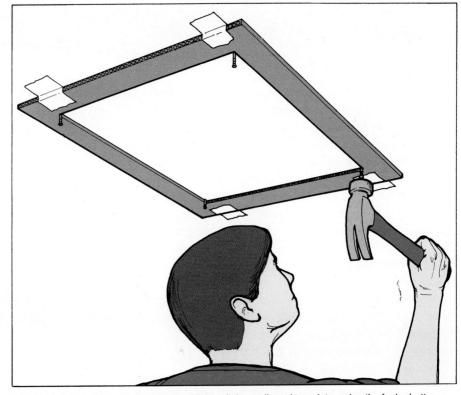

Prepare template for ceiling opening. Make a light cardboard template, using the fan's shutter as a guide. Then tape the template to the ceiling where you want to locate the fan. Drive nails through the ceiling material to locate joists in attic. You may have to reposition the template to correspond with joist spacing.

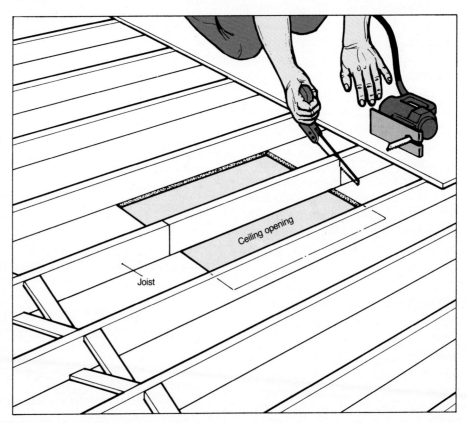

Cut the joists in the attic from a working platform. Make the initial cuts in the ceiling joists. Work from a 4 × 8-foot platform of plywood spanning several joists for support. Check your measurements twice before you make the cuts. You can cut the hole in gypsum-board ceiling material with a sharp utility knife from below.

SUPPORTING THE FAN

A frame made of the same 2-inch lumber as the joists is now constructed to hold the fan securely in the ceiling. You can build the frame separately, if you have room to move it up into the attic space after it is built. If not, you will have to build the frame in place in the attic. We suggest that you measure, mark, and cut the material outside the attic and then simply fit and nail it into position inside the attic. Lay out the material on the joists and mark them for cutting. You can design the framework to match the fan's depth (thickness) to the width of the joists. The fan can set on top of the joists or set on an elevated platform of 1 × 4s, as the illustrations show.

We recommend that you purchase 4-foot lengths of material that you will use to frame the opening. Pressure-treated fir is a good choice of wood. The shorter lengths usually are straighter and easier to transport than longer 8- to 10-foot pieces, even though the shorter ones may cost a bit more money.

STEP 3
FRAME THE OPENING

The frame fits between the joists. You nail the frame to the headers and joists with 16d box nails. Pick one of the framing configurations shown that best fits your circumstances.

Use a square to mark all saw cuts and take special care to make the cuts square. You want the butt joints to fit as tightly together as possible. Fit the headers into the opening and square them. Then nail the headers to the joists—three nails per joint. Stagger the nailing pattern and drive the nails at a slight angle for more holding power.

When you are finished, you should have a boxlike frame over which the attic fan sits. This opening must be square to fit the frame. At this point, bring the fan into the attic space and set it into the opening. If the fan does not fit properly, note the misfit and renail the headers.

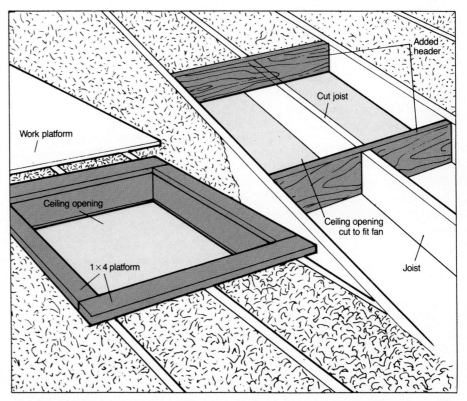

Supporting the fan. You can copy these framing details for the whole-house fan. Fan can recess between joists (right) or be elevated on a platform and recessed (left), depending on the fan's depth or thickness. The framework should be true and square; double-check your measurements.

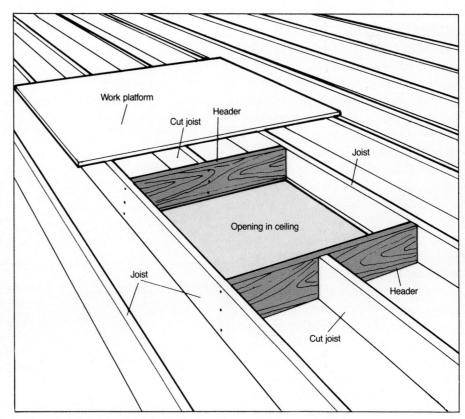

Framing the opening. Cut the headers outside the attic, if possible, then install them. Fasten them between side joists, against the cut joists to frame the opening as shown. Use three nails at each joint. The work platform can then be moved wherever needed for further work.

INSTALLING THE FAN AND CONNECTING POWER

After you have tested the fan in the opening for a perfect fit, you are ready to install it and connect it to the power source.

STEP 4
INSERTING THE FAN

Place the fan in position. Some fans have a rubber or plastic strip to minimize vibration. If yours does not, install strips of heavy weatherstripping or carpeting between the ceiling-mounted fan and the frame to minimize the transfer of vibration to the joists.

Do not nail the fan solidly in place. Secure it just enough to hold it in position. Wooden cleats are often used around the edges of the fan housing to keep the fan from moving sideways. This method will only work for ceiling-mounted fans. Those mounted in walls must be fastened more securely, but not so tightly that vibration is transferred throughout the house.

STEP 5
INSTALLING THE LOUVERS

The shutter (or louvers) is installed after the fan is in place. The shutter fits into the opening in the ceiling and is fastened with screws. Most shutters are designed to open automatically with air pressure when the fan is operating. Check the shutter for smooth operation. If louvers do not open completely, check for possible binding or twisting of the frame.

STEP 6
THE POWER CONNECTION

Mount the fan's operating controls in a convenient location in the living area. The accompanying drawing shows typical wiring for a whole-house fan. In this diagram, note the timer, which is mounted near the speed control. The speed control incorporates an on-off switch. Also shown is a high-temperature-limit switch, which turns off the fan in the event of fire in the attic or elsewhere in the house. This switch is located in the attic space.

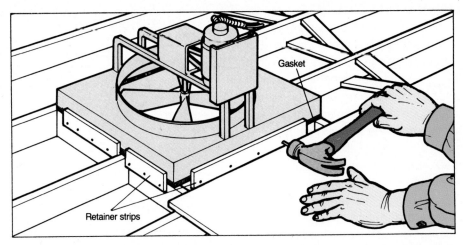

Inserting the fan in the ceiling framework. Set the fan into position on the framework you built for it. Then lightly nail the fan housing to the framework after you insert vibration pads between the fan housing and the framework. You can use wooden cleats to secure the fan in the opening. This keeps it from moving sideways.

Installing the louvers (shutter) in the ceiling. Screw the louvers (shutter) into place in the opening in the ceiling. Most shutters work automatically. Test the shutter opening; if it is sluggish, check for binding and realign. The louvers work on a spring device. For safety, wear goggles when installing the shutter in the ceiling.

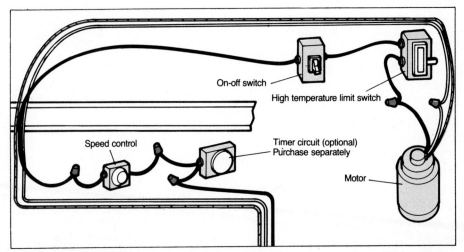

The power connection to the whole-house fan. This is a typical power connection for a whole-house ceiling fan. Leave the on-off switch in the high-temperature box in the ON position. A special switching link will automatically turn the fan off in the event of fire. Use wire nuts for all splices and wrap the nuts with electrician's tape.

Installing a Bathroom Wall Heater

You can power a bathroom heater from an existing outlet in the bathroom, or you can run cable for a new circuit, as explained here.

STEP 1
CUT HOLE AND FISH CABLE

First, purchase the heater. Then mark out its position in the bathroom between two wall studs.

Use the heater grille as a template to mark the wall covering for the cutout. Then cut the hole. Drill a small hole at the inside corners of the guideline on the wall so you can insert a keyhole or saber-saw blade.

Fish the new cable, AWG No. 12 gauge two-wire with ground, from the basement up through a hole in the bottom wall plate into the heater opening. If the heater is rated at more than 3,000 watts, use No. 10 gauge wire; if it is more than 4,000 watts, use No. 8 gauge wire. The heater package will list wiring requirements.

If you tap into an existing circuit be sure it can handle the extra load. Many local codes require a separate circuit for an installed heater.

STEP 2
CONNECT HEATER CABLE

Strip about 8 inches of outer insulation from the cable and connect the cable to the housing of the bathroom wall heater. You will need a two-part cable connector for this; the heater housing will have knockouts for the cable.

Insert the heater housing in the hole in the wall. The housing is fastened to the studs with screw holes provided in the housing. Make sure the housing is square in the opening and that the front edge of it fits flush with the surface of the wall covering.

You should hire a professional electrician to connect the other end of the cable to a new circuit in the main entrance panel.

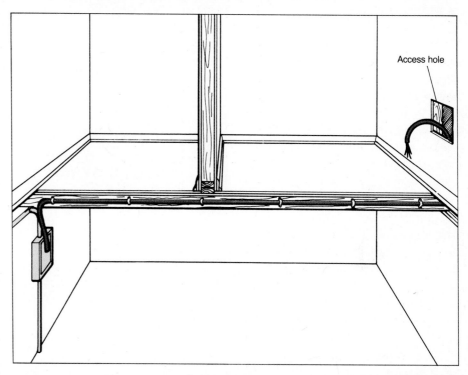

Cut hole and fish cable from service panel to heater. Creating a new circuit is usually best since a larger size cable is needed to meet the heater's wattage requirements. Cut a hole in the wall between studs for the heater. Then fish the wire up through the wall plate and floor into the opening. Use fish tape for this. Fishing cable is explained on pages 83–85.

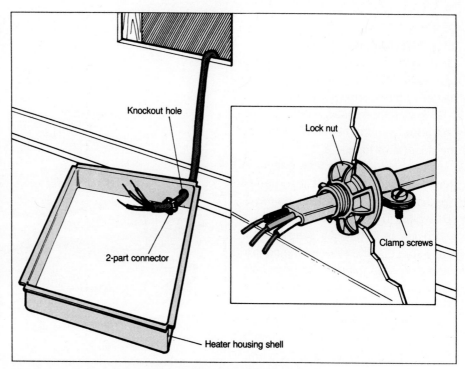

Connect heater cable to heater housing. Connect the cable to the heater housing with a two-part connector which may be furnished in the heater package. Strip about 8 inches of outer insulation from the cable and approximately ¾ inch insulation from the wires inside the sheath. Use wire strippers.

WIRING CONNECTIONS FOR WALL HEATER

Most wall heaters have a terminal box to which cable wires are attached. The heater is prewired.

STEP 3
CABLE TO TERMINALS

Connect the cable wires to the terminals on the heating unit. The black wire goes to the brass terminal and the white wire to the light-colored terminal. Loop the ends of the wires with long-nose pliers and hook around the terminal in the direction in which the screws tighten—clockwise.

Connect the ground wire to the metal heater housing. There may be a screw or clip provided for this. If not, simply drive a sheet metal screw through the housing and loop the ground wire around it. Then tighten the screw.

If the heater requires 240 volts of power, connect each cable wire to a terminal, wrapping the white wire with black electrician's tape to indicate that it's a power wire.

Then insert the heater assembly into the heater housing in the wall and fasten it with the screws provided.

STEP 4
THE FINISHING TOUCHES

Most heaters have a decorative frame and grille that are attached to the heater and housing with screws.

A switch/thermostat control shaft protrudes from the heater unit through the decorative trim.

Assemble the frame first, putting in the noise-reducing gasket, if the heater has this feature. Then attach the decorative grille to the heater unit. It screws into place or is held by special clips. Make sure that the shaft for the control knob protrudes through the grille hole punched for it. It should not bind in the hole.

Now attach the frame to the heater. It may push into place, or you may have to screw it to the heater and grille unit. Finally, install the control knob on the shaft and tighten the setscrew in the knob, if it has one.

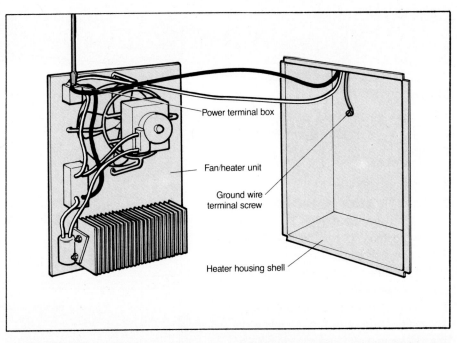

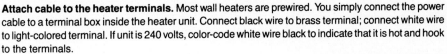

Attach cable to the heater terminals. Most wall heaters are prewired. You simply connect the power cable to a terminal box inside the heater unit. Connect black wire to brass terminal; connect white wire to light-colored terminal. If unit is 240 volts, color-code white wire black to indicate that it is hot and hook to the terminals.

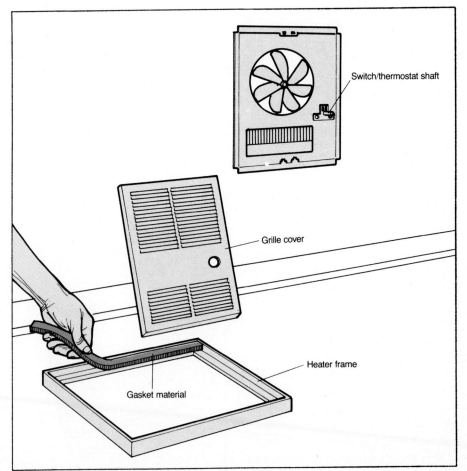

Assemble exterior parts. Depending on heater model, assemble the frame first and then attach the heater grille to the heater housing. Now install the frame. The control knob shaft protrudes through the grillework; place the control knob on the shaft as the final step.

Range-Hood Installation Basics

Installing a new range hood involves extending an electrical circuit and putting in ductwork, if your hood requires it. If you're replacing a range hood, the project involves little more than removing the old and inserting the new.

CHOOSING THE HOOD

Hoods come in two styles: ducted and ductless. A ducted hood removes the heated air from the room by exhausting it outdoors or, possibly, into the attic. A ductless hood filters odor and haze from the air and returns the air directly into the room.

The size of the hood depends on the size of the kitchen and the type of cooking done there. A duct longer than 10 feet requires at least a 400 cfm fan.

The rating of an average size hood ranges from 400 to 600 cubic feet per minute—the amount of air that the fan can move. A fan rated up to 400 cfm needs a 10-inch-diameter duct. Any hood rated above 400 cfm requires larger ducting. For example, a 1,000 cfm barbecue fan requires a round duct about 15 inches in diameter for best exhausting results.

PLAN THE DUCTWORK

Ducts come in several sizes and shapes to accommodate a variety of pathways. Either wall or roof caps are installed to finish off the outside opening. Although most ducting is made of sheet metal, flexible metal ducting also is available. You will need rectangular-to-round converters to connect the round ductwork.

INSTALLATION BASICS

The steps for installing a range hood vary from manufacturer to manufacturer. Specific instructions are given in each manufacturer's package. The standard installation procedures are explained below.

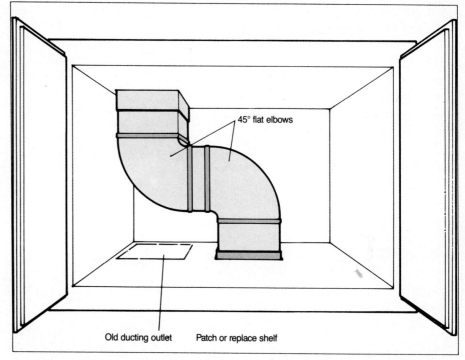

New hood ductwork can be connected to old. If you are exchanging a new range hood for an old one, you can use the existing ductwork, although you may need new elbow pieces to connect a new opening to the old ductwork. The ducts run through a cabinet space above the range hood and are easy to disassemble and reassemble.

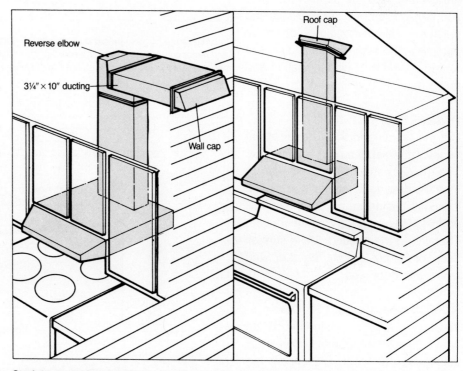

Straight-up ductwork is the most efficient. New ductwork can go out an exterior wall or up through the kitchen ceiling, attic space, and out the roof. A straight-up duct—through the roof—is the most efficient. Or you may opt to install a ductless range hood, which filters the air in the kitchen area instead of exhausting it outside.

RANGE-HOOD TYPES

A ductless range hood has a grease and odor filter and a fan and motor that pull the air through the filter. A ducted range hood is similar, but the air is expelled outdoors through ductwork.

The pathway you choose will depend on how the house is built and the hood's location. If the range sits against an exterior wall, the shortest path is straight out the back of the hood. If the hood is on an interior wall, avoid extremely lengthy and twisted paths. Go straight up through the wall space to the roof, if possible. If this path is obstructed by a second story, you will have to pass the ducting through the soffit to an outside wall.

CONNECTING OLD DUCTS

If the new hood is in the same position as (or similar to) the duct opening already in existence, you can connect the new hood to the old duct (page 125). If this is not the case, you may be able to use two pieces of elbow ducting to angle the channel over the old vent.

Sometimes new ducting is the best course, especially if the old duct is grease-laden. If you install new duct, you can (1) remove the old duct and patch the holes, or (2) screw down the damper in the exterior wall and caulk it closed, fill the duct with insulation and repair only the opening.

INSERTING THE DUCT

Cut the opening in the exterior of the house with a saber saw or keyhole saw. The opening should be slightly larger than the ducting. If local codes require it, install casing strips around a wall opening in a wood-framed house. Then insert the ducting. Make sure all duct joints are tightly together and taped with duct tape.

REMOVING AN OLD HOOD

You'll need a helper; range hoods are heavy. Turn off the power to the circuit that feeds the hood. Disconnect the wiring that powers the exhaust fan and hood light. Then disconnect the ducting and unscrew the hood in the opening and remove it.

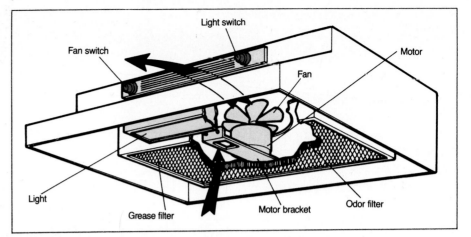

Ductless range hood filters the air. A ductless range hood is the easiest to install because there are no ducting problems. Air from the kitchen is pulled through filters by a fan and then circulated back into the kitchen. The odor filter contains charcoal pellets; the pellets should be changed at least once annually.

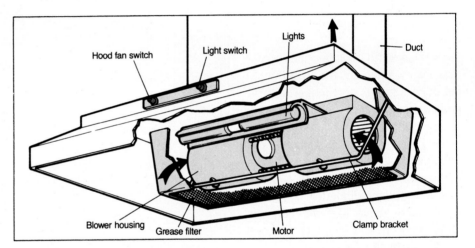

Ducted range hood expels the air outside. A ducted range hood also operates with filters and a fan and motor combination. The mechanics of the unit are almost the same as a ductless hood. You often can connect a new ducted range hood to the existing ducting without much bother. Running new duct can be a problem.

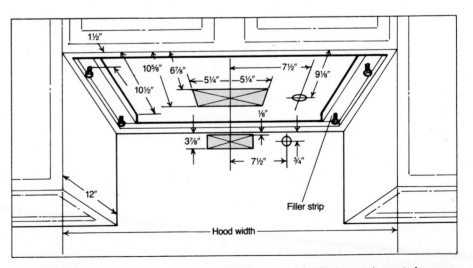

Put measurements/positions on walls and cabinets. Lay out the ducting requirements for a new range hood on the wall in back of the hood and the cabinet above it. Shown is a typical arrangement viewed from between cabinets looking up from the range. If the range is on an exterior wall, the duct can go straight through the wall to the outside, as crossed circles indicate.

CAPPING HOOD DUCTS AND CONNECTING TO POWER

How you handle the capping of the range-hood duct outside depends, of course, whether the duct comes through a wall, soffit, or the roof. The power hookup can be to an existing circuit or a new circuit. Have a pro connect a new circuit.

INSTALLING THE HOOD

The hood assembly simply fastens to filler strips underneath the bottom shelf of the cabinets above with screws and to the wall with screws or hollow wall fasteners, such as toggle bolts. Follow the manufacturer's instructions.

SEAL THE OPENING

If the duct comes through the roof, it should extend at least ¾ inch above the high side of the roof. Using asphalt roofing cement, completely seal the opening between the duct and the roof. Install the roof cap. Insert the high side edge under the shingles and apply roofing cement around cap.

If the duct comes out a soffit, embed the soffit vent in quality caulking compound. If the duct comes out the siding of the house, install a duct cap.

THE ELECTRICAL HOOKUP

The power must be off to make this connection. Fasten the cable to the hood with a connector locknut. Use wire nuts to splice the black cable wire to the black hood wire. Do the same with all white wires.

Finally, using the green ground screw, attach the cable equipment grounding conductor to the grounding bracket built into the hood. Comply with all local codes; regulations may vary. Then replace the wiring box cover and screw.

If you are tapping into existing power in a receptacle (outlet), hook the black cable wire to the brass-colored terminal and the white cable wire to the light-colored terminal on the unused terminals of the outlet. You will need a pigtail to connect the cable's ground wire to the grounding wire and screw attached to the metal outlet box.

Metal roof cap covers range-hood duct on roof. On the roof, let the duct extend over the shingles about ¾ inch. Cut the duct the same angle as the roof pitch. Flashing should go under shingles; you may have to cut them to fit. Coat the components with asphalt roofing compound for a seal. Use plenty.

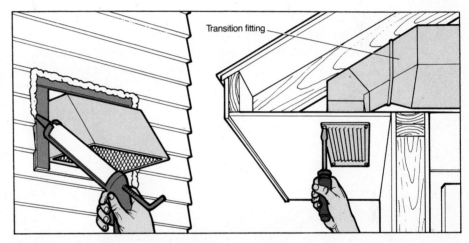

Seal vents at the soffit or on side of the house. If a soffit duct is used, embed the vent in caulking compound and screw the vent to the soffit with sheet-metal screws. If the duct comes out through the siding, install a wall cap over the duct and caulk the joints weathertight. Make sure the damper in the duct or cap isn't binding.

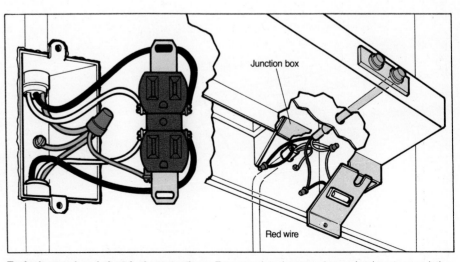

Typical range hood electrical connections. For range-hood power, you can hook up to an existing circuit or run cable for a new circuit to the main electrical service panel. Hood will be marked where wires go. At outlet, connect black wire to brass terminal; white wire goes to light-colored terminal. Hook ground to box.

Installing a Roof-Mounted Attic Fan

Heat buildup in an attic space can be awesome. Temperatures can climb to 120 degrees Fahrenheit and higher during the summer months. This heat can put a heavy load on air conditioning in the rooms below. One of the best ways to remove this heat is with a roof-mounted attic fan, which also can serve as a whole-house fan when you don't want to run the air conditioner. However, a whole-house fan in the attic floor will usually move more air than the roof model, which is ideally suited for lowering temperatures in the attic.

The capacity of the fan, that is, the amount of air it circulates in a minute's time, should be based on the space in the attic. Take your attic dimensions to the store; they'll advise you what size fan you need. For the fan to operate properly, the attic space should be vented through the soffits to create an air circulation pattern within the attic. As a rule of thumb, vents should be spaced at 3-foot intervals in the soffits along the eaves of the house.

INSTALLATION BASICS

Place a roof-mounted fan as close to the center of the attic as possible. Put it on the rear of the roof so it is not seen from the front of the house. Using a straight length of board as a guide, set the fan assembly on the roof so the top of the fan is level with the roof ridge. Measure this distance from the ridge to the center of the fan.

Use caution on the roof. If the roof is steeply pitched, let a professional handle the project.

Locate the center of the attic inside the attic and measure down from the roof peak to a point that corresponds to the desired location of the fan. Locate this point halfway between two rafters. Drive a nail up through the roof at this point so you can spot the nail on top of the roof. The illustration on this page shows the general procedures. The step-by-step basics are shown on the following pages.

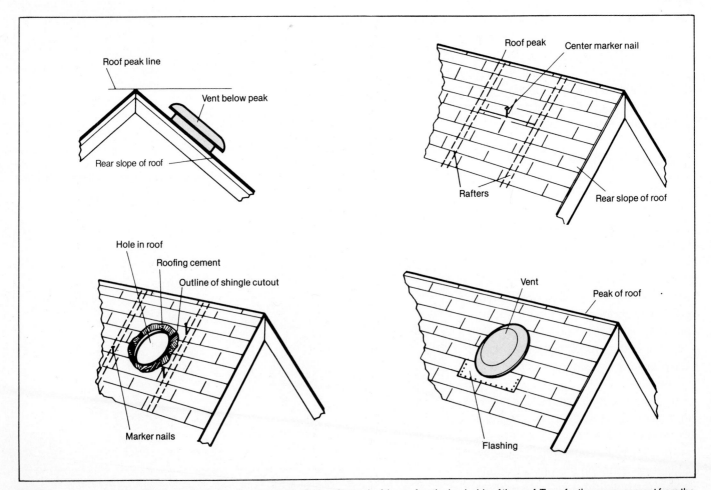

Typical sequence for installing a roof attic fan. Position the fan below the peak of the roof on the back side of the roof. Transfer the measurement from the peak of the roof to the fan to inside the attic. Measure down from the peak between the rafters. Then find the center of the rafters; drive a nail at this point through the roof so you can spot the nail on the roof. Make the cuts.

CUTTING THE OPENING FOR ATTIC ROOF FAN

After you determine the position of the fan on the roof, cut the fan opening.

STEP 1
DRAW A CIRCLE

On the outside of the roof, locate the marker nail. Using it as a center, draw a circle about 4 inches wider than the size of the hole specified in the instructions provided by the manufacturer.

With a utility or sharp hawk-nosed knife, cut around the circle, scoring the shingles as deeply as you can. Then remove the cut shingles. Continue making scoring cuts, removing the building felt underlayment and exposing the roof sheathing. At this point, double-check your measurements and make any adjustments needed.

STEP 2
MAKE THE HOLE CUT

Using the nail as a center point, draw another circle that is the size specified in the instructions. If this hole size is larger in diameter than the distance between the rafters, do not cut the rafters. Saw along their inner faces.

If you have a portable electric saber saw, cut through the sheathing in the roof, forming the circular hole for the fan. If not, use a keyhole saw to make the cut. You will have to drill a hole inside the cutting circle so you can insert the keyhole saw.

STEP 3
INSTALL THE HOUSING

About 6 inches above and below where the fan flashing will cover the roof, drive four nails into the roof to mark the location of the rafters. Then install the fan housing.

Remove any shingle nails within the area above the hole that would block the insertion of the fan flashing underneath the shingles.

Then apply a liberal amount of asphalt roofing cement to the exposed sheathing and the underside of the fan flashing. Slip the flashing under the shingles.

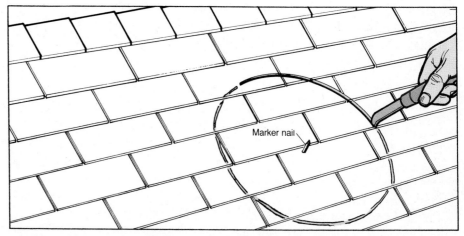

Draw a circle for a cutting guideline. Using the nail as a center point, draw a circle on the roofing. Then, with a sharp knife, score the shingles and remove them. Cut through the building felt to the roof sheathing. Double-check your measurements, using the nail as a guide. Make any adjustments necessary.

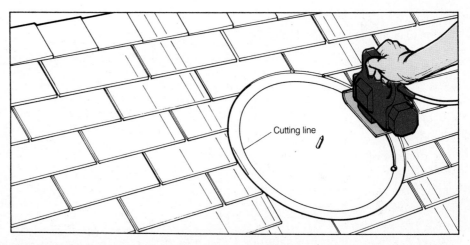

Make the hole cut in the roof for the fan. With a saber or keyhole saw, make the hole cutout in the roof. If the size of the hole overlaps the rafters, cut only to the face of the rafters. Do not cut the rafters. Even if the fan is oversize, the opening will be plenty adequate. Save shingle trimmings for patching later.

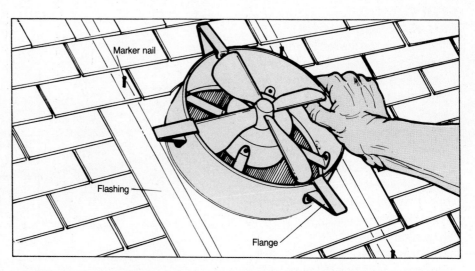

Install the housing and flashing on the roof. Slip the fan housing and flashing under the shingles over the hole in the roof. You probably will have to remove several shingle nails with a small pry bar to do this. Using the nails you drove into the rafters as a guide, fasten the flashing to the rafters with roofing nails.

STEP 4
ADD THE FAN CAP

Complete the work on the roof by installing the fan's screen and cover. It slides over the sides of the fan housing and is bolted to the rim of the housing.

ADDING SOFFIT VENTS AND CONNECTING THE FAN

To get the kind of ventilation that will benefit your home best, you will have to add soffit vents. First figure the square feet of attic space you have. The recommended ratio for every 150 feet of space is 1 square foot of net free area. For example, if you have an attic of 1,500 square feet, divide 1,500 by 150 to find the amount of free area. Here, it would be 10 square feet. The fan package usually has conversion tables.

STEP 5
ADD SOFFIT VENTS

Cut holes in the soffit for the vents. Space them at intervals in all eaves, locating them midway between the edge of the eave and the outside wall, and halfway between the lookouts that support the soffit. There are several sizes of vents, including continuous vents, that you can buy.

Make outside cuts with a saber or keyhole saw, using the vent as a template.

STEP 6
CONNECT THE WIRING

In the attic, fasten the fan thermostat to a rafter; make sure the temperature-sensing element is exposed to the air; it should not be in the fan's direct air stream.

You can tap into an attic junction box to power the fan. If not, you can run a two-wire with ground cable (or matching cable, probably No. 14 gauge two-wire) to a box in a room on the floor below. This procedure is explained on pages 85 and 89-90.

Connect the two-wire leads in the thermostat wiring box to the two cable wires, matching the wire color and fastening with wire nuts. Fasten the grounding conductor to the grounding screw on the thermostat.

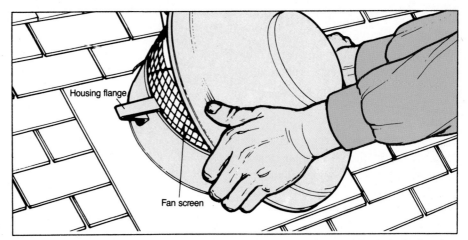

Add the fan cap to the fan housing on the roof. The fan cap is simply slipped over the fan housing on the roof and bolted into position. Check around the installation and trowel asphalt roofing compound in all cracks, joints, and over exposed nailheads. Use plenty of compound to make the roof watertight.

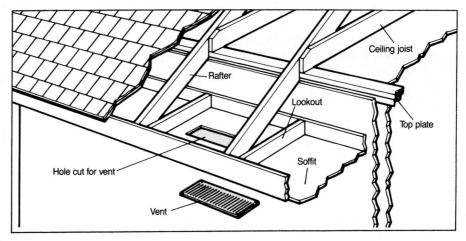

Install soffit vents for adequate air circulation. Soffit vents are easy to add. Use a template outline of the vent for saw guidelines. Push the vent into the soffit material and secure it with screws. The vents should be spaced evenly along the soffit, inserted between lookouts. You have a choice of vent sizes and styles.

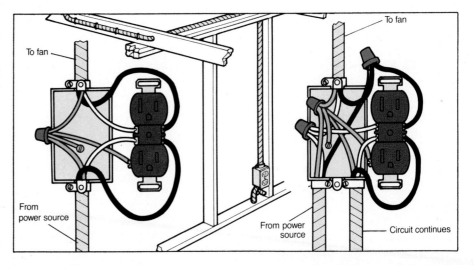

Connect the fan to a 120-volt circuit. At an end-of-run outlet (left) hook the black fan cable wire to a brass terminal, white wire to a silver terminal. At a middle-of-run outlet (right), hook black and white power source wires to like-colored fan cable wires and pigtails to the outlet. Pigtail grounding wires to the box. You can add a switch in the black line to the fan if you wish.

Installing a Gable-Mounted Attic Fan

You can install an attic fan in any gable of the house. The fan serves the same purpose as a roof-mounted one. The gable wall has to be opened and framed to support the fan and louver; this is an easy do-it-yourself job.

Start by purchasing the right-size vent for the attic's square footage. The store personnel can advise you. You will need a drill or brace to bore a starter hole for a keyhole saw and a crosscut saw to finish the cut. You'll also need a hammer, tape measure, carpenter's square, 16d hot-dipped common nails, and quality caulking.

Materials include 2 × 4 dimension lumber or lumber matching the house framing. We recommend pressure-treated lumber.

One vented gable end (not the one with the fan) must face the prevailing winds. Otherwise, you will not achieve the exchange of air that you need.

STEP 1
OPENING THE GABLE END

On the inside of the attic, outline the vent location. Try to mount it as high as possible directly under the center of the gable. Cut the siding and studs from the outlined area. Then cut an additional 1½ inches from the studs above and below the outlined area.

STEP 2
FRAMING THE OPENING

Cut and nail two 2 × 4 headers to fit horizontally between the studs on either side of the opening. Cut two cripple studs to fit between the headers to frame the vent. Then nail the cripples to the headers.

If you are fitting a triangular vent in the top of the gable end, cut a single header to fit across the top of the cut studs, and flush against the end rafters. Nail 2 × 4s to fit under the double end joists from the header to the ridge.

The vents are installed on the outside of the house.

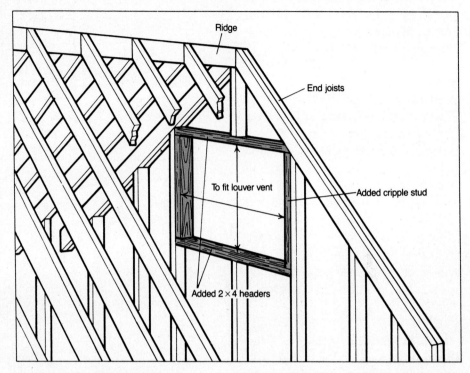

Installing a rectangular gable end vent. For a rectangular gable end vent, cut the central stud first. Then add 2 × 4 headers that are reinforced with cripple studs on either side. The studs around the opening will support the roof structure until you complete the fan framing. Before you cut, double-check your measurements.

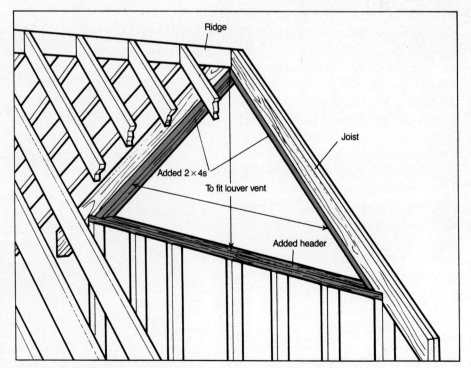

Installing a triangular gable end vent. For a triangular-shaped gable end vent, a larger opening may be required than for a rectangular vent. Place a header across the cut studs. Add reinforcing 2 × 4s to the end joists. Caulk all framing joints that you make as extra protection against the elements.

INSTALL OUTSIDE VENT AND MOUNT GABLE ATTIC FAN IN FRAMING

Once the framing is in position, the louver unit is installed on the outside. The fan is installed inside, mounted on the framing members.

STEP 3
INSTALLING THE VENT

From outside the house, lay a bead of caulking compound around the edge of the opening. Insert the louver unit, and nail or screw it through the siding and into the 2 × 4 framing. Most louver units are equipped with insect screening. If yours is not, staple screening to the louver framing on the inside of the attic, or fasten the screen in place with screen molding to keep the screen in position and to provide a neat edge.

STEP 4
MOUNTING THE FAN

The fan is fastened to the framing with flat washers and lag screws driven through the fan's mounting brackets and into the 2 × 4s. Make sure that the top of the fan faces up toward the roof. Attach the fan's thermostat and controls to a wall stud near the fan. Most fans are prewired from the thermostat to the fan, so you only have to connect the housepower to the thermostat.

For power, you can tap into an existing outlet or junction box inside the attic. Use UF No. 12 gauge two-wire with ground cable. At the source, connect the black-insulated cable wire to the black-insulated power wire. Splice the white wires together. Use wire nuts on both splices and wrap the nuts with electrician's tape. The grounding wire pigtails and connects to the box.

At the fan, connect black to black, white to white, and ground to ground, using wire nuts and plastic electrician's tape.

STEP 5
ENLARGE GABLE VENT

If the attic vent area is not large enough, you'll need to enlarge the opposite gable vent or add more vents to soffit area (see pages 130 and 132).

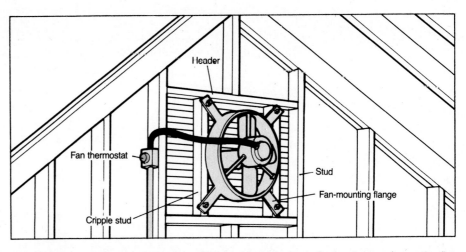

Mount the fan to the framing members this way. Mount the fan to the framing members using flat washers under the head of lag bolts (screws) placed through the metal flanges attached to the fan's housing. Since most fans are prewired, you only have to run housepower to the fan and make the connections at the thermostat.

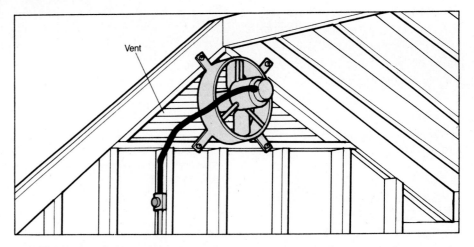

Mounting a fan over an existing triangular vent. In an existing triangular vent installation, the fan usually is fastened to the joist supports and the header at the base of the triangular cutout. Use lag bolts and washers to mount the fan; the brackets are slotted so you can level the fan in the opening. The wiring hookups are at the thermostat.

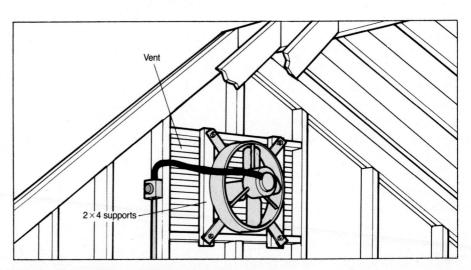

Add fan-mounting 2 × 4s to existing gable vent. If the fan is somewhat undersized for an existing vent opening, you can add vertical 2 × 4s to the framing and mount the fan to these members. Face nail them to the framing so you have plenty of bearing surface for the fan mounting brackets. The thermostat is the switching control.

Replacing an Existing Thermostat

If the existing thermostat in your home is malfunctioning and you want to exchange it for a new one of the same type and, perhaps, the same brand, it's an easy project to do: you merely hook up the new unit to the same wiring.

If, however, you want to move the location of the thermostat, you will have to extend the wiring from the furnace. This involves fishing the wires to the location, as explained on pages 83–85.

TURN OFF THE POWER

At the main service panel, turn off the circuit supplying the power to the furnace. Remove the thermostat cover, then remove the wires connected to the thermostat terminals. Remove the thermostat base from the wall.

STEP 1
MOUNT THE NEW BASE

When the old base is off, you will see two wires protruding from the wall. These run to the furnace. Mount the new thermostat base over these wires and pull them out of the wall about 3 inches. Drive in a couple of mounting screws, but don't tighten them.

With a plumb bob or small torpedo-style level, level the base on the wall. Then tighten the screws. The base must be level or the thermostat won't work properly.

STEP 2
MAKE THE CONNECTIONS

Note the terminal connections on the mounting base. If your system has just two wires, you can connect either wire to either terminal screw.

If the system has three wires, hook the wire with the white insulation to one terminal and the other two wires to the second terminal. If the base has three terminals and there are three wires, match the wires to the color codes on the terminals.

Complete the job by installing the cover on the mounting base.

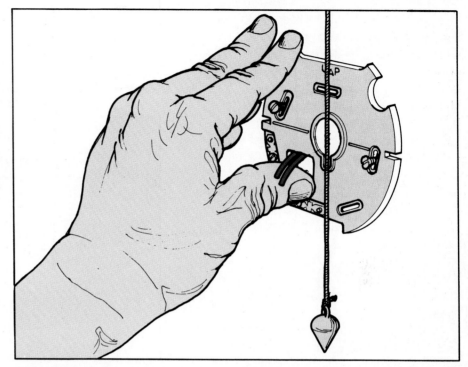

Mount the new base for the thermostat. Pull the furnace wires through the base, after you remove the old base. Then level the new base on the wall and fasten it tightly in position. The base must be level on the wall so the thermostat will operate properly. Do not use the old base for the new thermostat.

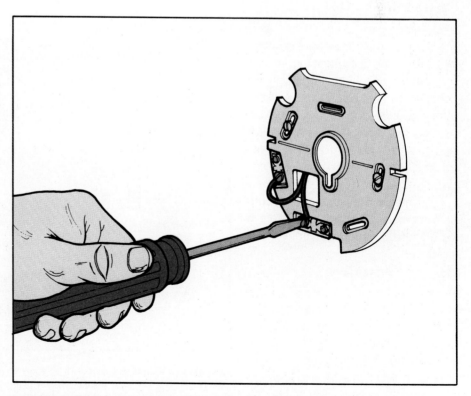

Make the connections from the furnace. Hook the furnace wires around the terminals in the direction that the screws turn—clockwise. You can hook either wire to either terminal. If there are three wires, hook the white wire to one terminal, and both other wires to the second terminal.

Adding a Programmable Thermostat

Thermostat manufacturers keep finding new and better ways to conserve electricity serving heating and air-conditioning equipment. Perhaps the biggest and most efficient innovation now on the market is the programmable thermostat. It can be set to adjust the temperature in your home automatically for waking and sleeping hours. The thermostat also may include indicators that set different temperature levels for those hours when the house is usually occupied and for those hours when it is not.

TYPES OF UNITS

Thermostats come in many different styles.

There are some units that replace heat-only thermostats that control only the furnace. Other units replace thermostats that control both heating and cooling, providing that the air-conditioning unit is mounted in your forced-air furnace.

Since energy-saving programmable thermostats vary considerably from one brand to another, be sure to get full installation and programming instruction with the unit when you buy it. For example, some thermostats require a complete week-long run-through to set the day and night temperature sequence where you want it. Others operate on pins that may be set in just one session.

If you misplace the instructions, don't try to improvise. Go back to the store or the manufacturer for the complete directions.

THE COMPONENTS

All models come with a wall plate that is fastened in place. The existing thermostat wires run through the plate. A subbase is attached over the existing wall plate and the programmable thermostat fits over this subbase. The contacts match exactly to make the hookup.

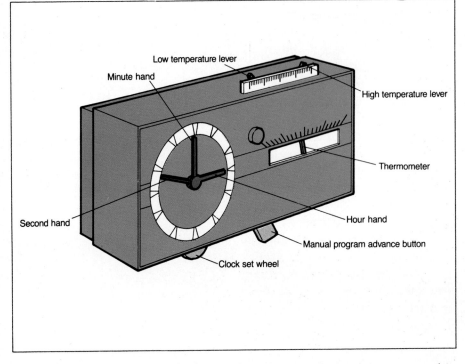

Programmed thermostat adjusts temperature. With a programmed thermostat, you can regulate the temperature in your home according to your schedule and lifestyle. The thermostats are an easy do-it-yourself connection, and they cost little more than a regular heating-cooling thermostat.

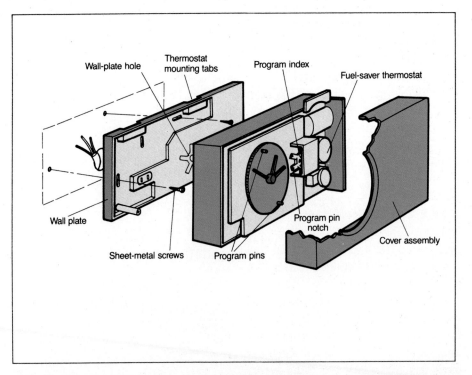

Programmed thermostat hooks to existing wiring. The wires from the heating-cooling unit are pulled through a wall base plate. Then the programmed thermostat is mounted to the base plate. Some programmed units use pins for heating-cooling settings. Others operate on a push-button system that sets the time and temperature.

INSTALLATION GUIDELINES FOR PROGRAMMED THERMOSTATS

Remove the old thermostat from the wall after you turn off the power to the thermostat circuit at the main electrical service panel. Lift off the cover plate and remove the wires from the terminals. Then remove the old base.

Pull the wires a short way out of the wall. You may want to tag the wires so you can match them to comparable identification marks on the new thermostat. Plug the hole through which the wires protrude with spackling compound or loose fiberglass insulation. This is important. Otherwise, a warm or cold draft through the opening could affect the operation of the new programmed thermostat.

INSTALLING THE NEW UNIT

The Honeywell thermostat shown in the exploded diagram on page 134 has a built-in clock that, coupled with programming, governs the heating and cooling cycle. The clock is run by a small battery that must be charged before the thermostat can function. From then on, the battery recharges while the thermostat is working.

CONNECTING THE PLATE

Pull the wires through the opening in the wall base and screw the plate loosely in place. Then level the plate and tighten the screws (see page 133).

CONNECTING THE WIRES

Fasten the wires to the terminals of the new unit. The white wire goes to the terminal marked W. The red wire goes to the terminal marked R. If the wire is black, connect it to the W terminal. If there are three wires, connect the white and black wires to the W terminal.

THE JUMPER METHOD

If your system has a single transformer for heating and cooling, strip enough insulation from the wire to connect the wire to terminals RC and RH. This connection will be so noted in the manufacturer's instruction package.

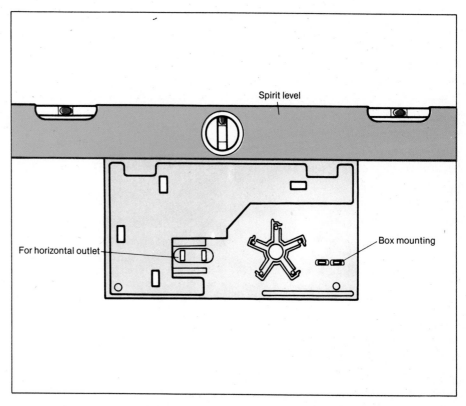

Connecting the wall plate for new thermostat. A programmable thermostat is controlled by a mercury switch. Therefore, the wall plate must be perfectly level for the thermostat to function correctly. Mount the wall plate to the wall, and then level it. Tighten the mounting screws and recheck level. Adjust if needed.

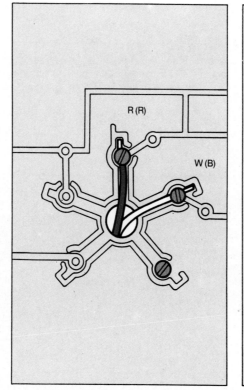

Connecting the wires. The wires must lie between the design ridges. This prevents interference with the thermostat mechanism.

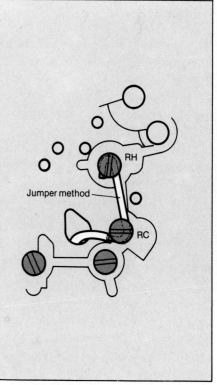

Using the jumper method. If your system has a single transformer, strip enough insulation from the wire to connect terminal RC with terminal RH.

THERMOSTAT SETTINGS

Once installed on the wall, the new thermostat has to be programmed.

THE HEAT ANTICIPATOR

Check the primary control or gas valve of the heating system to find out how much current it draws when operating. This is the heat-anticipator rate. On the lower right side of the thermostat base is a dial. Set this to the rating. If you can't find a rating, check the manufacturer's instruction sheet.

PROGRAMMING

Programming the Honeywell unit is accomplished by three interrelated components. Other brands are similar.

First is the clock, which has two twelve-hour sections, one light-colored for day, the other dark-colored for nighttime. The second component is two temperature levers. The blue one is for the lowest temperature level; the red is for the highest. The third component is a set of pins that fit into cogs on the clock wheel. The pins signal the control mechanism that the red or blue temperature level is required. The pins are color-coded.

Since it takes thirty minutes for the temperature to change from one level to another, two pins can't be closer to each other than one hour.

The thermostat probably can handle more than two pins. If the house is empty from 8:30 to 4:30 each day, set a blue pin at 8:30 and a red pin at 4. You'll have a warm house mornings and evenings.

On some thermostats that have a weekly cycle, you will have to program each day on a daily basis.

RECALIBRATING

You can recalibrate an inaccurate thermostat thermometer. Remove the thermostat cover and open the lens protector. Set a thermometer that you know is accurate next to the thermostat. After 30 minutes, insert a screwdriver into the slot in back of the thermostat and adjust the indicator until it matches the thermometer.

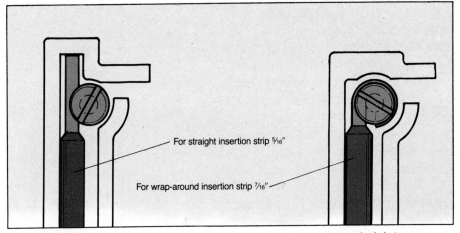

Connecting thermostat wires. You can fasten the wires to the thermostat terminals in two ways; as shown, the housing may dictate which way to use. (Left) You can insert the straight bare wire end on the left side of the terminal and tighten the screw. (Right) Or you can strip about 7/16 inch insulation from wire and hook it left to right around the screw. This method is probably best.

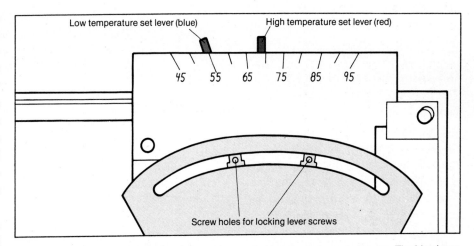

Programming the thermostat. The temperature control has two color-coded levers. The blue lever sets the cool temperature; the red lever sets the warm temperature. On some thermostats, you code warm and cool temperatures with a push-button arrangement. You may have to go through a week's cycle.

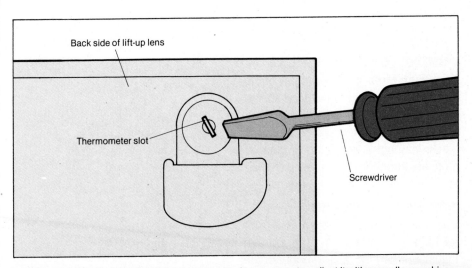

Recalibrating the thermostat. If the thermometer is not accurate, adjust it with a small screwdriver. The slot for this is built into the back of the thermometer. Turning the screw realigns the temperature indicator. Let the recalibrated thermometer sit a day or two, then make any additional adjustments needed.

10 Wiring for Small Appliances

Turn off the power before doing any work on the circuit.

REPAIRING AND INSTALLING DOORBELLS AND CHIMES

The circuit must be complete for a doorbell or chime to work properly. A break in the circuit may be caused by a broken wire, corroded door-button contacts, a burned-out transformer, or a defective signal device.

If your home has buttons at two doors and one sounding device serving both doors, there are two complete circuits that must be checked.

SIGNAL NOT LOUD ENOUGH

Check all terminals for cleanliness and tightness. Disconnect the wires and clean the terminals with sandpaper. Then wipe the terminals with a cotton swab dipped in alcohol. If this doesn't work, the trouble is with the push button, transformer, or sounding device.

Look for trouble at the push button first. The wires may be corroded or broken at this point. Clean them with abrasive and reconnect to the door button.

If a new device is barely audible or gives a dull sound, the problem may be in the transformer. Check the data on the new device and on the transformer. The voltage output marked on the transformer should be within 2 volts either way of the voltage requirement

marked on the sounding device. If mismatched, replace the transformer.

WHEN THE DOOR SIGNAL KEEPS ON SOUNDING

If the signal device won't shut off, the door button has shorted, probably because of corrosion. Clean the terminals and then reconnect, as explained on this page. If this procedure doesn't work, then replace the button.

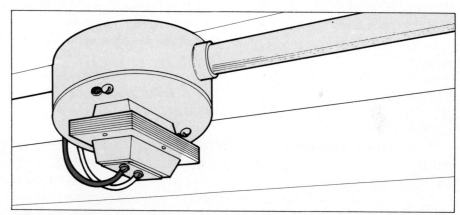

Transformer lowers house voltage. A doorbell or chime installation needs less than 120 volts of power to operate. Therefore, you will have to install a transformer to step down the house voltage to 24 volts. The actual hookup is easy (see page 138).

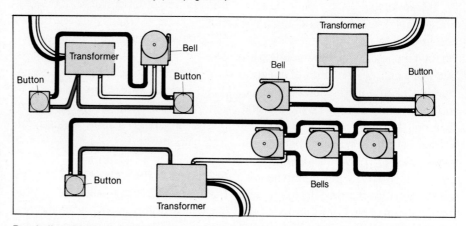

Doorbell or chime connections. A doorbell circuit must have three connections: transformer-button, transformer-bell, button-bell. Top right: one button controls one bell. Top left: two buttons operate one bell. Bottom: one button operates three bells; a stronger transformer may be needed.

Doorbell Installation

All door signal devices are installed about the same way whether they are buzzers, bells, chimes, or chimes that play tunes. The first step is to plan the job, selecting a location for the sounding device. Then locate a 120-volt power source so you can tap it for the transformer. The power source must not be switch-controlled.

The transformer may be wired directly into a junction box in a basement or attic above a dropped ceiling. Once the doorbell and transformer locations are determined, you can estimate the amount of low-voltage wire needed. Measure the entire distance in feet from the transformer to the sounding device and then from the device to each door button. Add another 15 feet for connections and turns in wire run.

The low-voltage wire that you buy should be rated at 300 volts. It will be designated as thermostat wire, No. 20 or larger AWG, or equivalent bell wire.

STEP 1
CUT OPENINGS AND FISH WIRE

First turn off the power to the circuit. Drill a ½-inch hole in the wall for the sounding device wire. Drill a ¾-inch hole in the floor or ceiling plate to run the wire to the transformer.

The openings for the door buttons should stand at waist height, about 4½ feet above the ground. Measure out about 4 inches to mark the opening so you won't drill into the studs at the door frame. Drill a ½-inch hole at the mark. In the sill plate directly below the first hole drill a ¾-inch hole.

Now fish the wire, as explained on pages 83–85. The wire should go from the transformer to the sounding devices, from the sounding devices to the door buttons, and from the door buttons to the transformer. Staple the wire, where you can, at 4-foot intervals with insulated electrical staples.

If you plan the project carefully, you may be able to run the bell wire behind baseboards, molding, and trim without fishing the wire. It will take more wire, of course, but the cost is not prohibitive when you consider the time it takes fishing wire through walls and ceilings.

STEP 2
WIRE THE TRANSFORMER

Most transformers have two wire leads that connect to the 120-volt power supply, and two terminals where the bell–button wires connect. Remove a knockout from a junction box and mount the transformer over it with the wire leads extending into the box.

Strip about ½ inch of insulation from the bell and button wires and connect them to the transformer terminals. You can connect more than one wire to a terminal, but do not mix bell and button wires on the same terminal. Then make all connections at the bells and buttons.

STEP 3
CONNECT POWER WIRES

At the junction box, connect the black wire of the prewired transformer to the black power wire. Connect the white wire of the transformer to the white neutral wire in the junction box. If the transformer is not prewired, the terminals will be marked POSITIVE and NEGATIVE. Connect the black wire to positive and the white wire to negative.

You probably will have to pigtail these splices. Cover the splices with wire nuts and wrap a layer or two of plastic electrician's tape around the wire nuts.

MAKING FINAL CONNECTIONS FOR DOORBELLS AND CHIMES

Once the wiring is in place and the wires are connected to the signal, door buttons, and transformer, you are ready to complete the job.

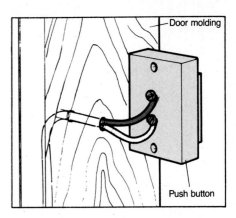

Cut openings and fish wire. Drill the holes for the bell wire connections and then fish the wire to the buttons and door signal. Terminals are labeled.

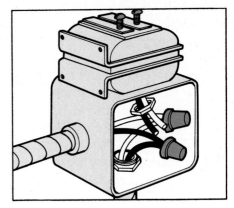

Mount the transformer. Punch out a knockout in the junction box and mount the transformer, slipping its wires into the box. Check all connections.

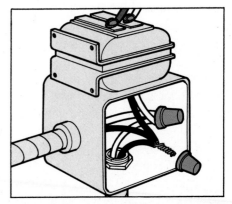

Connect the wires. Connect bell wires to the transformer terminals. Splice power wire leads of the transformer to housepower. Use wire nuts and tape splices.

STEP 4
MOUNTING PROCEDURES

Mount the sounding device with a wall anchor suitable for the job. If the wall is hollow (gypsum board), use toggle bolts or Molly anchors. If the wall is masonry, use lead or plastic shields and screws. Also mount the door buttons with wood screws.

TESTING THE SYSTEM

Once the installation is complete, turn on the power circuit. Check both door buttons to make sure they function. If the signal device responds to both buttons, the installation is okay.

If neither doorbell signal works, look for trouble at the transformer or in the wire from the transformer to the sounding device.

If one button functions but the other does not, the problem is either in the button or with the wires connecting the button to the transformer.

If the transformer doesn't hum when the door button is pushed, suspect a faulty transformer or dead circuit.

You can test the circuit with a voltage tester. Hold the probes of the tester to the ends of the circuit wires and have a helper turn on the circuit. The bulb should light. If it does, replace the transformer. If not, there are problems with the circuit wiring. Have a professional electrician check out the circuit.

If a new device is barely audible or gives a dull sound, the problem may be in the transformer. Check the data on the new device and on the transformer. The voltage output marked on the transformer should be within 2 volts either way of the voltage requirement marked on the sounding device. If mismatched, replace the transformer.

COMPLETE THE PROJECT

To finish the doorbell project, install all cover plates. Caulk and seal the outside wire entrance if the sill plate was penetrated. Also caulk around the door-button openings.

Make sure these openings and the trim plate or escutcheon around the buttons are sealed from weather.

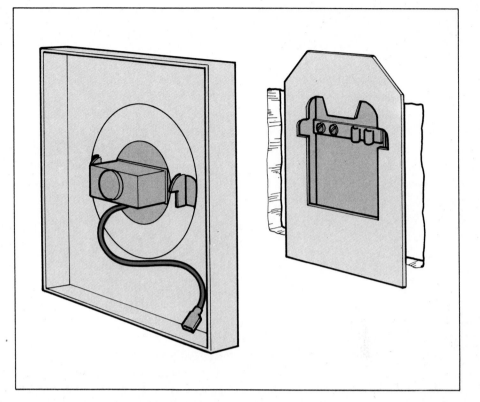

Mounting procedures for doorbell or chimes. This bell unit is mounted on a plaque that hooks into a frame attached to the wall. If the wall is hollow construction, use toggle bolts or Molly anchors. For mounting on masonry, use shields and screws.

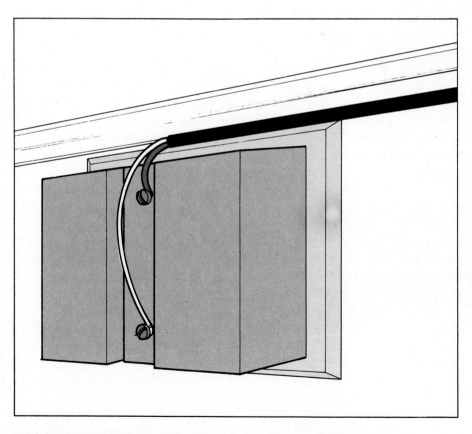

Behind-wall mounting is alternate method. Alternate method of mounting decorative chime units is behind the wall. Instructions for doing this will be included in the signal package. Musical chimes can be reprogrammed.

Low-Voltage Remote Switching

You can save a great deal of time, work, and money when you install new wiring by using *low-voltage remote control*. Standard 12- or 14-gauge cable is used only between the main panel and the outlet or fixture boxes. Switches are wired with low-cost 18- or 16-gauge wire that does not have to run in conduit, and the switches do not have to be mounted in boxes (unless local codes require it). The lightweight wires are easy to run, strip, and connect. You can use any number of switches, at many locations, to control a light or outlet. And you can install a master unit that switches everything individually from a single location. The power in the switch wires is only 24 volts, so there is no shock hazard in those runs.

SYSTEM COMPONENTS

In addition to low-gauge wire, you need three kinds of devices for a low-voltage remote control system: a transformer, switches, and relays. They can be bought individually, or in complete packages for systems of various sizes.

One transformer supplies switching power for the entire system. It requires 120- (or 240-) volt primary power, and supplies 24 volts to the system, like a bell transformer. Its two 24-volt terminals connect to a terminal board, which may be mounted anywhere nearby; no special mounting precautions are necessary. The terminal board has a rectifier that converts the 24-volt power from alternating to single-direction flow; this avoids relay damage. Wires of two colors run from terminal board to the system components: a blue wire to each relay, and a white wire to each switch (color coding may vary with manufacturer; check the package).

The switches are rocker type: pushing ON sends a momentary pulse to a relay that closes the power circuit at the fixture or outlet. Pushing OFF sends a pulse that breaks the power circuit. When a switch is not being pushed, it is in a center, off (no-pulse) position. A switch has a mounting strap that matches a standard box, or a bracket for boxless mounting in a small opening cut in the wall. Each switch has three terminals, one for the white wire from the transformer terminal board, and two for wires to the relay, usually red and black. Always connect the same color wire to the ON terminal of each switch in a system, the other color to the OFF terminal.

Each relay has a small rectangular box portion that encloses the contacts that open and close the power circuit. The box has two terminals, one for the hot wire from the 120-volt power cable, the other for a full-gauge jumper to the fixture or receptacle. (The white wire in the power cable connects directly to the device controlled, never to a relay.) A cylindrical barrel attached to the relay box contains an electromagnet that operates the circuit contacts whenever it receives a pulse from its remote control switch. A relay mounts in an outlet or fixture box so that the barrel extends through a standard ½-inch knockout hole to the outside. Spring clips on the barrel snap-lock the relay in position. The relay barrel has three color-coded leads or terminals, which connect to the incoming low-voltage wires: red and black to matching-color switch wires, blue to the blue wire from the transformer terminal board. A single relay can be connected to several switches so it can be controlled from many locations; simply connect all like-colored wires together. Make connections with small-gauge wire nuts.

Low-voltage remote control switching is especially easy to install in open framing, as in new construction before the walls are closed up. It can also be used to supplement an existing system. However, low-voltage wires must not run into or through a box with 120-volt cable connections—only to the external connections on a relay barrel.

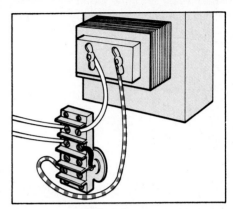

The transformer mounts on a covered junction box. A white wire and a color-coded wire connect it to the terminal board.

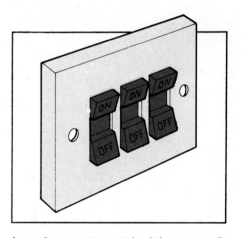

Low voltage remote-control switches are usually rocker-arm switches. Larger panels contain controls for the entire house.

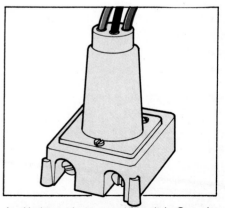

A relay is an electromagnetic switch. One wire goes to the transformer terminal board, two wires to the remote control switch.

BASIC HOOKUP FOR LOW-VOLTAGE WIRING

The basic system connections are described here. Your system may differ.

1. FIXTURE CONTROL

A typical hookup to turn a fixture on and off is shown (right). Your system may vary in details; check the instructions.

The transformer is mounted on a covered junction box with the 120-volt connections inside. A color-coded wire runs to one rectifier terminal and a white wire to a board terminal. Note the rectifier to terminal board jumper shown. From the terminal board, a white wire goes to the switch and a blue wire to the relay. Connections to other switches in the system are the same.

Red and black wires from the switch go to like-color terminals on the relay. Fixture box connections are shown below, right. Incoming 120-volt hot wire goes to one relay terminal; a jumper goes from the other terminal to the fixture. The white wire goes directly to the fixture, the grounding wire to the box.

2. OUTLET CONTROL

For outlet installation, gang two boxes together (or use a double-width box). For an end-of-run, fully switched outlet (not illustrated), run low-voltage wires to the relay just as for a fixture. In the box, connect the incoming hot wire to one relay terminal and a jumper from the other relay terminal to one brass outlet terminal. Run the white wire to a silver outlet terminal.

The hookup shown at far right is for the middle of a run, with the top outlet switched and the bottom outlet always hot. Break off the connecting link between the brass terminals on the receptacle. The incoming hot wire connects to the outgoing hot wire to provide power further on in the circuit. It is also pigtailed to the relay and to the lower brass outlet terminal. The power jumper from the relay goes to the upper brass terminal. The white wires connect to the silver outlet terminals (link not broken off). The grounding wires are connected and pigtailed to the box.

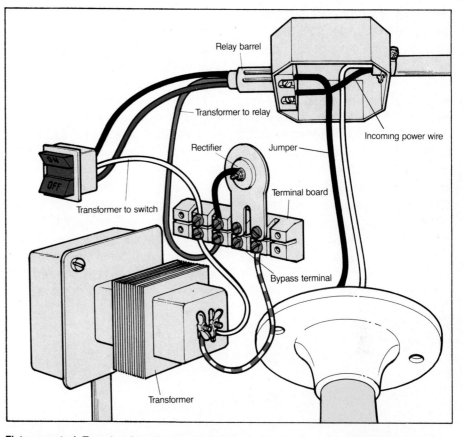

Fixture control. Two wires from the transformer supply 24-volt power to the terminal board. From there a white wire carries power to the switch, a colored wire carries power to the relay. Red and black wires connect the switch to the relay. A single relay can be connected to several switches.

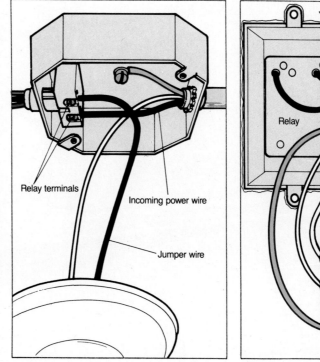

Fixture box connections. Incoming hot power goes to relay, jumper connects relay to fixture. White wire goes directly to fixture.

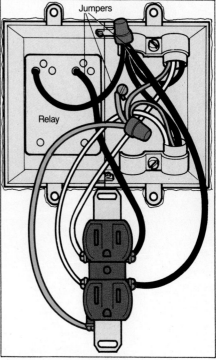

Outlet control. Wiring for one switched, one hot outlet is shown. Link between brass terminals must be removed, but not silver.

ADDING MASTER CONTROL TO LOW-VOLTAGE SYSTEM

A master control panel can give you control over eight or twelve switches from one location. The panel can be located almost anywhere you want, such as in an entryway near the front door, in a master bedroom, or the kitchen. The eight-switch panel has eight low-voltage switches. The twelve-switch panel has two numbered, circular dials, one controlling the ON signal, the other controlling the OFF signal. Both panels have provisions for a directory to the switches and pilot-light indicators.

The master control panel illustrated on this page, as well as others which are similar, have provisions for a directory of the switches and for the pilot-light indicators, if you choose to add them to the system.

A master control panel may be added to existing construction. However, the system is easiest to install in walls and ceilings that have not been finished—brand-new construction such as a room addition. Fishing wires through finished walls and ceilings can be a very time-consuming job.

As you go shopping for the system, also keep in mind that the system can be modified to control all the electrical devices in your home. It can automat-ically, for example, turn on in sequence a coffee maker, space heater, and the lights. Or these appliances may be individually turned on with a switch installed in the room.

And you can add motor-driven master controls that can operate electrical devices while you are away from home. For example, you can set the timers to turn on the lights at a specified time after dark. Then the lights can be programmed to turn off at a later hour.

As you might suspect, the wiring connections are complicated, although they are within most homeowners' skills. Instructions usually are furnished with products.

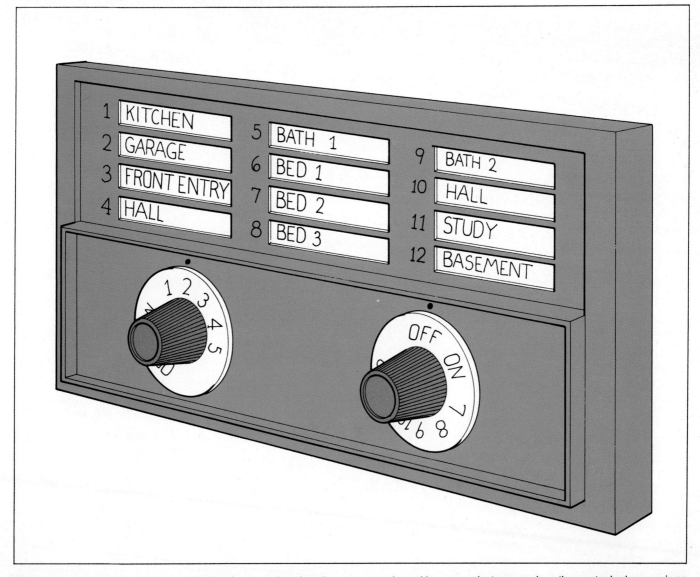

Master panel lets you control house lighting from one location. A master control panel in a convenient area such as the master bedroom or in an entryway near the front door can provide you with control at one location over all the low-voltage circuits in the house. The low-voltage system is extremely easy to install in open framing, such as brand-new housing or remodeling for a room addition.

How to Wire a Smoke Detector

Whether codes in your area require it or not, it's just smart business to equip your home with smoke detectors. The equipment is not prohibitive in cost and is easy to connect to housepower.

Before you install a smoke detector, be sure to read the manufacturer's suggestions for installation. You also can get information concerning smoke detectors by writing to the National Fire Protection Association, Batterymarch Park, Quincy, MA 02269, and by consulting your fire department.

If you don't want to wire in a detector, you can buy battery-operated models. Here are the procedures for installing a wired-in smoke detector:

1. Decide where you want to position the smoke detector. The best location is the center of a ceiling area or on a wall 10 inches down from the ceiling. A hallway at the top of a staircase is a good spot to place the unit, and so is a hallway off a kitchen or at the top of the stairs in a basement entrance.

2. Make a hole in the ceiling or wall and install the mounting plate. You can use a drill for this.

3. Select a nearby junction box to tap for power. Turn off the power to that particular circuit. Then run a length of No. 12/2 UF cable from the power source to the location of the smoke detector. Splice the black cable and power wires together and the white cable and power wires together. The power source should not be controlled by a switch. You must have constant power to the detector.

4. Connect the cable wires to the detector: black to black, white to white. Wire nut the splices and wrap the nuts with plastic electrician's tape.

5. Screw the detector to the mounting plate and snap on the cover.

6. Turn on the power and test the detector by using the test button, or by blowing smoke on the detector.

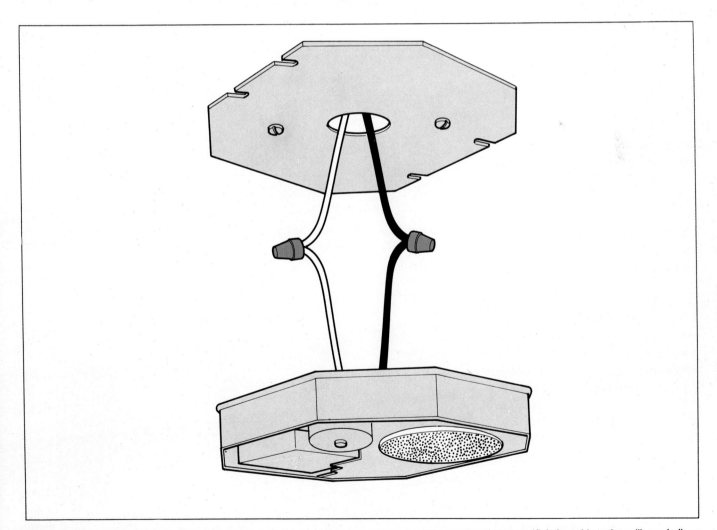

Smoke detector connects easily to house power. A cable-powered smoke detector is easily connected once you fish the cable to the ceiling or hallway wall location you've chosen. Black wires and white wires are spliced with wire nuts. Cost of the equipment is not prohibitive, and it has been proved that detectors save lives. Detectors are now required by codes in many areas.

Installing Remote-Control Audio

Remote-control speakers can supply music in a room above, below, or beside your audio equipment. You can even run speaker lines outside to the patio and enjoy music at poolside without subjecting your equipment to the effects of temperature, humidity, and weather. It takes a bit of doing to make the connections, but they are well within do-it-yourself skills.

INSTALLATION GUIDELINES FOR A REMOTE HOOKUP

With a length of two-conductor cable, you can add two speakers in another room to a stereo amplifier and suffer no loss in sound quality. Select No. 18 wire if the run is less than 20 feet. Use No. 16 wire if the run is 20 feet or more.

Some speakers and amplifiers may require soldered connections; most do not. Follow the directions given by the manufacturer of the equipment. Do not work with the amplifier on.

1. Select the speaker location and drill a ½-inch hole at the baseboard level behind each speaker. Drill a 1-inch hole behind the amplifier at baseboard level.

2. Examine the back of the amplifier. You will find two sets of terminals, one right and one left, labeled REMOTE. Each set of terminals probably will be labeled positive (+) or negative (−). Some setups use a color-coding system. Red means positive and black means negative. The back of the speakers have terminals labeled positive and negative.

3. Determine what color-coding system is used in your cable. Strip ½ inch of insulation from each end of the cable, and fish the cables between the amplifier and each of the speakers. See pages 83–85.

4. If your amplifier has screw terminals, attach the positive wire to the plus terminal and the negative wire to the minus terminal.

If your amplifier has spring-clamp terminals, you must tin the wires before you insert them in the clamps. Twist the strands tightly together. Heat the wire with the soldering iron, and then touch the solder to the wire. When they're cool, insert the wires into the clamp.

5. Hook the wires to the individual speakers to complete the project.

INSTALLING A REMOTE VOLUME CONTROL

A remote volume control can add to the utility of remote-control speakers, since the sound can be heard only in the room in which you desire it. This installation requires three-conductor cable, which connects the volume control to the amplifier, and two-conductor cable, which connects the volume control to each speaker. You will also need an autotransformer-type volume control that is compatible with the amplifier and small wire nuts.

Guidelines on how the system is connected are explained on page 145.

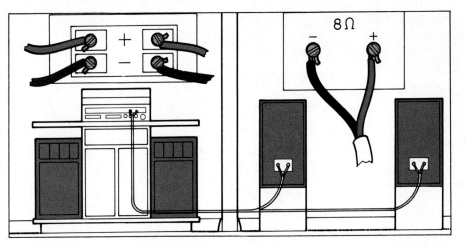

Remote terminals for speakers in another area. By using the remote terminals on an amplifier, you can connect a set of speakers in another location. The terminals are usually marked positive and negative on the back of the amplifier.

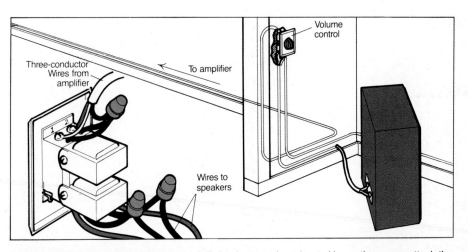

Wiring plan for a remote volume control. To hook up a volume control in another room, attach the white wire to input 1, and the red wire to input 2. Splice the black amplifier wires with the black volume wire as shown in the inset.

REMOTE VOLUME CONTROL HOOKUP

First, cut a rectangular opening to house the volume-control device. Drill 1-inch access holes at baseboard level behind amplifier and speakers.

1. Fish three-conductor cable between the amplifier and the volume-control opening. Fish two-conductor cables, one to each speaker, from the volume control.

2. Make the amplifier hookup. The three-conductor cable will have a red, black, and white wire. Attach the black wire to the left negative terminal; attach the white wire to the left positive terminal; attach the red wire to the right positive terminal.

3. Find the side of the volume control that is labeled INPUT. The amplifier wires go here. Fasten the white wire to input 1, then fasten the red wire to input 2. Splice the two black amplifier wires with the two black control wires.

4. Remove ½ inch insulation from the two speaker cables. Attach the positive wires to the numbered terminals. Match each neutral wire to the corresponding black control wire. Splice with wire nuts and install the cover plate.

INSTALLING SPEAKERS MOUNTED IN THE CEILING

A ceiling-mounted speaker can be a convenient installation.

1. Determine the location. Be sure there is adequate space between joists for speaker units.

2. Make a template of the speaker. Then draw around the template on the ceiling and cut the opening in the ceiling for the speaker. Position the speaker.

3. Fish two-conductor cable between the opening and the amplifier. Then install the speaker housing, pulling the cable through a center knockout.

4. Strip the wires ½ inch and put on crimp connectors if required. Slide the positive wire onto the positive connection. Do the same with the negative wire to the negative connection.

5. Install speaker in housing.

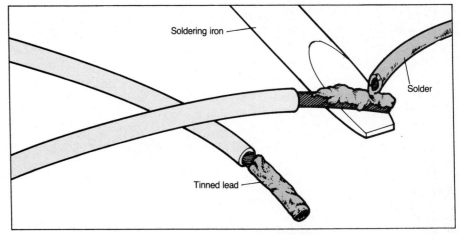

How to tin a wire for more positive contact. To tin a wire for more positive contact, twist the strands of wire together with your fingers. Then heat the wire and hold noncorrosive solder to the wire. Don't heat the solder.

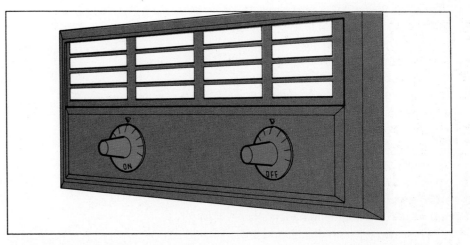

Master control unit puts sound where you want it. A master switch such as this one gives you control of remote fixtures. The system has dials for on and off. You simply dial the area and then push the button to get the sound.

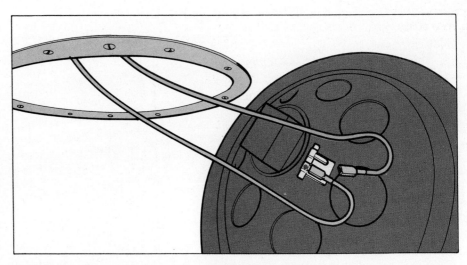

Follow color codes when wiring ceiling speaker. To wire a ceiling speaker, attach the light-colored wire to the terminal coded with either a red dot or a plus sign. You will need just two-conductor cable from the amplifier to the ceiling speaker.

INSTALLING A SPEAKER JACK

If you want to move the speakers to various locations from time to time, you can attach plugs to the speaker cables and install speaker outlets with phone jacks in the locations you want. This gives the system plenty of flexibility without a lot of added cost.

You'll need ¼-inch phone plugs for the speaker cables and lengths of No. 18 two-conductor cable. The cable will be color-coded. Here is the basic assembly:

1. Remove the plug jacket and slip it over the cable ends. Split the cable about 2 inches. Find the copper wire (in gold insulation) and cut the wire ½ inch longer than the silver-colored wire. Then remove ¼ inch of insulation from each wire and tin the ends with noncorrosive or rosin-core solder.

2. The connections in the plug will be different sizes. Attach the copper wire to the longer connection. Attach the silver-colored wire to the shorter connection. Then slip the jacket over the connections and hook the speaker to the cable.

INSTALLING THE OUTLET

You will need a soldering iron, noncorrosive solder, a 1-inch drill bit and drill, and needlenose pliers.

1. Drill a hole in the wall. Then fish cable between the opening and the amplifier.

2. Split the cable about 2 inches and strip about ½ inch of insulation from the wires.

3. The back of the outlet has a spring contact and sleeve contact. Loop the silver-colored wire through the spring contact. Hold the wire in place and heat it and the spring contact with the soldering iron. Then touch the connection with solder. The solder must be smooth. If not, reheat the solder. The solder will almost automatically smooth itself. Don't try to spread it out evenly with a knife or other tool.

4. Solder the gold-colored wire and the sleeve contact the same way.

5. Fit the outlet into the opening and then fasten it in position with screws.

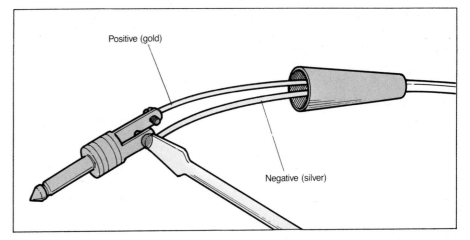

Split the cord. Split the cord and attach the silver side to the short terminal of the plug. Attach the gold side to the long terminal for the plug connections.

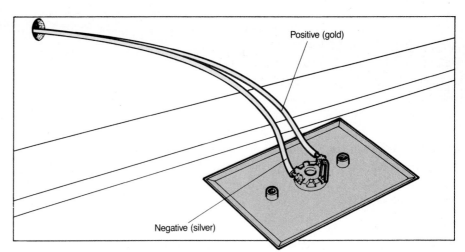

Wall plate connection. Solder the gold side to the sleeve contact and the silver side to the spring contact. Use noncorrosive (rosin) solder.

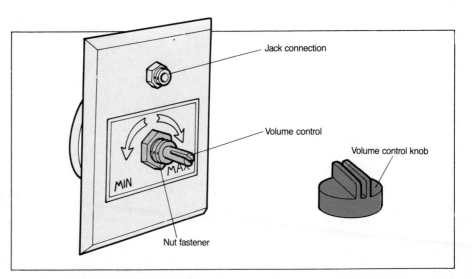

Locknuts secure jacks. The jack (top) and the control shaft are fastened to the cover plate with locknuts. The control knob slips over shaft.

EARPHONE HOOKUP

You will need a 4-inch-square standard blank double-gang plate for a switch, an L-pad volume control (stereo), a three-conductor stereo headphone jack, soldering iron, noncorrosive solder, continuity tester, three-conductor cable 18 inches longer than the distance between the amplifier and hookup, wire nuts, and two 330-ohm two-wall resistors.

1. Drill ⅜-inch openings, centered between each pair of screw holes on the switch plate.

2. Insert the volume-control shaft through one hole. Slide the volume-indicator plate over the shaft; secure the volume control with a locknut. Then install the jack in the other opening.

3. The volume control has two sets of three terminals. Cut three 4-inch jumper wires of red, white, and black insulation. Each will be soldered to a terminal. The black wire goes on base No. 1, white on base No. 2, and red on center No. 2.

4. The jack base has three terminals and three contacts. Attach the continuity tester to one of the contacts. Touch the terminals with the probe until the bulb lights. Mark the plate indicating what the terminal matches up with. Do this for each contact. Then solder the loose jumper ends. Connect the black jumper to the terminal that matches the sleeve contact; connect the white jumper that matches the long spring contact; connect the red jumper to the short spring contact.

5. Strip 3 inches of insulation from a three-conductor cable. Strip ¼-inch insulation from the red and white wires and 1½ inches from the black wire.

6. Connect black wire to both No. 1 terminals on volume control. Connect the white wire to base terminal No. 3 on the control, red to center No. 3.

7. Cut the hole for the earphone plate. Splice the amplifier cable to the like-colored wires of the earphone plate. Attach resistors to the left and right terminals of the amplifier's remote terminals. Then connect the red, white, and black wires as shown.

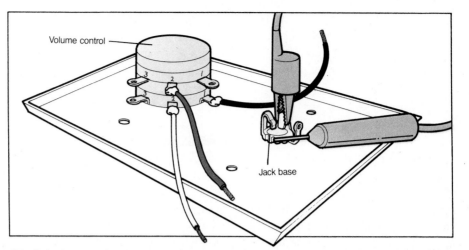

Volume control

Jack base

Attach the jumper wires to the marked terminals. First, attach jumper wires to the terminals of the two levels of the control in the order shown. Then test the contacts and the terminals to find the matching parts. Use a continuity tester.

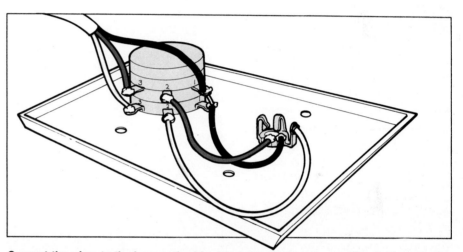

Connect the wires to the base and cable. Attach the wire from the amplifier. Solder each wire carefully, especially the black wire, which must hook to the lower terminal. Then attach the cable. Use noncorrosive solder.

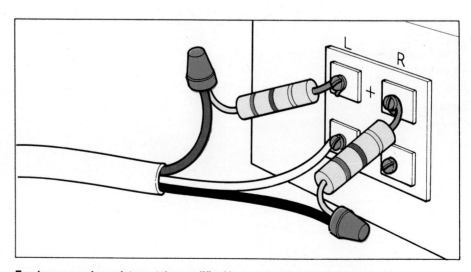

Earphones require resistors at the amplifier. You must install resistors at the amplifier when you are wiring an earphone jack. You will have to cut a hole in the wall for the plate and fish the cable between the amplifier and the jack.

INSTALLATION BASICS FOR AN OUTDOOR HOOKUP

An outdoor hookup for an audio speaker can add enjoyment to a patio or a swimming pool area. You must install three-conductor cable that is approved for outdoor use. Be sure to check and follow all the local codes regarding the use of cable and conduit. The store where you buy the materials will be able to advise you. Also check information on pages 150, 151, and 152. UF-type cable usually is specified for outdoor and underground use.

TOOLS AND MATERIALS

An outdoor hookup is housed in an outdoor receptacle box. You will also need three pieces of ½-inch steel pipe: one 6- and one 12-inch length, and one T connector. In the receptacle box will be a switch plate, cut to fit, and two jacks. The final hookup requires three wire nuts and plastic electrician's tape. You also will need a ⅜-inch metal drill bit, drill, a hacksaw, a hammer or baby sledge, soldering iron, and noncorrosive solder.

INSTALLING THE HOUSING

1. Connect the 6- and 12-inch pipe with the T connector. Screw either end of the 6-inch pipe into the receptacle housing.

2. Dig a hole 4 inches deep at the spot where you want the receptacle. Make sure it doesn't obstruct a traffic pattern or block an area where you might want to place furniture or an outdoor grill.

3. Using a piece of scrap lumber to protect the receptacle housing, pound the pipe into the ground up to the base of the T connector.

4. Run the cable to the box in a trench, as discussed on page 152. If the local code requires conduit, however, use it instead. To go under a walk or driveway, you can improvise a water ram with a garden hose. Dig a hole on each side of the obstruction. Secure a garden hose to a length of stiff molding. Stick the hose in the hole and turn on

the water full blast. Then wiggle the hose under the obstruction until it meets the hole on the other side. Tie the cable to the hose and pull the hose back out of the hole the water ram made under the obstruction.

CREATING THE PLATE

Use a hacksaw to cut the size of the switch plate to measure 2 × 4 inches. Measure ⅞ inch in from the mounted openings. At these points, drill ⅜-inch openings for the jacks. Use a metal drill bit.

Insert the jacks into the plate and secure with locknuts. Cut 6-inch jumpers, one red, one white, and two black. Solder the black jumpers to the right-hand terminals on each jack. Then solder the red and the white jumpers to the left-hand terminals.

INSTALLING THE PLATES

In the gasket, there will already be some mounting openings. But they will not align with the openings in the adaptor plate. Use the plate to mark the positions on the gasket and drill in the new openings as required. Use a metal bit.

Use wire nuts to splice the cable wires to the like-colored wires of the jacks. Wrap the nuts with plastic electrician's tape. Insert the plate in the box, then slip the gasket into position. Fasten the receptacle cover in place. Finish the installation by hooking up the amplifier wires.

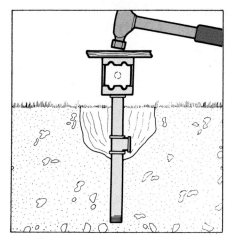

Protect receptacle. An outdoor speaker outlet is housed in an outdoor receptacle box. Protect it as you hammer down the post.

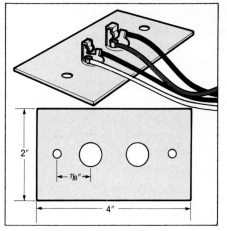

Drill holes in plate. Use metal bit in power drill to punch necessary openings in blank switch plate. Then solder amplifier wires to jacks.

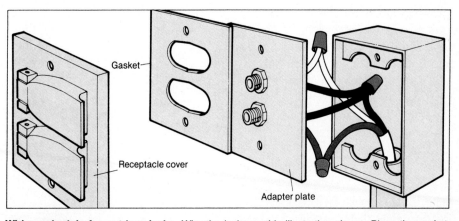

Wiring schedule for outdoor jacks. Wire the jacks as this illustration shows. Place the gasket between the adaptor plate and the receptacle cover in order to maintain a dry, safe installation. Wire nut and wrap all splices with tape.

11 Outdoor Wiring

There are lots of good reasons for putting in outdoor wiring. Lighting probably is the primary one. Power for appliances may run a close second in a long list of purposes.

But before you start an outside electrical project, contact the municipal building inspector to determine the requirements that have been established for your community concerning outdoor wiring. In some communities, only a professional electrician can make the final hookups. In other areas, the work must be inspected before it can be put into operation. You will have to find out whether the municipal electrical code permits the use of Type UF cable, or if it specifies Type TW wire and conduit.

Generally, local codes require that outdoor wiring be protected by conduit whenever it is installed aboveground. If the wiring is to be buried, most codes allow Type UF cable. However, some require that Type TW wire and conduit be used.

Always, without fail, turn off the power at the main electrical service panel before working on a circuit.

OUTDOOR LIGHTING TYPES
Outdoor lighting falls into two general categories: functional and decorative. Functional lighting illuminates high-use areas, such as steps, stairs, gates, walkways, and patios. Decorative lighting adds dimension and mood to exterior space. In some cases you will find that, with modification, functional lighting can be decorative.

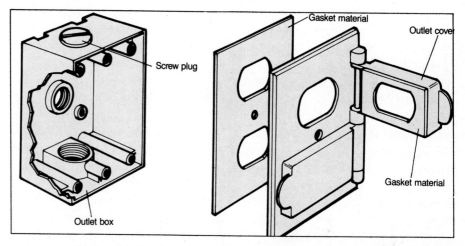

Outside receptacles are made of extra thick metal with screw fittings and gaskets between faceplates and openings to the outlets. In stores, you may find these products in the lawn and garden department.

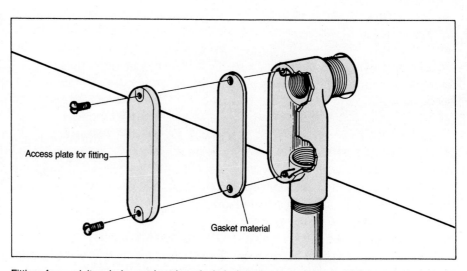

Fittings for conduit and wire used outdoors include these basic products. An LB fitting is L-shaped and has a back opening for conduit. The fittings have weatherproofing gaskets.

Outdoor Wiring Rules and Products

Whether you plan to light the walkways or paths for safety, or spotlight a lawn feature, it's a good idea to draw a plan of the wiring scheme you want. This will save you plenty of time and help you estimate the materials needed. Follow these guidelines as you plan your installation:

1. Provide enough light to meet the needs, but do not overlight. Too much light can ruin the atmosphere of an exterior space and can cause surface glare. Several strategically placed small lights should replace several large ones.

2. Try to place the lighting fixtures so only the light is seen, not the source.

3. To achieve a visual effect that is seldom available in any area, backlight architectural or landscaping features. This technique creates shadow and depth.

4. Position lighting with efficiency in mind. A series of lights can extend the interior lights bordering a backyard or patio. Exterior lighting should complement interior lighting.

5. Try to keep the distance between lights to a minimum. The more spread out the lighting, the more costly the installation.

6. For safety, provide at least 5 lumens of light at all walkways, ramps, and stairways.

7. Stairway lights should shine down toward the risers so that the treads will not be in shadow.

PATHS FOR CABLE

As you plan, try to place all fixtures and receptacles so that they are easily accessible, both for installation and for future maintenance. Keep the total distance between fixtures to a minimum.

If you have to dig to bury cable, contact the local utilities first. They will need at least three days' notice to plot underground wiring and plumbing for you. *Do not dig until you contact the utilities.* Driving a spade blade through an electrical cable can be dangerous.

EQUIPMENT

Outdoor electrical equipment, such as fixture boxes and receptacles, is especially manufactured to meet codes and resist the elements. You also should use weatherproof light bulbs in outdoor fixtures. These resist shattering when the temperature drops.

Do not use electrical products specified for indoor use outdoors.

CONNECTORS AND FITTINGS

An LB fitting (shown on page 149) is a right-angle connector that is used with a conduit to bring cable through the wall of a house. The fitting routes cable toward a trench that has been dug from the house to the area where the electricity is needed.

LB fittings are threaded on both ends. Conduit passing through the house wall to the outside is screwed to one end. Conduit leading down the side of the house to the trench is screwed to the other end. Thus, cable is enclosed in the metal to provide an efficient seal from the time it leaves the house to the time it enters the ground. LB connectors are outfitted with thick gaskets and metal cover plates.

Box extenders are used when tapping an existing outdoor receptacle or fixture junction box for power. The extender may have a nipple and a 90-degree elbow so that the wires may be brought from the fixture, through the conduit, to the point where power is wanted.

OUTDOOR CONDUIT

Three types are available, but check the codes before you buy.

Rigid aluminum and rigid steel conduit provide equal protection to the wires that pass through them. Rigid aluminum is easier to work with, but if it is going to be buried in concrete, first coat it with bituminous paint to keep it from corroding.

Both types of metal conduit come with a variety of fittings, including elbows, offsets, bushings, couplings, and connectors. If offsets and elbows do not provide the necessary turns in rigid metal or EMT conduit, you will need a bending tool called a hickey.

Nonmetallic conduit is made from either polyvinyl chloride (PVC), which is normally used aboveground, or high-density polyethylene, which is suitable for burial. If PVC is going to be exposed to direct sunlight, it must be labeled as suitable for use in sunlight. But before you purchase nonmetallic conduit, be sure you check local codes. Don't assume that it's approved. An inspection might require you to replace the nonmetallic materials with another product; this can be very costly and time-consuming.

OUTDOOR ACCESSORIES

Stores offer a wide variety of electrical accessories manufactured especially for outdoor use.

These include all types of lighting fixtures, such as spotlights and lampposts as well as outdoor cooking appliances, pool lights, and devices to control insects. Most of the accessories run on regular 120-volt housepower, so connecting power from your home to the devices is fairly easy to do and within do-it-yourself skills.

In general, you just have to tap into power inside the house and run a cable through the wall to the exterior. Then make the connections. About the hardest part of the job is digging wire trenches.

Extending Power Outside the House

There are two main ways to extend electricity from the house to the outside. You can run the power cable through the basement—or basement crawl space—or through the attic.

THROUGH THE BASEMENT

Follow these procedures for a basement exit:

1. Locate the exit point for the cable. It may be near a water pipe that extends through the wall or at a corner. The spot where you go through the wall should be at least 3 inches from a joist, sill plate, or floor to allow clearance for a junction box.

2. Outside, measure from the common reference point to the spot selected for the exit. If the spot is on the foundation, make sure the spot does not fall on a joint between concrete blocks or where two pieces of siding join. The spot has to provide a firm base for the LB fitting. At this point outside, drill a small hole through the wall to verify that the path is clear. If the hole is in a block wall, don't drill through the top block. Blocks below the top have a hollow center; top blocks often are filled with concrete.

3. Use a star drill and baby sledge hammer to cut the opening for the extender in masonry. Wear safety glasses and gloves while working.

4. Back inside, open one of the knockouts from the back of a box and mount the box so the hole matches the hole through the wall. The box is mounted with masonry shields (anchors) and screws.

5. Outside, dig the cable trench.

6. Onto an LB fitting screw a nipple long enough to extend from inside the box through the hole to the outside. Outside, attach conduit to the LB fitting and run the conduit down the side of the house to the trench. Then seal the joint around the fitting with quality caulking compound. Inside, secure the

nipple to the box with a connector. The opening is now ready for the cable.

THROUGH THE ATTIC

To bring power through the attic and an eave, you will need an outdoor outlet box, nipple, 90-degree corner elbow, and a length of conduit to extend down the side of the house to the trench.

1. Hold the assembly against the overhang of the roof so the box and nipple are against the soffit and the conduit is against the wall. Try to run the conduit near a downspout to make it inconspicuous.

2. Mark the soffit where the cable will pass through the soffit into the box. Use a 1⅛-inch bit to drill a hole through the soffit for the cable. Then remove a knockout to correspond with the hole, and fasten the box to the soffit with screws.

3. Run the cable from the attic power source and out the hole in the soffit. Clamp the cable to the box. With conduit straps, strap the nipple and conduit into place and complete the installation by running conduit down the side of the house. The path is now ready for the cable installation. Be sure to check the codes for the type of cable and/or conduit you can use.

THE CONNECTION

You will have to pull the cable through the pathway you have made for it. Then the cable can be connected to the power source inside the house. The best plan is to complete the entire project first—hooking up the outside lights and appliances—before connecting to power. If you are creating a new circuit, have a professional electrician connect the cable to the main service panel. If you are connecting to an existing outlet, make sure the circuit has enough amperage to handle outdoor demands for power. How this is figured is discussed on page 9.

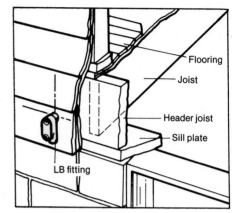

The access point. Place hole through wall for cable at least 3 inches from joists, sill plate, and flooring. LB fitting goes on outside wall.

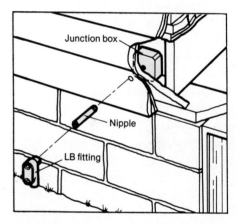

Box location. Mount box inside. Nipple goes through wall and screws into box. LB fitting screws onto nipple; conduit screws into fitting.

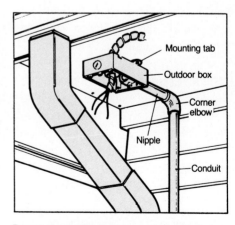

Box at the soffit. Cable runs from attic to box fastened to soffit exterior. Conduit drops to trench on ground. Run conduit next to downspout, if possible.

Installing Power Cable Outside

Running the cable from the house out to the yard, pool, garden, or wherever you want it involves digging a shallow trench and building an anchor for each receptacle. Here's how:

DIGGING A TRENCH

First, call the utility company for a plot of pipes and wiring that may be running underground on your property. In some areas you are required by law to do this. Check your local code on depth requirements. Generally, cable not in conduit (but with proper insulation, see page 26) must be buried at least 24 inches deep, with expansion loops as shown at far right. Put intermediate metallic conduit at least 6 inches deep, rigid nonmetallic conduit at least 18 inches deep.

TRENCHES UNDER SLABS

If the wires have to go under a walkway or driveway, you can use this technique: Dig the trench up to the obstruction. Then continue the trench on the other side of it. Cut a piece of conduit 10 inches longer than the span. Hammer a point on one end of the conduit. Now hammer the conduit under the obstruction. When it appears on the other side, cut off the point with a hacksaw. You now can connect another piece of conduit to it or run the cable through the conduit under the obstruction. Also see page 148 for another technique.

INSTALLING RECEPTACLES

The receptacle should be at least 12 inches above ground level and anchored underground. Do this by laying the cable or conduit either through the center opening of a concrete block or through a coffee can filled with concrete.

Since so little cement is required for this job, we suggest that you buy already-mixed concrete mix sold by stores in 80-pound bags.

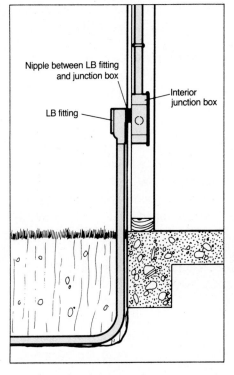

From house to trench. Here's the hookup for outdoor wiring as it leaves the house on its way through a trench to a receptacle or appliance in the yard area

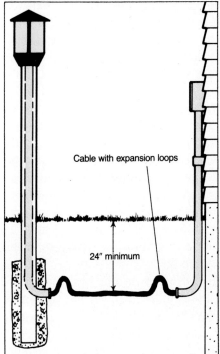

Bury cable at least 24 inches. Bury the cable at least 24 inches underground—or according to local code requirements. Loop the cable as shown to allow for expansion.

Concrete block anchor. Lower a concrete block over the positioned receptacle and conduit/cable for an anchor. Fill space with concrete.

Tin can anchor. You can use a large tin can as a receptacle anchor. Cut both ends open and lower the can over the box and into the ground. Fill with concrete.

How to Install a Lamppost

A lamppost must be buried at least 2 feet deep for stability and protection from frost heave. Some posts are adjustable. They come with an opening for UF cable. If you are using conduit, extend the opening in the lamppost.

1. Mark guidelines, 18 inches long and ⅞ inch apart, on the post. To cut out the outlined strip (see illustration), use a hacksaw that has a blade-type grip. Once the sides are cut, bend out the strip and saw it off, using a file to smooth sharp edges. If the post has a middle-of-the-run hookup, cut another slot in the direction that the cable continues.

2. If you're using conduit throughout, measure and cut a piece that extends from the already-positioned conduit at the house to the top of the locknut of an adjustable post or to the top of a nonadjustable post.

3. Dig the trench and attach the conduit capping it with a plastic bushing to protect the cable.

4. Once all the receptacles, lights, and other features are in place, fish the wire through the conduit. Hook up all wiring as you would for conventional systems.

5. Dig the posthole 2 feet deep and about 8 inches wide. Position the conduit, if needed, as described above. Position the post over the conduit, or thread UF cable through the cable opening.

6. It's a good idea to set the post in concrete, although you can lay down alternating layers of dirt and large gravel around the post. Tamp and compact the fill after every addition.

If you are creating a new circuit for the lamppost, run the cable to the main electrical service panel. Then have a professional electrician make the power hookup after you complete the rest of the lamppost project. If you tap into an existing power source inside (or outside) the house, make sure that the circuit can handle the extra power load.

THE CONCRETE MIXTURE
At home-center and building-material outlets, you can buy already-mixed concrete in 80-pound bags. You simply add water to the mixture and stir. One bag of concrete mix will yield about two-thirds of a cubic foot of concrete. For a lamppost, you may need two bags of material.

After the mixture is dumped into the hole with the post in position, round off the top of the concrete in a crowned configuration with a trowel. The crown will help drain water away from the lamppost. Then brace the post with a length of 2 × 4 to steady it until the concrete sets—a couple of days is best.

ABOUT WIRES AND CONDUIT
The wires you pull through conduit must be insulated, but they may be single strands since the conduit takes the place of cable insulation.

The neutral wire must be coded white. The other wires may be black or one red and one black.

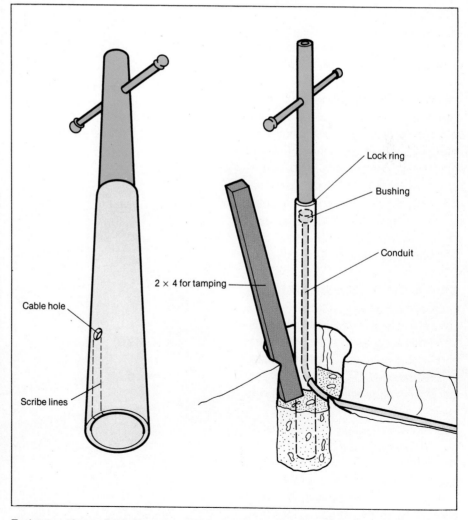

Cable hole

Scribe lines

2 × 4 for tamping

Lock ring

Bushing

Conduit

To slot a post for conduit (left), mark 18-inch-long lines, ⅞ inch apart, on the post. Extend beyond the opening for UF cable. Cut along the lines with a hacksaw. To anchor the post (right), dig a hole 2 feet deep and 8 inches wide. Bend the conduit to come up in the middle of the hole, almost to an adjustable post's lock ring or a fixed post's full height.

Adding a Single Exterior Outlet

This project shows how to install a single exterior outlet to provide power for appliances and tools.

GOING THROUGH SIDING

If at all possible, locate the exterior outlet directly opposite an interior outlet. This way, you can use the same power source for both outlets.

1. Shut off the power to the circuit that operates the interior outlet. Remove the faceplate and the outlet. Then with a long ¾-inch drill bit, drill a hole through an opening in the back of the box through the sheathing and siding.

2. Outside, locate the drilled hole. Then with a keyhole or saber saw, cut away the sheathing and siding to fit the exterior box that you will install in the exterior wall. Set the saw so the blade won't enter the interior box.

3. Remove the back knockout on the cast metal box and screw this box into the house with the knockout hole aligned with the hole in the wall. Insert a 10-inch length of cable in the hole.

4. Connect the cable inside to the terminals of the receptacle and the cable outside to the new GFCI receptacle. Then install a waterproof gasket and faceplate over the outside outlet.

THROUGH MASONRY WALLS

Outline the shape of the box on the concrete block with masking tape. Then drill a series of holes within that border with a masonry bit in a power drill. Clean out the area with a cold chisel and baby sledge. Wear safety glasses and gloves.

Drill a hole through the wall, matching a knockout in the back of the box. The cable will run through this hole to a junction box on the interior wall.

Adjust the ears of the exterior box so the box will extend about ¹⁄₁₆ inch from the block. Then cement the box in place. Connect the outlet and install a weatherproof cover as shown.

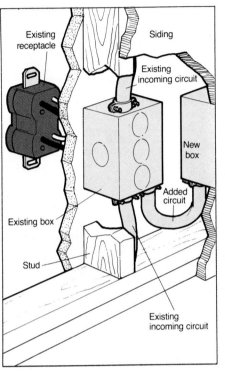

Tap into existing outlet. Turn off power and remove existing outlet from interior box. Drill hole through back of box to exterior. You will tap this outlet.

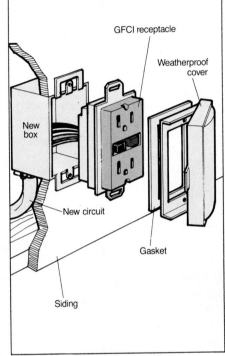

Install outside box. Cut hole in siding and sheathing from outside and insert exterior box. Run cable through knockout to inside box and make power hookup.

Drill and chisel hole. Drill series of holes in concrete block for exterior box. Remove back knockout, insert box, and drill hole to interior for power cable.

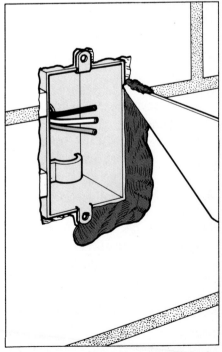

Mortar box into block. Mortar exterior box in place. Connect outlet to power in interior junction box, which may be surface-mounted to block with masonry shields.

Glossary

AC Alternating current. The type of current found in most home electrical systems in the United States.

AWG American Wire Gauge, a system of sizing wire.

Ampere, amperage, amps A unit of measurement that describes the rate or strength of electrical flow. Amperes are measured in terms of the number of electrons flowing through a given point in a conductor in one second when the electrons are under a pressure of one volt and the conductor has a resistance of one ohm. Conductors are rated by their **ampacity**, the current in amperes they can carry continuously under conditions of use without exceeding their temperature ratings.

BX cable Electrical cable wrapped in a protective, flexible, metal sheathing. BX contains at least two conductors. Some codes limit its use.

Back-wired Type of receptacle or switch in which wires are inserted into openings and secured by clamps rather than by terminal screws.

Ballast Device that controls the current in a fluorescent light.

Bare wire In a cable, the wire that has no insulation and functions as an equipment grounding conductor. See Green wire.

Bar hanger Support installed between the joists or rafters of a ceiling to support a junction box.

Black wire In a cable, the wire that functions as a hot wire.

CSA Canadian Standards Association. See National Electrical Code.

CO/ALR Marking that designates switches and receptacles that may be used with aluminum wiring.

Cable Two or more wires grouped together inside a protective sheathing of plastic or metal.

Canopy Dishlike structure of a ceiling fixture that covers the wiring, box, and ceiling opening.

Cartridge fuse Cylindrical fuses that are rated to carry higher voltages and current levels than plug fuses. Two types: with and without blade contacts.

Channel The metal support base of a fluorescent fixture that holds the starter, ballast, and lampholders.

Choke ballast The ballast found in small fluorescent fixtures. These ballasts lack the transformers necessary for larger tubes.

Circuit breaker A protective device that opens a circuit automatically when a given overcurrent occurs. Can also be operated and reset manually.

Circuit map A diagram that indicates (1) the locations of all wall switches, receptacles, and major appliances and (2) designates in some fashion the circuit which feeds the electrical items. Useful for determining the actual load level on a given circuit and tracing circuit problems.

Collar The finishing locknut on a ceiling fixture.

Common The identified terminal on a three-way switch. Usually has a dark-color screw; may be marked COM.

Conductor A metal wire, bar, or strip that offers minimum resistance to the flow of electricity.

Conduit Metal or plastic tubing designed to enclose electrical wires.

Continuity tester A device that indicates when a complete electrical patch exists between two points. *Never* used with circuit on, or to determine the presence of power. See Voltage tester.

CU/AL Marking that designates receptacles and switches that may be used with copper or copper-clad aluminum wire.

Current The flow of electrons through a conductor.

DC Direct current. The electrical current supplied by a battery and often an engine-driven generator.

Dimmer switch A switch that can vary the intensity of the light it controls. There are two styles: Hi-Lo and rotary.

Double-pole switch A switch with four terminals that controls a single major appliance. The toggle is marked ON/OFF.

Duplex receptacle Receptacle holding two outlets.

EMT Electrical metal tubing, sometimes called thin-wall conduit.

Elbow connector Right-angle piece used in a raceway and conduit runs.

End-of-the-run Box with its outlet or switch at the final position in a circuit. Only one cable enters the box.

End-wired Type of switch that has terminals on the top and bottom of the switch housing.

Energy efficiency rating (EER) A number indicating the relative amount of energy consumed by a given appliance. The higher the EER, the more efficient it is.

Faceplate The decorative plate installed over a switch or receptacle. The plate also covers the wall opening and thus protects the wiring.

Filament The thin wire in an incandescent bulb that glows to produce light.

Fish tape Flexible metal strip used to draw wires and cables through walls, raceway, and conduit.

Four-way switch One of three switches controlling one outlet or fixture. The other two switches are three-way switches. A four-way switch has four terminal screws. The toggle is not marked ON/OFF.

Front-wired Type of switch with terminal screws facing the front of the switch.

Fuse A safety device designed to protect house circuits. A metal wire inside the fuse melts or disintegrates in case of overload or short circuit, thus shutting off the current. See also Cartridge fuse.

GR Terminal screw for a ground wire.

Ganging Joining two or more switch boxes for greater capacity.

Green wire In a cable, the wire that functions as an equipment grounding conductor. See Bare wire.

Ground Fault Circuit Interrupter (GFCI) A safety circuit breaker that compares the amount of current entering a receptacle on the hot wire with the amount leaving on the white wire. If there is a discrepancy of .005 volt, the GFCI breaks the circuit in 1/40 of a second. The device is usually required by code in bathrooms, kitchens, and outdoor areas that are subject to dampness.

Grounding electrode conductor (Ground wire) Wire that carries current to earth in the event of a short circuit. The ground wire is essential to the safety of your house wiring system and of its users.

Hickey Bracket-shaped adaptor that screws to a threaded stud; a threaded nipple screws into the other end and is secured by a locknut. Also a conduit bender.

Horsepower Designation of power requirements often used for electrical tools, such as power drills. One horsepower equals about 746 watts.

Incandescent light Light created by passing electric current through a thin wire called a filament. The glow of the filament is called incandescence.

Incoming wire Hot wire that feeds power into a box.

Internal saddle clamp A fitting that screws into the inside of a box to hold cable in place. The clamp secures the cable, not the wires.

Jumper wires Short lengths of single conductor wire that are used to complete circuit connections.

Junction box Metal box inside which all standard wire splices and wiring connections must be made.

Kilowatt A kilowatt (kw) equals 1,000 watts.

Kilowatt hour (kw/h) A kilowatt hour equals 1,000 watts used for one hour.

Knockouts Perforated pieces of metal in a box that are removed with a punch and hammer to permit insertion of wire.

LB fitting A right-angle connector used to bring cable through an exterior wall.

Locking switch Switch that must be unlocked before it can be turned on.

Lumen Unit of illumination given off by a light.

Major box Another name for a junction box.

Malibu light Low-voltage lights designed, usually, for outdoor use.

Middle-of-the-run Box with its outlets or switch lying between the power source and another box. Cable(s) enters and leaves this box.

Mounting slots Slots that permit the position of a switch or receptacle to be adjusted so it is straight in relation to a wall or ceiling surface.

Mounting strap Metal structure on a switch or receptacle with slots at the top and bottom through which screws are driven to attach the device to a box. Also a metal strip that fits over a ceiling box to help support a ceiling fixture.

NM cable Economical cable permitted for use in normally dry locations.

NMC cable Like NM cable but also usable in moist or corrosive locations.

National Electrical Code Body of regulations spelling out safe, functional electrical procedures. Local codes can add to but not delete from NEC regulations.

Neutral bus bar Common connection between the neutral wire coming from the utility company, the neutral and equipment grounding conductors of the house wiring, and the equipment grounding (bare or green) conductor. Connects to a grounding electrode, often the cold water entrance pipe.

Overload Too great a demand for power made on a circuit.

Pigtail A short piece of wire used to complete a circuit inside a box.

Plaster ears Adjustable ears on a receptacle's mounting strips that let you recess the box to allow for a flush-finished installation.

Polarized plug Plug with an equipment prong longer than the two blades, one of which is wider than the other.

Polarized receptacle Outlet with prong openings that accommodate polarized plugs.

Programmable thermostat Thermostat that maintains a home's temperature between preset high and low limits.

Quiet switch Most common type of toggle, or snap, switch. It is quieter than older switches, but still makes some noise.

Raceway Surface wiring that adds outlets, switches, and fixtures without extensive structural work.

Recoded wire White-insulated wire that has been taped or painted black. The recoding indicates that the wire now carries power.

Red wire In a cable, the wire designated as a hot wire. Usually used as a switch wire in three-way switches.

Relay Electronically powered switch that turns lights and outlets off and on in a remote-control low-voltage system.

Romex Plastic-sheathed cable containing at least two conductors.

Rotary dimmer switch See Dimmer switch.

Service panel The point at which electricity provided by a local utility enters your house wiring system.

Short circuit A fault that occurs when a hot or ungrounded wire touches a grounded (white) or grounding (bare or green) wire. This causes an overcurrent that will trip a protective device (circuit breaker or fuse).

Side-wired Type of receptacle or switch having four terminal screws mounted on the receptacle. In a switch, the terminal screws are on the sides of the switch housing.

Single conductor Wire purchased individually rather than combined in cable; used, for example, to create jumper wires.

Single-pole Type of switch with only two terminals.

Spacer plate Plate added to increase the depth of a box to make room for wires and splices. Used for installation of such devices as raceways and GFCIs.

Starter A switch in a fluorescent light that closes the circuit only when sufficient power is available.

Switch loop Installation in which a ceiling fixture is installed between a power source and a switch. The power bypasses through the fixture box to the switch. The switch then sends power to the fixture itself.

TW wire Type of wire most often used in home circuits, raceway, and exterior conduit.

Three-way switch One of two switches controlling a single outlet or fixture; it has three terminals.

Transformer Device designed to convert the voltage in a circuit from the normal 120 volts to a lower level; for example, to supply 12 volts to low-voltage exterior lights or 24 volts to a doorbell transformer.

Traveler wire Transfers electricity from one three-way switch to another.

UF cable Cable for use in wet, outdoor and underground locations; also used inside.

UL, Underwriters Laboratories Independent organization that tests electrical products for safe operation and conformance with published standards under various conditions. Products that pass may display the UL logo.

Volt, voltage Unit of measurement of the electromotive force of a current. One volt equals the amount of pressure required to move one ampere through a wire that has a resistance of one ohm. Volts multiplied by amps give the wattage available in a circuit (V × A = W).

Voltage tester A device that measures the voltage of an electrical current flowing through a circuit. See Continuity tester.

Watt, wattage Unit of measurement of the amount of electrical power required or consumed by a fixture or appliance. See also amps and volts.

White wire White-insulated wire that forms a circuit with a power wire.

Wire nut Plastic cover for a wire splice. The inside is threaded metal.

Wire stripper Tool designed to remove the insulation from a wire without damaging the wire itself.

Zip cord Line cord designed with a thin section between the insulating coverings of the wires. The cord easily splits when pulled down the middle.

Index

Metric Conversion Charts

LUMBER

Sizes: Metric cross-sections are so close to their nearest Imperial sizes, as noted below, that for most purposes they may be considered equivalents.

Lengths: Metric lengths are based on a 300mm module which is slightly shorter in length than an Imperial foot. It will therefore be important to check your requirements accurately to the nearest inch and consult the table below to find the metric length required.

Areas: The metric area is a square metre. Use the following conversion factors when converting from Imperial data: 100 sq. feet = 9.290 sq. metres.

METRIC SIZES SHOWN BESIDE NEAREST IMPERIAL EQUIVALENT

mm	Inches	mm	Inches
16 × 75	$^5/_8$ × 3	44 × 150	$1^3/_4$ × 6
16 × 100	$^5/_8$ × 4	44 × 175	$1^3/_4$ × 7
16 × 125	$^5/_8$ × 5	44 × 200	$1^3/_4$ × 8
16 × 150	$^5/_8$ × 6	44 × 225	$1^3/_4$ × 9
19 × 75	$^3/_4$ × 3	44 × 250	$1^3/_4$ × 10
19 × 100	$^3/_4$ × 4	44 × 300	$1^3/_4$ × 12
19 × 125	$^3/_4$ × 5	50 × 75	2 × 3
19 × 150	$^3/_4$ × 6	50 × 100	2 × 4
22 × 75	$^7/_8$ × 3	50 × 125	2 × 5
22 × 100	$^7/_8$ × 4	50 × 150	2 × 6
22 × 125	$^7/_8$ × 5	50 × 175	2 × 7
22 × 150	$^7/_8$ × 6	50 × 200	2 × 8
25 × 75	1 × 3	50 × 225	2 × 9
25 × 100	1 × 4	50 × 250	2 × 10
25 × 125	1 × 5	50 × 300	2 × 12
25 × 150	1 × 6	63 × 100	$2^1/_2$ × 4
25 × 175	1 × 7	63 × 125	$2^1/_2$ × 5
25 × 200	1 × 8	63 × 150	$2^1/_2$ × 6
25 × 225	1 × 9	63 × 175	$2^1/_2$ × 7
25 × 250	1 × 10	63 × 200	$2^1/_2$ × 8
25 × 300	1 × 12	63 × 225	$2^1/_2$ × 9
32 × 75	$1^1/_4$ × 3	75 × 100	3 × 4
32 × 100	$1^1/_4$ × 4	75 × 125	3 × 5
32 × 125	$1^1/_4$ × 5	75 × 150	3 × 6
32 × 150	$1^1/_4$ × 6	75 × 175	3 × 7
32 × 175	$1^1/_4$ × 7	75 × 200	3 × 8
32 × 200	$1^1/_4$ × 8	75 × 225	3 × 9
32 × 225	$1^1/_4$ × 9	75 × 250	3 × 10
32 × 250	$1^1/_4$ × 10	75 × 300	3 × 12
32 × 300	$1^1/_4$ × 12	100 × 100	4 × 4
38 × 75	$1^1/_2$ × 3	100 × 150	4 × 6
38 × 100	$1^1/_2$ × 4	100 × 200	4 × 8
38 × 125	$1^1/_2$ × 5	100 × 250	4 × 10
38 × 150	$1^1/_2$ × 6	100 × 300	4 × 12
38 × 175	$1^1/_2$ × 7	150 × 150	6 × 6
38 × 200	$1^1/_2$ × 8	150 × 200	6 × 8
38 × 225	$1^1/_2$ × 9	150 × 300	6 × 12
44 × 75	$1^3/_4$ × 3	200 × 200	8 × 8
44 × 100	$1^3/_4$ × 4	250 × 250	10 × 10
44 × 125	$1^3/_4$ × 5	300 × 300	12 × 12

NOMINAL SIZE	ACTUAL SIZE
(This is what you order)	(This is what you get)
Inches	Inches
1 × 1	$^3/_4$ × $^3/_4$
1 × 2	$^3/_4$ × $1^1/_2$
1 × 3	$^3/_4$ × $2^1/_2$
1 × 4	$^3/_4$ × $3^1/_2$
1 × 6	$^3/_4$ × $5^1/_2$
1 × 8	$^3/_4$ × $7^1/_4$
1 × 10	$^3/_4$ × $9^1/_4$
1 × 12	$^3/_4$ × $11^1/_4$
2 × 2	$1^3/_4$ × $1^3/_4$
2 × 3	$1^1/_2$ × $2^1/_2$
2 × 4	$1^1/_2$ × $3^1/_2$
2 × 6	$1^1/_2$ × $5^1/_2$
2 × 8	$1^1/_2$ × $7^1/_4$
2 × 10	$1^1/_2$ × $9^1/_4$
2 × 12	$1^1/_2$ × $11^1/_4$

METRIC LENGTHS

Lengths Metres	Equiv. Ft. & Inches
1.8m	5′ $10^7/_8$″
2.1m	6′ $10^5/_8$″
2.4m	7′ $10^1/_2$″
2.7m	8′ $10^1/_4$″
3.0m	9′ $10^1/_8$″
3.3m	10′ $9^7/_8$″
3.6m	11′ $9^3/_4$″
3.9m	12′ $9^1/_2$″
4.2m	13′ $9^3/_8$″
4.5m	14′ $9^1/_3$″
4.8m	15′ 9″
5.1m	16′ $8^3/_4$″
5.4m	17′ $8^5/_8$″
5.7m	18′ $8^3/_8$″
6.0m	19′ $8^1/_4$″
6.3m	20′ 8″
6.6m	21′ $7^7/_8$″
6.9m	22′ $7^5/_8$″
7.2m	23′ $7^1/_2$″
7.5m	24′ $7^1/_4$″
7.8m	25′ $7^1/_8$″

All the dimensions are based on 1 inch = 25 mm.